# Conceptual Mind and Computing Paradigm
Al Galvis

## Conceptual Mind and Computing Paradigm

The author and publisher make no expressed or implied warranty. No liabilities are assumed arising out of the use of the information or software contained herein, including responsibility for potential errors or omissions. Every effort has been made to provide appropriate trademark information about all the companies and products mentioned in this book.

Printed in the United States of America
ISBN 978-0615862552

*In the memory of my loving Mother and grandparents who made this work possible.*

# TABLE OF CONTENTS

# PREFACE

Conceptually, our mind is an entity of beautiful simplicity designed for the single function or purpose of *processing information*. This is a book about the mind's conceptual framework and its application to software engineering challenges. Concepts are straightforward entities that can be readily grasped. For instance, the concept of messaging represents the interchange of information between individuals like you and me. This book isn't an introduction to programming or software design. It assumes that you are reasonably familiar with at least one programming language and basic software design techniques.

Concepts can be implemented using any arbitrary computer language. They are also highly reusable entities that can be applied to solve a variety of common problems in the real world. Concepts can streamline software and make it more flexible, reusable, understandable, timely, and cost-effective. They can improve overall quality while saving a considerable amount of effort and resources dedicated to building complex software applications. The world around us exhibits inherent solutions and associated design in response to specific problems. Conceptualization entails the extraction of concepts, relevant to the problem domain, from natural and man-made reality. In doing so, the problem at hand can be effectively solved by mirroring the concepts involved as part of preexisting solution and design. A realistically accurate representation and solution are also achieved.

The book seeks to achieve a healthy compromise between theory and application. The theory is illustrated by presenting plenty of examples and working applications. There is no much in terms of involved mathematical formulations; mainly some demonstrations presented for completeness sake. In agreement with Occam's razor, Concepts and the associated computing paradigm represent entities of striking simplicity:

"Nature does not multiply things [Concepts] unnecessarily; that she makes use of the easiest and simplest means [Concepts] for producing her effects; that she does nothing in vain, and the like." Galileo Galilei.

In writing this book, I also tried to pursue Occam's razor as related to content and presentation. Mother Nature always seems to know best. In general, it is probably how good software and writing should be: simple.

1

On the other hand, for the sake of clearness and better understanding, certain key ideas are repeated as needed.

For better understanding, the book substantially relies on the reader's intuition and reasonable common sense. While reading this book, we ought to think in conceptual terms, which our minds are perfectly capable of doing. Also, the natural language represents the ultimate tool for conveying information, in the form of concepts, as related to expressiveness, conciseness, and power – a match for the conceptual mind that hosts it.

In order to fully understand certain ideas, you may need to rely on other disciplines such as philosophy, psychology, and cognition. They will be referenced when appropriate. Concepts and the conceptual mind have been studied from many perspectives that can be leveraged while reading the material.

If you would like to provide your expert review of this book, we would love to hear from you. Criticism and comments for improvement are always welcome; especially in terms of areas that were missed or require additional work. I apologize in advance for any potential mistakes or omissions.

# ROADMAP

The book consists of the following main parts:

**Realistic Information Model (REAL):** describes several relevant aspects behind Concepts including philosophical, psychological, and cognitive aspects.

**Concepts (C):** information is processed by the mind in the form of concepts.

**Conceptual Design (CD):** discussion on elements, principles and methodology of conceptual design; in particular, the extraction of relevant concepts from natural and man-made reality via conceptualization.

**Information/Conceptual Machines:** introduces a Turing-complete mathematical model for the conceptual paradigm. The mathematical foundation is straightforward and therefore leveraged to explain ideas and principles covered by subsequent chapters.

**Family of Concepts:** collection of the main Concepts, extracted from nature, related to information processing. The specification of Concepts is very similar to the specification of Design Patterns. On the other hand, there are key differences between both software abstractions (see comparison with related software models).

**Conceptual Framework:** Concepts are leveraged for the specification and design of a complete component framework applicable to the implementation of arbitrary information technologies.

**Design Pattern Implementation:** covers how concepts can be leveraged for the reusable implementation of common design patterns.

**Distributed Component/Service Model:** Concepts are applied to the design and specification of a complete component/service model. In turn, such model can be utilized for the implementation of a Service Oriented Architecture (SOA).

**Comparison with related software models:** the proposed paradigm is compared to several software models including object-oriented models, design patterns, and component-based software engineering (CBSE).

**Natural Language of Concepts (NATURAL):** application of the model to computer languages and related AI/Cognitive architectures.

**Model Evaluation and Metrics**: evaluation of the conceptual model and proposed metrics.

**Applications**: there are several chapters discussing the application of the proposed paradigm. A complete Conceptual framework is one of the applications included. It features the implementation of a distributed component and service model. The implementation of well-known pattern is also discussed.

**Paradigm Comparisons (Appendix):** the conceptual paradigm can be applied to solve a wide variety of problems in multiple technology areas. Comparisons with a wide variety of models, architectures, and technologies are discussed as part of the appendix. A detailed comparison with traditional application interfaces (APIs) is also included.

It is recommended that you start by reading the introductory chapters: a) Realistic Information Model (REAL) b) Concepts (C) c) Conceptual Design (CD) d) Live or Animated Entities and e) Messaging. They should give you the basis for understanding of all the other chapters. The conceptual paradigm is applicable to a wide range of information technologies. After reading the aforementioned chapters, you will be in a position to start reading specific chapters of interest to you. To grasp the motivation and many benefits derived from the application of the proposed paradigm, please read the chapter dealing with the state of the art.

The family of concepts represents a large portion of the book. You can read them all at once, or one at a time, on as needed basis. Several other chapters make reference to specific concepts in the collection. One chapter covers the application of the paradigm to the specification and design of a Conceptual computer language: NATURAL.

If you are interested in the mathematical foundations, I hope you will enjoy the relevant chapters: a) Mathematical Model – Information and Conceptual Machines. b) Information Machines and Turing completeness. They provide the mathematical model behind the conceptual paradigm. Like me, you may also derive satisfaction from the fact that all the qualities of the proposed paradigm are a direct consequence of its straightforward mathematical foundation. The mathematical demonstrations presented require basic knowledge of Algebra, Set theory, and Logic.

After reading the introductory chapters, you can directly dive into the chapters dealing with applications. Once the applications become more advanced, you will also need to rely on chapters that cover the conceptual framework. Most of the applications are built on top of it. The Jt conceptual framework is a reference implementation of the presented model. It supports Java and Android. The complete source code of the framework is part of the accompanying materials. Most mainstream technologies are fully integrated with the framework including Apache Axis (SOA), JDBC, EJB, Java Mail, JMS, Servlets, JSPs, and XML

The sample applications are mainly written using Java and Android. However, the conceptual paradigm and framework can be implemented using any arbitrary computer language. The transparent integration of heterogeneous platforms, technologies, protocols and computer languages is one key benefit derived from the paradigm. A basic knowledge of Java and/or Android is recommended for the understanding of the chapters dealing with applications.

# CONCEPTUAL PARADIGM

Biomimetics is the examination of nature, its models, systems, processes, and elements to emulate or take inspiration from, in order to solve human problems. The term Biomimetics comes from the Greek words bios, meaning life, and mimesis, meaning to imitate. Applications of Biomimetics have led to innumerable advances in science and engineering. The Computer Science field is no exception.

The human mind represents the pinnacle of natural creation. Nothing else in the known universe comes close. This conceptual engine is designed, literally, for a single purpose or function: *processing of information*. Computer systems are information processors, like our minds. In consequence, computer systems can be significantly improved by mirroring the conceptual paradigm and model leveraged by the mind. Concepts can be employed to represent all aspects of reality. They can also be applied to communicate ideas, learn, understand, and efficiently solve arbitrary problems. Information is the fundamental abstraction that defines our perceived reality.

Conceptually, the natural mind is an entity of beautiful and mathematical *simplicity*. Only *three* concepts are involved as part of the mind's 'computing model': a) Information machine (mind itself). b) Single function expressed by the information primitive ($f(m)$). c) Information represented by a single Concept construct ($I$). The aforementioned abstractions also represent a streamlined and complete set of natural concepts applicable to the comprehensive implementation of arbitrary information processes and technologies – including cognitive processes like memorizing, learning, logical reasoning, and natural language processing. The natural concept of messaging is ubiquitous. Realistically, it also represents the only mechanism of communication between the mind and its environment.

Information comes in the form of messages which are processed via the primitive – like a sentence, for instance. The conceptual engine (A) can be defined mathematically as $A = (processInformation\ (message),\ I)$. As mentioned earlier, it has a single function to perform (primitive): *processInformation(message)*. The symbol $I$ represents the information (i.e. concepts) already known (learned) by the engine. A is Turing complete, fully implementable, and features the same processing power of a computer. A can also be expressed as $A = (f(m),\ I)$, where $f$ represents any computable function. Furthermore, based on George Boole's Laws of Thought, the conceptual engine is also capable of *logical* reasoning:

"The truth that the ultimate laws of thought are mathematical in their form, viewed in connexion with the fact of the possibility of error, establishes a ground for some remarkable conclusions. If we directed our attention to the scientific truth alone, we might be led to infer an almost exact parallelism between the intellectual operations and the movements of external nature. Suppose any one conversant with physical science, but unaccustomed to reflect upon the nature of his own faculties, to have been informed, that it had been proved, that the laws of those faculties were mathematical; it is probable that after the first feelings of incredulity had subsided, the impression would arise, that the order of thought must, therefore, be as necessary as that of the material universe. We know that in the realm of natural science, the absolute connexion between the initial and final elements of a problem, exhibited in the mathematical form, fitly symbolizes that physical necessity which binds together effect and cause."

George Boole.

Mathematical laws and remarkable conclusions indeed: $A=(\beta\ (m),\ I)$, where the function $\beta$ represents logical processing of information, applied to incoming messages (m), as defined by Boole's Algebra of Logic (!).

As a consequence of the proposed paradigm based on natural concepts and associated computing model, software engineering processes are improved in terms of overall complexity, level of abstraction, true correspondence with reality (Realism), communication gap between man and machine, logical abilities, interoperability, quality, cost, timeframe, and so forth. Mother Nature solution to the "software problem" and associated complexity is in character as expressed by Occam's razor:

"Nature does not multiply things unnecessarily; that she makes use of the easiest and simplest means [Concepts] for producing her effects;" Galileo Galilei.

Simplest Concepts indeed: $(A=(\beta(m),\ I))$.

# 1.    REALISTIC INFORMATION MODEL (REAL)

Our reality is defined by a single concept: *information*. The Latin roots of the term mean "to give form to the mind". In turn, the ancient Greek word for form was used in the philosophical sense to denote the ideal identity or essence of an entity in reality. In other words, information is the 'substance' or essence that shapes our minds and allows us to conceptualize our reality. Our thinking minds and patterns consist of this single concept.

Information is a fundamental concept, a cornerstone of human activity, societal interaction, and existence. Without the ability to process information, a variety of living beings and specifically people would not be able to cope with reality, adapt, and therefore survive. Critical functions like thinking, moving, walking, talking, reading, hearing, decision making and internal body functions would not be possible.

The human mind represents the pinnacle of natural creation when it comes to information processing. Nothing else comes close to this conceptual engine. Conceptually, computer systems are information processors, like our minds. As a consequence of the Biomimetics principles, computer systems can be improved by mimicking the conceptual framework used by the mind. Information is organized and processed based on concepts. Concepts are abstract entities, general notions or ideas. Our logical minds process and understand information in a conceptual fashion. People constantly use concepts to transmit ideas (information), solve problems, and make decisions.

The Realistic Information Model (REAL), based on the fundamental information concept, *mirrors* reality and seeks to provide a complete and accurate model of the real world. Nature has already done the work, set the standard, and successfully solved information challenges via proven solutions. The proposed realistic model attempts to faithfully examine and mirror nature's information model, processes and solutions. In addition, it attempts to understand and mimic the conceptual paradigm used by the mind, part of the natural realm.

A realistic information model includes the following *concepts*, mirrored from nature, and part of the information pattern family: a collection of

8

independent entities or individuals, some of which are *Live or Animated Entities*, interacting with each other and/or interchanging information via *Messaging* within the context of information *Dialogs and Processes*. *Live* or *Animated* entities are able to process information and exhibit independent behavior. The aforementioned concepts are often organized into more complex entities represented by the *Group* concept. In reality, these ubiquitous concepts mirror nature and the world around us. Therefore, they can be found everywhere: communities, organizations, companies, human body processes, applications consisting of local and distributed components interchanging information and working cooperatively within the context of a process, etc.

Consider an organization or process where multiple entities, or groups of entities, work cooperatively to achieve specific common goals. The survival and development of such organizations have depended on finding solutions for information and process challenges. For instance, communities of individuals have developed sophisticated ways of communication (i.e. messaging). Human speech, and in general communication between members of the same species, would be an example. The interchange of information is vital to the survival of every organization and community. Societies have built sophisticated information infrastructures and frameworks to carry the messaging required for communication and decision making purposes. Communities and organizations have been able to deal with fault tolerance challenges by providing individual, message, and process redundancy.

Since information is the fundamental concept that defines our reality, the proposed model also consists of a single information primitive. Our minds are designed, literally, for a single purpose or function: *processing of information*. In case you are wondering about this single information primitive and how it works, look closely. You are doing it right now while you read (process) this document. You are processing information sentence by sentence: each sentence represents the message being processed. Not to mention all the processing of information that has taken place in order for the information to reach its destination: networks, computers, email systems, visual system, nervous system, etc. Each one of these systems is conceptually an information system designed for the single purpose of information processing. *Keep in mind* that most of our thinking patterns or thoughts contain information in the form of concepts.

9

It has been recommended that in order to fully describe the proposed model, I will need to rely on conceptual models studied by several disciplines including philosophy, knowledge representation, ontology, and linguistic. They will be mentioned when appropriate. Philosophical realism needs to be included which states that reality exists independent of the observer and that the *truth of a representation is determined by how it corresponds to reality (The Correspondence Theory of Truth [30])*.

Notice that other models and technologies achieve various degrees of realism (accurate correspondence with reality) even though they were created without that guiding principle or goal in mind. Distributed artifacts for instance, although artificial, achieve communication and therefore a limited level of realism when compared with the Messaging abstraction: the *real* thing.

Ideally, complete results can be achieved when the overriding design mindset, abstractions, principles and goals are governed by the deliberate and faithful pursue of a model that mirrors reality without any artificial deviations, which generally result in shortcomings, weaknesses and/or inefficiencies. For example, a model for an artificial heart or limp is able to achieve several degrees of realism based on how close it mimics the real organ and its functions. An ideal model consists of a complete and accurate representation which includes all the critical concepts (i.e. realistic).

Nature is wise, its processes present many qualities:  simplicity, completeness, accuracy, robustness, efficiency, versatility, and so forth. Other critical aspects are also part of natural processes, including redundancy, fault tolerance, and so on. A realistic model that mirrors nature absorbs these traits and characteristics. As a consequence, software engineering methodologies and techniques can be improved by mirroring the models, abstractions, processes and solutions found in nature and the real world. Keep in mind that nature processes have evolved and improved during long periods of time through natural selection. These processes are fine-tuned entities able to provide redundancy, efficiency, and fault tolerance.

10

Nature and its natural selection processes have already addressed and solved, in very robust and simple ways, the main challenges faced by distributed/concurrent component systems and models. Specifically, in the area of concurrent and distributed information processing. There is no need to reinvent the wheel so to speak. We just need to mimic the models, processes and solutions found in nature and the real world. Models and technologies that fail to accurately mirror relevant reality, and its natural concepts, are inherently artificial, incomplete and limited.

The information pattern family provides several examples of concepts including Live or Animated entities, Messaging and Information Process. These concepts can be applied to model a wide variety of problems in the real world. Notice that the concept of Live or Animated entity refers to several classes of physical objects: person, computer system, automated machine, living being, etc. The same concept applies to many different classes of physical objects.

The terms object and component are often used interchangeably hereafter. Conceptually speaking, a component, like a CPU chip, also represents an object. Physical objects often become components of more complex structures (car part or arm). From an information perspective, the fundamental aspect is whether the object or component is able to process information in the real world. If so, the object or component is called an Animated/Live entity or Animated/Live component. In reality, most entities are unanimated objects or components, unable to process information.

On the other hand, we should distinguish between the concept use to represent the entity, inside our minds, and the entity or physical object being represented. Although tightly related, they are two separate and decoupled entities. Concepts are mental representations based on information and separate from the actual entities or physical objects being represented: Kant called it the "thing-in-itself" or the "thing per se" [30]. In other words, concepts constitute just a representation inside our minds. For instance, the physical entity called 'mind' is able to process information. The concept 'mind' cannot, since it only exists inside our mind. The concept and the actual entity are separate.

The position stated in the previous paragraph does not contradict a *moderate* realistic position. It is also consistent with a compromised approach known as *conceptualism*, which presents itself as a middle ground between nominalism and realism: asserting that universal concepts exist, but they exist in the mind, rather than real entities existing independently of the mind. 'Exaggerated' realism holds that universal things exist in nature which is viewed as going against common sense.

The term conceptualism and the associated philosophy fit nicely with the conceptual approach and paradigm being proposed. A realistic/conceptual model is based on solid philosophical grounds expressed by the ideas behind moderate realism, conceptualism, and the associated correspondence Theory of Truth [30]. Notice that the philosophical ideas being discussed are in harmony with scientific and engineering disciplines where models/concepts are usually measured based on the accuracy of the representation (correspondence) and the tangible results produced by their implementation. The same principle applies to computer science and related technologies.

Concepts are utilized by the mind to represent all aspects of reality. Obviously concepts are not limited to the representation of physical objects. They are mental representations able to convey and encapsulate information about every aspect, including physical objects. For instance, Gravity, Force, Energy and other natural laws are concepts. They do not represent objects or design patterns. Reality is made of more than these two well-known abstractions. There are many other concepts that are involved. A complete and realistic information model of reality must include *every* concept. Concepts can also be used as a mental representation of processes in the real world such as messaging: transference of information. In summary, our minds use concepts to represent all aspects of reality including physical objects, living entities, natural laws, processes, and so on.

## 2.    Concepts (C)

### 2.1    Intent

A concept consists of information about a specific aspect of reality. This abstraction allows the conceptualization, communication, and processing of information. A precise definition can be found in the dictionary: "an idea of something formed by mentally combining all its characteristics or particulars; a construct". A concept is the group of associations (information associations) that represents such characteristics or particulars. Concepts improve reusability, decoupling, encapsulation, and scalability by separating the fundamental information aspect from all other aspects such as how the information is stored, represented, transferred, secured, processed and so forth. Concepts are also fully decoupled from the entities that process them. Entities (sender/receiver), concepts and processing mechanism are decoupled entities, fully independent. Consider that there is clear separation between a concept and the mind (or entity) that communicates and processes it.

### 2.2    Applicability

Every single aspect of our reality can be expressed as a concept. As demonstrated by our mind, concepts are applied to represent and tackle every problem found in daily life.   The mind uses concepts to understand, communicate and process arbitrary aspects. A conceptual paradigm is widely used by the human mind in order to process information and adapt. Actually, concepts define a significant part of our perceived reality.

Concepts are highly reusable abstractions. The same concept can be applied (reused) to solve a variety of problems. This is an effective and efficient mechanism that allows our mind to do more with less so to speak. The mind is able to reuse a specific concept to frame, understand, and solve problems in a variety of contexts. Once our *minds get or grasp the concept*, that is. Our minds can apply the same concept to similar problems which seems a perfect match for adaptation purposes. A changing environment brings forth new problems and situations. A conceptual and versatile mind, able to apply learned concepts to new problems, is probably a suitable match for such survival and adaptation challenges.

For instance, the concepts that belong to the information pattern family [2,4,5] have wide applicability: messaging, animated/live entity, memory, group, association, dialog, and information process. They can be used to model and solve a variety of problems. These concepts apply to countless processes in nature and the real world: communities, organizations, families, human body processes, social networks, colonies of insects, your banking system, BPM/BPEL processes, a collection of local and distributed components interchanging information and working cooperatively within the context of a process, etc. These are just some examples of the scenarios that can be modeled using the information patterns. All these scenarios share common challenges, and problems: reliable and secure communication between entities, redundancy, fault-tolerant considerations, process reliability, concurrency, interoperability, scalability, and the need for an accurate and complete information model.

The concept of message is another example. It can be applied to countless entities in reality: a number, an email message, a document, a spoken sentence, energy, biochemical message, and so on. In general, all types of information can be associated to this concept. Since information can be used to represent everything, a message can be used to transfer information about every single aspect of reality. Information, message, and messaging are very broad concepts and therefore broadly reusable.

Another example would be the concept of a reservation. We can use this concept to convey information about multiple aspects: hotel reservation, computer reservation, airplane reservation, parking reservation, etc. The concept of a reservation can be applied in multiple contexts. Notice that the information related to each particular class of reservation will be different. The information needed for a hotel reservation is not the same as the one required for an airplane reservation, although both scenarios share exactly the *same concept*. Concepts are very versatile and dynamic entities with wide applicability.

## 2.3   Motivation

As mentioned earlier, the implementation of traditional O-O multithreaded and distributed applications/services is a complex

14

undertaking, expensive and prone to error. Complexity, budget overruns and quality issues are usual in the context of these software development projects. Challenges include communication, reusability, reliability, fault tolerance, redundancy, monitoring, interoperability, quality, scalability, and so on.

Consider for example, the design and implementation of a document manager for mobile devices using traditional O-O multithreaded/distributed technologies. This application is designed to provide basic capabilities for accessing, displaying, and updating the information contained in documents. The documents can come in many formats (PDF, HTML, plain Text, MS Word, XML, etc.). The mobile application should also provide remote access via web services or comparable capabilities since the documents may be stored remotely. In general, mobile applications are highly interactive. The target application fits the profile. Multiple threads of execution are required. No single thread is allowed to monopolize the cpu for long periods of time, otherwise the offending thread may be forced to stop. Consider that multiple functions may be happening concurrently: speech synthesis, voice recognition, music, graphical user interface updates, phone calls, text messages, notifications, alarms, GPS, and so.

The conventional solution for general purpose O-O applications, and in particular for the proposed mobile application, will present a variety of challenges and limitations including:

a) Strong coupling which ties the solution to a specific platform, protocol, multithreading/distributed technology, document format, device characteristics and/or computer language.

b) Lack of reusability which usually results from strong coupling, lack of encapsulation and the inability to provide reusable threading/distributed functionality as part of a framework. Reusability limitations are also caused by overlooking concepts and the conceptual interfaces found in reality, which happen to be highly reusable entities (see Conceptual Interfaces).

c) Lack of encapsulation usually associated with not relying on the messaging concept as the communication mechanism between participant components. The threading mechanism is usually artificially implemented as a separate object. A single thread may also be artificially associated with multiple components which hinders encapsulation.

d) Complexities dealing with distributed/SOA technologies based on distributed artifacts such stubs, IDLs, WSDLs, RPCs, or similar. Distributed artifacts are also a source of interoperability limitations.

e) Complexity dealing with multithreaded and distributed technologies related to thread management, thread synchronization, race conditions, deadlocks, and so forth.

f) Complex quality issues brought about by the previous challenges which get compounded and harder to manage as the number of threads, remote interfaces and/or team members increases.

g) In general, the solution is tied to specific device configuration, or data format. For instance, HTML pages displayed by your computer may need significant changes to be displayed on the mobile device. Such device dependencies are a direct result of not using a conceptual approach and solution. Concepts on the other hand, are independent of the computer technology/device and data format being employed. Animated/Live components using a conceptual interface are able to reformat the page layout on the flight to meet the device requirements.

h) Scalability and interoperability limitations associated with several of the previous challenges.

i) Complexity incorporating remote and local components/services into BPM/BPEL processes derived from the lack of messaging as the communication mechanism and underlying realistic abstraction. This specific challenge applies when BPM/BPEL tools are used as part of the implementation.

The challenges and limitations get compounded when additional real-world production aspects are considered such as security, access control, scalability, and fault tolerance. All the aspects outlined above have a negative impact on software cost, overall complexity, maintainability, quality, timelines, and risk.

## 2.4    Participants

In formal terms, a Concept (C) can be defined as an n-tuple of information associations:

$$C = \{a1, a2, ..., an\}$$

$ai$ is an information association of the form $(xi, yi)$, meaning that $xi$ is equal or associated to $yi$ $(xi = yi)$. A Concept (C) can be recursively expressed as:

$$C = \{(x1,y1), (x2,y2), \quad , (xn, yn)\}$$

- $xi$ represents a concept as defined by C or a sequence of symbols in the alphabet: $xi = (b1, , bn)$; $b_i \in \sum$; $i = [1 .. n]$
- $yi$ represents a concept as defined by C or a sequence of symbols in the alphabet: $yi = (b1, , bn)$; $b_i \in \sum$; $i = [1 .. n]$

The simplicity of the Concept representation can be deceiving. Arbitrary aspects of our reality can be expressed as information in the form of a Concept (C). All the conceptual information accrued until the present day, expressed by spoken or written sentences, can be represented using this conceptual form (C). Stated in plain terms, a Concept is a group of *information associations*. For instance, a spoken sentence (or message) is a concept. A sentence contains one or more associations of information: verb, subject, adverb, and so on.

The sentence "please make a reservation" is a concept that consists of the following group of associations:

$$S = \{a_1, a_2, a_{3,} a_4\}$$

17

a1, a2, a3, and a4 are information associations:

S can be expressed as follows:

S={(1,please), (2,make), (3,a) (4,,reservation)}

An alternative representation may consist of grammatical associations:

S={(adverb,please), (verb,make), (article,a) (object,reservation)}

adverb = please
article = a
verb = make
object = reservation

A third representation may be in the form of a predefined application message intended for a computer component:

S={(operation, make), (what, reservation)}

The example can be generalized to represent any arbitrary sentence. A sentence is a concept. Multiple representations are possible. Similar to human and component communication, the main aspect is that the involved parties agree on syntax and semantics. Notice that the sentence S is also a message. Messaging is the abstraction used to transfer concepts. Our minds receive conceptual information via verbal or written communication in the form of messages (sentences). An arbitrary message (M) is also a concept that can be expressed using the concept notation employed above:

$M = \{(x1,y1), (x2,y2), \quad , (xn, yn) \}$

As discussed earlier, concepts do not have any information processing capabilities. In a sense, they are 'passive' entities responsible for the single purpose of conveying information. Another entity needs to process the information conveyed by the concept, using the information primitive:

### *processInformation (M)*

This primitive represents the mathematical function required to process information, in the form of messages. The entity receives the message (M) and processes it, which mimics what the brain does after receiving conceptual information in the form of verbal or written messages. The same concepts (literally) apply to local and/or distributed live components interchanging information and performing computations. Arbitrary aspects of reality can be expressed using a single abstraction or language construct: Concept. For instance, every unanimated physical object modeled by a traditional O-O language can be represented as a Concept (C). The attributes of the object can be expressed in terms of information associations. On the other hand, representing a Concept (like a message for example) using a typical object is difficult and restrictive because its attributes are not fixed. The object representation is just not a good fit (correspondence). Messages can have all kind of structures although they correspond to same concept: Message (M).

Two concepts are said to be semantically equivalent (C1 = C2) if they have the same meaning. In particular, a concept is equivalent to its definition:

$$C = Definition (C)$$

For instance, messaging is defined based on other concepts as "transference of information":

$$Messaging = Definition (Messaging) = \{(transference), (of), (information)\}$$

In turn, each concept part of the definition has its own definition. An expanded graph of information associations can be built. Notice that a simplified notation is utilized to represent the concept: $C = \{(y1), (y2), , (yn)\}$. This representation can always be transformed to use the conceptual notation shown previously.

## 2.5    Structure

In reality, concepts are processed by other entities. The concepts themselves do not have any information processing capabilities. Concepts only contain information. Let us consider the concepts in the mind, from the standpoint of the information aspect. They do not process any information. They only convey information. Our mind acts as a conceptual engine able to process concepts.

There is also a wall of separation between the information (Concept) and the entity processing it. Both entities are fully decoupled. Concepts can be viewed as passive entities that only serve the purpose of conveying information. Concepts are like the information stored in database tables although they do not consist of a fixed number of attributes. In general, a third party component or system is required to process the database information. There is clear separation between the information and the components/systems responsible for processing it. Concepts are transferred, in the form of messages, via the messaging abstraction.

## 2.6    Information Machines

A mathematical model for the conceptual approach can be summarized as follows:

a) **Information machine (A):**  An automatic machine able to perform computations via the information primitive which defines the machine's single function (or purpose). A is defined by a two-tuple $A= (processInformation(message), I)$. The machine A is Turing complete. It can also be expressed as $A= (f(m), I)$, where $f$ represents any computable function.

b) **Information primitive**: Single function *processInformation (message)* where the message represents conceptual information (C).

c) **Information (I, C)**:  information stored (i.e. known) by the machine and represented by $I = (C1, Cn)$, where $C1, ,Cn$ are concepts. Each

20

concept (C) can be expressed by a single language construct, C = {a1,a2, ,a$_n$} where a1,a2, ,a$_n$ are information associations.

Information Machines (A-machines) are fully encapsulated, independent, and decoupled from other entities. The ubiquitous concept of messaging (M) represents the only realistic mechanism of information exchange between the machine and its environment. However, it is not an intrinsic concept part of the machine itself.

One straightforward implementation of the Information Machine is via an encapsulated and decoupled OO component, consisting of a single method with a single parameter (message). The method may return information in the form of a concept (C). A component that implements the Information Machine abstraction is called a Live or Animated component. It can be visualized as a computer (mini-computer) since both have equivalent processing power.

A complete version of the model is covered as part of a separate chapter (see Mathematical Model). The mathematical concepts (3) found in the model deliberately mirror the ones part of the conceptual mind: a) Entity or machine with a single function or purpose. b) Processing of information expressed by single function (primitive). c) Information in the form of Concepts (C). This represents a streamlined and complete set (Turing Complete). It also illustrates the broad scope and applicability of natural concepts: a compact set of them (3) can be applied to solve, in a comprehensive fashion, an otherwise complex problem. No additional abstractions or primitives are required as part of the straightforward model based on nature. In agreement with Biomimetics ideas, complexity and redundancy are effectively removed from the formulation. Conceptually, the mind represents an entity of mathematical and beautiful simplicity – naturally.

## 2.7    Consequences

The following consequences are directly tied to the model's mathematical formulation based on natural entities.

**Reusability:** Concepts improve reusability. Actually they are highly reusable entities. Our minds are able to reuse the same concept to understand, frame, communicate and solve diverse problems. For instance, the concepts of reservation and message can be utilized in a variety of scenarios. Efficiency is gained by doing more with less so to speak. The same concept can be reused to convey information in multiple scenarios.

There are many examples that can be presented to illustrate how concepts improve reusability. The concepts part of the information pattern family, provide reusability improvements. A generic implementation can be achieved. The functionality provided by these concepts can be reused across arbitrary application domains. The reusable functionality is usually provided by a conceptual framework. The information pattern family also improves and encourages reuse because components can be integrated from multiple platforms, languages and technologies. In other words, technologies, languages, protocols can be freely mixed and matched within the context of the information pattern family.

Processes implemented based on the proposed abstractions can be reused as part of more complicated processes. The proposed abstractions can also be leveraged to provide reusable implementations of design patterns[2]. For instance, the implementation of a reusable Proxy to access remote components is feasible. A reusable Animated/Live proxy can be utilized for any remote component implemented based on the common messaging interface. A generic implementation of the Proxy design pattern can be achieved. The same principle applies to the reusable implementation of other design patterns.

**Decoupling:** Concepts improve decoupling. There is absolute separation between the concept itself (information) and the entity that process it. Both concerns can be altered independently. Concepts also separate the fundamental information aspect from other aspects such as how the information is stored, represented, transferred, secured, processed and so forth. Concepts are passive entities that only serve the purpose of conveying information.

Consider the concepts part of the information pattern family. Sender, receiver, message (Concept) and messaging mechanism are decoupled entities, encapsulated and fully independent. Each of these aspects can be changed independently without impacting the others. Our minds and the concepts that it contains are totally decoupled. Two completely separate entities are involved.

**Simplicity**: Concepts are uncomplicated entities that only contain information. No information processing mechanism is required. The proposed model relies on straightforward abstractions to represent arbitrary aspects of reality:

a) Information expressed as Concepts:
$$M = \{(x1, y1), .. , (xn, yn)\}$$

b) Components able to process information based on a single information primitive (Turing Complete): processMessage(M)

In particular, the information pattern family consists of straightforward abstractions that mirror the real world. The implementation is simplified as well, since it requires a few abstractions and single information primitive.

**Interoperability**: Concepts help improve interoperability. As discussed earlier, concepts of the form C = {(x1, y1), , (xn, yn)} can be freely transferred between systems and components regardless of technologies, languages, protocols, and data representation. The same principle applies to any arbitrary concept (C). In a sense, concepts are *fluid* abstractions that can be interchanged between heterogeneous technologies, systems, components and applications.

A process, based on the family of information patterns, can transparently incorporate components and applications that use multiple technologies, languages, platforms, protocols, and so forth. As stated earlier, concepts separate the critical information aspect from how such information is stored, represented, transferred and processed. All these aspects can be altered independently without impacting the actual information.

Concepts and the information primitive are independent from a specific language, technology and/or protocol. Platforms, languages, technologies and protocols can be freely mixed and matched within the context of a process. For instance, the information remains the same (semantics) regardless of what communication technology or protocol is being used: sockets, .Net, HTTP, RMI, REST, SSL, EJBs, etc. All these technologies and protocols can be readily incorporated as part of an integrated information process.

**Realism**: it should have become clear that realism is a relevant concept when dealing with computer systems, models and technologies. Therefore the concept of realism should be proposed and formalized as related to computer technologies. Obviously the realistic model is based on such concept. There are many other notions that are familiar in the engineering realm like encapsulation, decoupling, reusability, and so forth. Realism refers to the faithful pursue of system models, designs, and implementations that mirror reality without any artificial deviations, which usually result in shortcomings, weaknesses and/or inefficiencies. As a consequence, the overriding model mindset must be based on design, concepts, assumptions, primitives that accurately mirror the reality being represented. Obviously an ideal model and implementation must be as close as possible to the real entity or process being modeled (correspondence Theory of Truth).

In regards to computer systems and technologies, it should be said that a realistic model must be based on the fundamental information concept which defines reality. The world around us is divided into two categories based on the information concept: a) entities that can process information (Components) and b) Entities that cannot (Concepts). The concept of Realism is consistent with the principles of Biomimetics. On the other hand, reality also includes man-made entities, processes, and concepts that need to be considered and modeled as part of computer systems. Also, human beings, use a unique conceptual interface and framework to communicate information, which also needs to be part of a realistic information model.

Models, systems and technologies that fail to adhere to realism principles and concepts are unable to provide an accurate representation of reality. Therefore they are intrinsically incomplete and limited. Distributed artifacts and Multithreading are examples of artificial abstractions that fail to achieve a realistic and accurate representation. The concepts of Messaging (M) and Live or Animated Entities (A) are the realistic abstractions found in nature. Notice that other software engineering notions can be associated with the concept of realism. For example, the notions of encapsulation and decoupling correspond to how entities exist in reality: fully encapsulated and decoupled from other entities.

**Encapsulation:** Concepts improve encapsulation. Components, Concepts and Messages are self-contained and encapsulated units. Messaging is the only mechanism of communication between independent components. Components and processing mechanism (information primitive) are realistically encapsulated as part of a single unit represented by the abstraction of Live or Animated Entity.

**Conceptual Framework:** As a best practice, it is recommended that a framework implement the concepts part of the information pattern family. Although a framework is not required to implement the concepts involved, it is strongly encouraged because of multiple considerations including reliability, reusability, quality, implementation cost, security, exception propagation, and so forth. Software engineers are able to concentrate on the business logic. The information infrastructure (plumbing) is provided by the framework.

Traditional frameworks based on distributed artifacts, traditional APIs and multithreading inherit the limitations and shortcomings of the associated model and abstractions. In general, it is more difficult, and usually unfeasible, to build a comprehensive framework of reusable components and concepts to deal with the communication, security and concurrency functionality. For instance, in general, it is not possible to provide a reusable implementation of Proxy applicable arbitrary distributed components or services. Each remote API, based on distributed artifacts or similar technology, requires a separate implementation which hinders reusability.

**Mobile applications:** Since Live/Animated components are fully decoupled and encapsulated, they can be reused at the component level.

The utilization of concepts is a main contributor to the decoupling and encapsulation qualities exhibited. A single Animated/Live component or package can be reused as part of a completely new application, which is efficient and minimizes the size of the executable image. This becomes necessary, especially for mobile applications where there are specific resource constraints to follow. Traditional O-O components usually dependent on many other components and/or packages creating a web of coupled interdependencies. It is difficult or unfeasible to extract a particular component or package for reuse, especially when the component/package has been built by someone else. A whole library of components (or jar) needs to be added as part of the application which has an impact on the overall application size. Creating, maintaining, and using several versions of a traditional library also hinder the process.

Obviously, reusability improves quality, overall cost, delivery timeframes, executable size, and so on. Animated/Live components can be acquired or purchased. A market for these components is feasible and probably recommended. Reusability extends to heterogeneous computer languages since Animated/Live components can be reused across computer languages and technologies.

The information pattern family can be reused across the board, because as mentioned earlier, information is a highly reusable concept. The information patterns are applicable to a wide variety of technologies and architectures: ESB, SOA services, REST, Android, design pattern implementations, BPEL/BPM technologies. All these technologies deal with the fundamental concept of information. Such level of reusability also helps improve quality, overall cost, delivery timeframes, and so on. In the specific case of mobile applications, it also improves executable size which needs to be kept under control due to specific resource constraints.

**Versioning:** Conceptual interfaces offer backward compatibility. Consider an arbitrary modern human language. After evolving for a long period of time, human communication has become a very efficient, flexible and versatile mechanism of transferring information. New words and terms are being added constantly. Take for instance, the new term 'smartphone'. Some words become archaic and progressively fade away, being replaced by newer words or concepts. A 'new version' of the language, so to speak, is being constantly created to meet changing information requirements. The messages, part of the language, are constantly evolving without having an impact on the mechanism of communication itself (fully decoupled).

The same principles apply to conceptual interfaces based on messaging. New messages or updated messages with new associations can be methodically added to the interface without having an impact on the independent messaging mechanism. As a consequence, the need to create, maintain, and merge several versions of the software, which quickly becomes time consuming, difficult, and error-prone, is minimized or eliminated. The need for versioning is also minimized because of the reduction in the overall number of application components required for a conceptual implementation – most of the entities are realistically represented as Concepts.

**Conceptual paradigm and learning curve**: The conceptual level represents a higher level of abstraction. In order to take full advantage of concepts, people need to think in terms of abstractions: concepts such as *Animated/Live entity, messaging, group, association, memory, information process, and information itself.* Learning time and training may be required.

Although the proposed conceptual approach is natural, intuitive, and consistent with the real world, traditional approaches are based on unrealistic artifacts like multithreading and method/procedure invocation (both local and remote). Keep in mind that the proposed model and abstractions inherit many qualities derived from their natural contra parts. It is challenging to find drawbacks or trade-offs, which is unexpected within the context of design patterns. A similar situation occurs when we look at other real-world concepts that may be part of our software model, like gravity, energy and force.

**Overhead:** Transferring messages between components introduces a small overhead when compared with traditional method/procedure invocation. As computers become faster and faster the involved overhead becomes a non-issue. Also, the benefits of messaging and concepts outweigh the small performance cost.

## 2.8    Known Uses

**Design patterns.** Concepts have been used to implement and/or facilitate the implementation (i.e. reusable implementation) of well-known design patterns like Gang of Four design patterns (GoF), DAO, MVC, J2EE Design patterns, Master-Worker, and so forth [2]. Keep in mind that pattern implementations need to deal with information and concept interchange between participant components. Therefore the pattern implementation can use concepts as the basis for a realistic and comparable solution, while at the same time improving, reusability, interoperability, encapsulation, cost, overall complexity and so on.

**Conceptual Component Frameworks**: Concepts have been leveraged for the implementation of a complete component framework able to handle, in a very *natural* fashion, complex information challenges like concurrency, asynchronous messaging, versioning, native interfaces, seamless distributed component/service access, interoperability, exception propagation, BPEL/BPM component integration and so on.

The members of the information pattern family are fully implementable and reusable abstractions able to provide the information framework required for building robust applications. Since they can be utilized over and over again, a reusable framework improves maintainability, overall quality, cost, and timeframe delivery. Frameworks and component implemented based on the information patterns are also able to operate at a higher level of abstraction: conceptual level. In order to accurately mirror nature processes and the thinking patterns of the mind, a conceptual framework is needed.

**Distributed Component and Service Model (SOA)**: Concepts are well suited for the implementation of a complete distributed component/service model (Turing complete) able to handle complex real-world considerations such as security, redundancy, interoperability, fault tolerance, concurrency, scalability, etc. Conceptually, communicating with a remote component/service is not different from communicating with a local one when realistic information concepts are being used.

In particular, the information pattern family provides transparent access to distributed components/services regardless of technology, platform, language, data representation, communication protocol, and so on. They also help deal with a complex set of problems related to remote access and multithreading in the context of distributed applications.

**UML/BPM/BPEL processes and technologies.** Concepts have been used to model arbitrary business processes in a realistic and accurate fashion. In particular, the information pattern family can be used for the comprehensive implementation of business process technologies (BPEL/BPM), frameworks, and applications [10]. The information process abstractions can also be readily incorporated into UML/BPM/BPEL diagrams in order to design and implement applications with comparable functionality to traditional business process applications. There is a direct correspondence between the proposed abstractions and specific modeling diagrams and tools.

## 2.9    Implementation

Arbitrary computer technologies can be used to implement concepts. Notice that the object abstraction is implemented via a language compiler or interpreter. There is no reason why concepts cannot be implemented using similar capabilities. The concept $C = \{(x1,y1), , (xn, yn)\}$ can be constructed and manipulated using a hypothetical conceptual computer language or technology as follows:

C->x1 = y1;
C->x2 = y2;
....
C->xn = yn;

The semantics of "->" is similar to "." for Objects. It expresses the information association (or attribute). However, concept associations are dynamic as opposed to fixed object attributes. Additionally, the Concept construct (C) represents *pure* information: in reality, it does not need to implement any methods.

For example, consider the sentence: "please make a reservation":

```
Concept Sentence = new Concept ();
Sentence->proverb = "please";
Sentence->verb = "make";
Sentence->article = "a"
Sentence->object = "reservation"
```

Sentence->verb is the verb associated to the Sentence. Notice that the same concept (Sentence) can be used to represent any arbitrary sentence. Although every sentence is associated to the same concept, sentences can have all kind of structures. They may combine verbs, adjectives, adverbs, prepositions, and so on. The number of possibilities seems endless. A similar situation applies to the concepts of reservation and message.

Messages can have all kinds of forms. A traditional object, with a fixed number of attributes, is not a good fit to represent such dynamic entities. The issue comes down to the fact that not every concept represents a physical object. Like sentences, concepts do not consist of a fixed number of information associations. Concepts and objects are two separate abstractions – with different representations.

On the other hand, every physical object can be represented as a concept. Information associations are used to represent the attributes of the object. The mind works with mental representations of physical objects in the form of concepts. This discussion also helps illustrate another limitation of conventional APIs. A complete information model, such as the proposed model, must be able to accurately represent every single entity that exists in reality which consists of more than physical objects. Design patterns partially help bridge such gap because not every concept is a design pattern.

Since there is no conceptual computer language just yet, another mechanism needs to be created. Consider the human mind. Concepts are *manufactured* within our mind. There is a clear separation (decoupling) between the concept and the entity processing it. When the mind is building a concept or idea in the form of a sentence, it associates information to each part of the sentence (verb, proverb, etc). In a sense, the mind acts as a concept factory.

The same concept can be applied to computer software. A factory component can be responsible for creating (manufacturing) and managing the concept construct. The implementation of the Factory design pattern is suitable for this purpose. The factory needs to provide capabilities to create, read, update and delete information associations.

For convenience, the following primitives should be provided:

```
// Create or Update an information association
factory.setValue (Concept, attribute, value);

//Read an information association
value = factory.getValue (Concept, attribute);
```

The Sentence example would look like:

```
JtConcept Sentence = new JtConcept ();

factory.setValue(Sentence, "adverb", "please");
factory.setValue (Sentence, "verb", "make");
factory.setValue (Sentence, "article", "a");
factory.setValue (Sentence, "object", "reservation");
```

The second implementation is not as clear and compact as the one proposed earlier. On the hand, it can be implemented using any computer language.

The factory component will have to handle arbitrary Concepts: C= {(x1, y1), , (xn, yn)}. There are several potential implementations depending on the target language and the data structure chosen for the representation of the group of associations: array, list, hashtable, etc.

Notice the simplicity of the conceptual approach, every concept can be represented as a single language construct: Concept. No internal processing mechanism is required. A concept can be visualized as 'pure' information. A third party creates and manages the information associations. A concept is independent of language, platform, technology, data format, and so on.

## 2.10   Related Work

To fully grasp the proposed conceptual paradigm, you may need to rely on ideas from disciplines like philosophy [30], natural language processing [27, 35], knowledge representation [27, 24, 28], cognition [29, 30, 32, 33, 34] and artificial intelligence [25, 28]. These disciplines study concepts from several different perspectives and application domains. The proposed approach is mainly focused on the application of concepts to software engineering processes, technologies, and methodologies within a realistic information model. Some AI applications are covered as well. Also, the conceptual approach is different in several areas including overall realistic approach, abstractions, information model, single information primitive, mathematical model, assumptions, implementation, and consequences.

Computer technologies may use the term 'Concept' in a variety of scenarios. However it is usually employed vaguely to refer to general notions like in "software concepts". It may also be used with different semantics from the one presented. The term 'Concept', and its associated construct, have a precise mathematical definition within the context of the described realistic information model. Some of the problems related to traditional APIs (procedure calling and parameter passing) have been discussed by authors with expert knowledge of the matter [26]. The lack of "conceptual usefulness" is also discussed, in regards to "concepts that help us to formulate and reason about processes".

# 3.     Conceptual Design (CD)

A conceptual design is tackled from the information standpoint. Conceptualization is the key step of the design methodology which extracts all the concepts relevant to the application or problem domain. A conceptual design involves the following elements, principles, and methodology:

## 3.1     Elements

a) **Information (I):** the concept of information is a fundamental one. Our reality is defined by it. Computers are information processors like our minds able to store and process it. *Information* technologies need to view *every* aspect from the information standpoint. As a consequence, the universe of entities is divided into two categories: a) Entities that can process information (Animated/Live entities) b) Entities that cannot (Concepts).

b) **Animated/Live entities (A):** entities able to process information via the single information primitive: *processInformation (Message)*. They interact with other entities (animated/unanimated) as part of real-world processes. Animated or Live entities often utilize an independent processing mechanism. A memory subcomponent usually provides information persistency capabilities.

c) **Concept (C):** single language construct, based on information associations, that mimics the way in which conceptual information is represented and processed by the thinking mind. A Concept, represents pure information, and has a precise mathematical definition: $C = \{a1, a2, ,an\}$. Conceptual information is represented using this single construct. The information pattern family represents a complete and compact set of concepts. It also provides a classification for conceptual information.

d) **Information Association (a):** basic building block of information. A concept consists of a group of information associations: $C = \{a1, a2, , an\}$

e) **Information primitive:** primitive (*processInformation (message)*) that mimics the single function of the mind: processing of information.

f) **Messaging (M)**: ubiquitous natural concept that represents the interchange of information between Animated/Live entities. All modalities of messaging are modeled including synchronous, asynchronous and streaming. Messaging can be classified into two major categories depending on the type of information (i.e. message) being exchanged: conceptual and non-conceptual.

g) **Unanimated Objects (O).** Physical objects unable to process information. All of them can be represented as concepts (C).

h) **Process.** Animated/Live and unanimated entities interact and/or interchange information (i.e. messaging) in the real world, as part of natural or man-made processes. Such processes are modeled and simulated using the information process abstraction. In some instances, physical laws or concepts like Gravity and Force need to be modeled as part of real-world processes.

i) **Group (G).** Abstraction that represents a collection of concepts: $G = \{C1, C2, ,Cn\}$. It allows the grouping or organization of concepts into more complex information structures.

j) **Dialog.** Interchange of messaging between two or more Animated/Live entities. Usually, the interchange is accomplished in the form of concepts: conceptual interface. A conceptual interface represents a higher level of abstraction in terms of the messaging being exchanged. Human languages represent examples of conceptual interfaces. Advantages of conceptual communication, that can be mirrored, include efficiency, completeness, conciseness, expressiveness, and true realistic correspondence [30].

## 3.2    Principles

a) **Biomimetics.** The principle of Biomimetics is associated with the examination of nature, its models, systems, processes, and elements to emulate or take inspiration from, in order to solve human problems. An ideal design should faithfully include *all* natural concepts part of the reality being modeled. All the elements above are consistent with the principle of Biomimetics. Each one of them is mirrored from nature. This principle is fundamental because nature provides the golden standard in terms of unparalleled efficiency, effectivity, completeness, resiliency, and so on.

b) **Realism.** The concept of realism refers to the faithful pursue of a design, and associated implementation, that mirror reality without any artificial deviations, which usually result in shortcomings, weaknesses and/or inefficiencies. As a consequence, the overriding mindset must be based on design, concepts, assumptions, primitives that accurately mirror the reality being represented. An ideal design must be as close as possible to the real entity or process being modeled (correspondence Theory of Truth). Obviously, the proposed model is based on Realism which is consistent with Biomimetics principles. Realism also considers man-made processes and entities.

c) **Correspondence.** Based on the previous two principles, the conceptual design and its implementation should faithfully correspond to the reality being modeled which is in agreement with the philosophical correspondence Theory of Truth [30]. The principle of correspondence is consistent and tightly intertwined with the principles of Biomimetics and Realism. Keep in mind that physical entity, mental representation (Concept), and software implementation are three different aspects related to the same real entity. Ideally, all three related aspects should be in perfect correspondence with each other. Consistency and accuracy are concepts related to correspondence. There must be consistency/accuracy between how concepts appear in reality and the design.

d) **Completeness.** Based on the previous principles, an ideal design, and associated implementation, should include *all* the concepts relevant to the particular problem or area of reality being modeled. The concepts part of the information pattern family represent a complete set (Turing Complete) that can be leveraged for the comprehensive implementation of *arbitrary information* technologies. Notice that all information patterns (7) are part of the elements of conceptual design.

e) **Unity.** The principle of unity refers to the harmonic relationship among all the involved concepts that allow them to work cooperatively as a unit. Unity gives a sense of oneness. It also refers to the idea of cooperation between entities. All relevant concepts should fit together as part of a holistic Universe.

f) **Conceptual paradigm.** Computers are information processors like the conceptual mind, nature's pinnacle in terms of information processing. Based on the previous principles, we need to mirror the mind's conceptual approach and framework in order to gain substantial improvements. All the elements and principles above are consistent with a conceptual paradigm.

g) **Information perspective.** As stated earlier, information is the fundamental concept. An ideal design must be tacked from the standpoint of information. In particular, concepts carrying information, flows of information (i.e. messaging), and entities processing those concepts need to be identified as part of the design process. All the elements and principles of a conceptual design are related in one way or another with the fundamental concept.

## 3.3    Methodology

The conceptual design methodology consists of the following steps:

1) **Conceptualization.** Identify all the concepts (i.e. information items) relevant to the problem domain and application. All of them can be represented using a single language construct (Concept).

2) **Information Classification and Partitioning** (divide and conquer). Classify the information into smaller groups of related concepts, if required by the size of the problem/application domain. The responsibility for processing each group of related concepts is assigned to an Animated/Live component.

3) **Communication of Information (Messaging).** Identify the flows of information between the Animated/Live entities and design the associated conceptual interfaces (CI).

4) **Evaluation (optional).** Identify the group of concepts use to evaluate the design. If the design principles have been faithfully followed, natural qualities will be inherently part of the design: efficiency, effectivity, completeness, unity, correspondence (consistency), and so forth. Correspondence with natural elements will also ensure efficiency and efficacy. Other aspects will be readily absorbed from nature as well, including fault tolerance and reliability capabilities.

5) **Prioritization (optional).** Assign priorities to the concepts identified during conceptualization depending on the system requirements. Due to budget, timeframe, or technical constrains, you may need to assign priorities.

Notice that the design methodology happens to be consistent with the way in which the mind solves arbitrary problems: conceptualization, classification, communication, evaluation, and prioritizations are key aspects of the problem-solving process.

Conceptualization is the key step of the design methodology which extracts all the concepts relevant to the application or problem domain. The Conceptual Design approach is in harmony with standard software design methodologies. On the other hand, it introduces several key improvements including Biomimetics principles, software Realism, true correspondence based on Philosophical/Scientific grounds, Concept construct (C), single information primitive, conceptual paradigm, and information pattern family.

The aforementioned aspects represent main differentiators from traditional design approaches. In particular, the wall of separation between component and concept from the information standpoint: Animated/Live components are the only real entities able to process conceptual information. All the other entities are realistically represented as concepts (C) – pure information, without behavior. The small number of realistic concepts required for typical implementations (perhaps optimal) should also be emphasized since it significantly streamlines software design (i.e. conceptual design) and development processes.

All the improvements are a direct consequence of the mathematical model on which the conceptual paradigm is based. Also, we should carefully consider that nature and natural processes already have an inherent design to them. In order to achieve true correspondence and realism, we must mirror it as part of the software design. Obviously, there is no point in 'reinventing' a design that already exists as part of natural creation. Also, improving on nature's design is probably unrealistic.

On the other hand, imitation of the natural design via conceptualization is an attainable goal, consistent with Biomimetics, which produces substantial benefits in terms of software engineering processes and methodologies. A similar principle applies to man-made processes which already have and inherent design and may need to be automated as part of computer systems. Conceptualization incorporates the extraction of realistic concepts, relevant to the application, from natural and man-made reality.

It can be argued that some of the elements, abstractions, and principles above are already part of design methodologies. It is true up to a certain point. On the order hand, there are several key differences in terms of elements, principles, and methodology. In particular regarding realistic correspondence, consistency, completeness, and unity.

Design patterns are ubiquitous concepts. On the other hand, not every concept is a design pattern or an object. Although concepts can be specified and studied using design pattern methodologies, there are several key differences between both abstractions. The conceptual paradigm has an impact on how design patterns are conceptualized and implemented specifically in terms of pattern participants/collaboration: components, concepts (pure information), and messaging/conceptual interfaces.

Several examples will be presented where technologies designed using more traditional methodologies are unable to achieve correspondence with the principles and elements outlined above – and therefore with reality. As a consequence, drawbacks and limitations become evident:
1) Traditional OO APIs
2) Distributed artifacts like IDL, WSDL, RPC, descriptors, and stubs.
3) Multithreading
4) Business Process Technologies (BPM/BPEL)

Consider the following quote: "We can note in passing that one of the **biggest problems** in the development of object-oriented SW architectures, particularly in the last 25 years, has been an enormous over-focus on objects and an under-focus on messaging (most so-called object-oriented languages *don't really* use the looser coupling of **messaging**, but instead use the much tighter *gear meshing of procedure calls* – this hurts scalability and interoperability)." Alan Kay et al.

As a rule of thumb, if the abstraction is not part of the *natural* language, it is probably a redundant artifact that is not really necessary or beneficial. Tradition APIs based on "gear meshing of procedure calls" fail to meet several of the principles above including Biomimetics, realism, unity, and correspondence. Obviously, they also fail to recognize and incorporate a ubiquitous design element: the concept of messaging.

As a consequence of the lack of messaging, distributed artifacts present disadvantages, limitations, and redundancy. They are also based on *"gear meshing of procedure calls"*. Again, the principles of correspondence, realism, Biomimetics, and completeness are not met. Distributed artifacts although artificial, achieve communication and therefore a limited level of realism when compared with the messaging abstraction: the *real* concepts. The implementation should also mirror the reality being represented. The term messaging is often employed loosely in the context of distributed technologies. On the other hand, the term is not used accurately since such technologies are fully or partially based on distributed artifacts: *gear meshing of procedure calls*.

The term 'multithreading' is not part of the natural language. It is an artificial abstraction (artifact). The principles of Biomimetics, realism, and correspondence are not met. The realistic concept is concurrency. Animated/Live entities operate independently and concurrently. From the information standpoint, these entities are able to process information concurrently (in parallel).

We should also note that the concept of concurrency is tightly intertwined with the concept of Animated/Live entities (unity, correspondence, completeness, and so on). In other words, concurrency usually happens when there is a group of entities working cooperatively. In such cases, Animated/Live entities must be part of a realistic design and implementation. Messaging is also related to concurrency and Live/Animated entities since it is the only realistic mechanism of communication: information is transferred via messaging in order to be processed.

Traditional BPEL/BPM process technologies are based on multithreading, distributed artifacts, and traditional APIs which bring forth shortcomings and limitations[2,4]. They are also based on artificial primitives that do not correspond with natural reality and introduce unnecessary redundancy. As stated earlier, several design principles are not met. In particular, the ones discussed previously. The information process, part of the information pattern family, provides a realistic solution.

The technologies above should illustrate the improvements provided by using the conceptual design methodology, elements, and principles. A conceptual design would have identified the natural concepts and avoided artificial abstractions. Artifacts would have never been considered as part of the design and subsequent implementation. A model missing key concepts, like messaging, would not be acceptable: *incomplete model.*

The provided examples should clearly illustrate key differences between conceptual design and traditional design methodologies. Specifically, in terms of key elements and principles. The simplification in terms of the software components should also be mentioned. In reality, most entities are unable to process information and should be realistically represented as pure information using a single language construct (Concept).

Assume for a moment that you are assigned the task of designing a new OO technology or framework. One of the software requirements would probably look like the following.

**Requirement:** the system needs to provide communication capabilities between local and remote components/applications. SOA service capabilities need to be implemented as well.

As part of the first step of the design methodology, let us conceptualize the requirement by relying on the information provided. A key concept here is "communication". If you look in the dictionary, you will find the definition to be related to the idea of interchanging information: *messaging.* By studying the requirement, the problem can be conceptualized and the ubiquitous/natural concept of messaging extracted which meets the principles of conceptual design.

40

In general, every time that "communication" or similar concepts are found, messaging must be included as part of the conceptualization step. From the information standpoint, "communication" refers to communication of information: messaging.

Conceptually, SOA services are covered as well because a *service is provided by a remote component*. Obviously, from the information standpoint, a service is a concept. There needs to be an associated component (Animated/Live entity) to provide a specific SOA service. The concepts of service and Animated/Live entity (service provider) are tightly intertwined. By meeting the first part of the previous requirement, SOA service capabilities are also provided [2]. In general, any Animated/Live component can be transparently exposed as a SOA service. Strictly speaking, and since a service represents a concept, any Animated/Live component can be exposed *to provide* a SOA service. Faithful correspondence to reality is required when describing how the different elements are related to each other (principles of Correspondence and Unity).

**Requirement:** components should be able to process information concurrently. In other words, tasks should be able to be performed in parallel.

Implicitly, tasks need to be performed by an active party: Animated/Live entity. Both concepts are tightly intertwined (Unity, Correspondence). From the information standpoint, we are talking about concurrent processing of information by Animated/Live entities. Obviously, based on the principles of conceptual design, we should observe how concurrency occurs in nature. Specifically, in the context of the problem and/or application at hand.

In order to conceptualize an arbitrary problem, it is good idea to rely on the classification of concepts provided by the information pattern family. You should be able to quickly assign a category or class to a specific concept. It also provides you with a complete set of concepts to choose from while conceptualizing a particular problem, application, or technology. The information family can be used as a checklist to identify and classify the concepts relevant to the problem domain.

**Requirement**: design a banking system.

From the information standpoint, a banking application needs to deal with many entities, all of which can be represented as concepts: accounts, transactions, statements and so forth. Few components are required in order to process the involved concepts, which substantially simplifies design and implementation. No redundant abstractions and primitives are required. Heterogeneous banking systems are able to transparently exchange information represented as concepts (C).

**Requirement:** add the concept construct (C) to your programming language or technology of choice.

Based on CD principles, in order to implement the abstraction you should attempt to mirror the concepts used by the mind. First of all, you should recognize that in reality a concept represents pure information (mental representation) without any information processing capabilities. One *single* construct is required to represent arbitrary conceptual information.

Since the mind acts like a factory of concepts, the language construct should be manipulated via a Factory implementation or similar component. A Concept has a precise semantics and mathematical definition: $C = \{a1, a2, , an\}$. It consists of a group of information associations. The proposed sketch design meets all the principles of conceptual design: Biomimetics, Realism, Correspondence, Completeness, and so on. In particular, the design has been performed from the standpoint of *information*.

Sometimes during the conceptualization process, you can find key concepts as part of the problem statement. Some of the problems related to traditional APIs (procedure calling and parameter passing) have been discussed by authors with comprehensive insight into the matter [26].

**Problem:** The lack of "conceptual usefulness" exhibited by traditional programming in regards to "concepts that help us to formulate and reason about processes" [26].

If you think conceptually, the problem statement contains the key to its solution. They key words are "conceptual" and "concepts". Concepts and the associated conceptual paradigm represent the solution to the problem. Also, as part of a solution, the idea of a conceptual computer language should be discussed. Consider the following requirement:

**Requirement**: implementation of a new conceptual computer language.

Bear in mind the wide variety of applications for such conceptual language: user interfaces, AI, robotics, health care systems, IVR, information search engines (web, DB), mobile, and so on. In general, such language can be applied to a large variety of automated devices and computer systems.

As usual, nature has already provided the best available model and solution: natural language. Based on Biomimetics, the challenge becomes accurately mirroring it. Conceptually, the way we instruct computers and robotic systems to perform tasks do not need to be different from how intelligent beings are instructed. The same concepts apply to both scenarios: information, messaging, conversation subject, context, message, procedure, task, and the other concepts found in reality. Obviously, both situations are conceptually equivalent or isomorphic. Consider that procedures and concepts represent pure information and therefore they represent something that you *learn*. In other words, conceptual knowledge (information) is acquired by *learning* new concepts and procedures based on associations with concepts already mastered. Based on the principles of correspondence and unity, the concept of procedure is associated with the concept of learning.

Within the previous context, the proposed approach represents a paradigm shift since a procedure is not a method/function that needs to be implemented but information that can be learned based on concepts already known. You do not program the system, you *teach* the system via the proposed conceptual language. Such language would have a significant impact on many areas of computing. A language is also a 'living entity' that keeps evolving by incorporating new words and concepts based on existing ones. The same principles can be applied to computer and robotic systems by mirroring the conceptual approach taken by natural languages.

43

A conceptual computer language is discussed in detail as part of another chapter, based on the following Turing-complete mathematical model:

a) **Information primitive**: Single Turing-complete function *processInformation (message)* where the message represents information in the form of a Concept (C)

b) **Concept**: Single language Construct C = {a1,a2, ,an} where a1,a2, an, are information associations.

An Information/Mathematical machine is a Turing-Complete automatic machine (A) able to perform computations via the information primitive which defines the machine's single function or purpose.

**Requirement**: design a machine able to process information – a computer.

Although somewhat vague, the requirement provides a *good idea* of what is needed. *If* we think in conceptual terms, and follow the CD design methodology, we should be able to derive the mathematical model directly from the requirement written in the natural language. It should give you a sense of the expressiveness, conciseness, and power of the natural language as the ultimate tool for transferring information – a match for the conceptual mind that hosts it. Based on Biomimetics and Realism principles, you should realize that information is processed in the form of packets of information (i.e. messages). In other words, the concept of information is tightly associated with the concepts of messaging and message because they represent how information is transferred in the natural world (Correspondence and Unity).

The requirement can be made as specific and complete as needed by adding more information to it.

**Requirement**: design a machine able to process information – a computer. Information is communicated through messaging (message form). It can be processed based on the following operations: store, retrieve, update, delete, logical processing.

The requirement can be conceptualized based on the proposed elements, principles, and methodology. It contains all the relevant concepts: machine, information, processing of information, message, messaging, concept (C), and operations. Notice the realistic one-to-one correspondence between the extracted concepts and the mathematical model. A complex problem has been *reduced (i.e. conceptualized)* to a compact and complete set of implementable concepts by relying on the proposed methodology. No redundant abstractions or primitives are included. Actually, the same concepts are required for the implementation of any arbitrary *information* technology or computer system. The solution and associated computing model can be expressed with mathematical simplicity, precision, and completeness – naturally. The scenarios presented should also illustrate the qualities of a conceptual design, and the conceptualization step in particular.

Thinking conceptually, when it comes to computer technologies, may require practice and training. However, the mind is especially 'engineered' for such purpose. Obviously, you must think in terms of abstractions. The conceptual level represents a higher level of abstraction. People may need to get started by relying on the elements, principles, and methodology provided. If your mind has fully grasped the concept, welcome to the conceptual paradise … sorry, I meant conceptual paradigm. It exists inside your mind. Have fun with it. By the way, the principles, methodology and some of the elements discussed are not limited to the realm of software engineering or computing. They can be leveraged for meeting design challenges in arbitrary domains, and engineering in particular – outside the current scope. Concepts are applied by the mind across the board.

All the examples above illustrate the impact of an approach based on the conceptual paradigm and the associated Turing-complete mathematical model.

# 4.    MATHEMATICAL MODEL  (Information and Conceptual Machines)

There are three (3) main concepts involved as part of the mathematical model which was initially introduced as part of a related paper [8].

a) **Information Machine (A):** An automatic machine able to perform computations via the information primitive which defines the machine's single function (or purpose). The machine A is defined by a two-tuple A= *(processInformation(message)*, I). A is Turing complete. It can also be expressed as *A= (f(m), I)*, where *f* represents any computable function*).

b) **Information (I, M):** processed in the forms of messages (M), also called information packets or chunks (IC). A message (M) is expressed by a n-tuple M= (b1, , bn) where b1, , bn are symbols in a finite set of symbols (alphabet $(\Sigma)$). Information machines include a memory subcomponent able to store and retrieve information. The information stored (i.e. known) by the machine is represented by I = (IC1, ,ICn), where IC1, ,ICn are information chunks (or packets). ICi = $(b_{i1},$ , $b_{in})$; $b_{i1},$ , $b_{in} \in \Sigma$; i = [1.. n].

c) **Information  primitive**: *processInformation  (message)* represents a function *f*: $\Sigma^* \to \Sigma^*$

Information machines (with memory), also known as A-machines, are Turing complete. Additionally, information machines can have several modalities.

a) **InformationMachine/Component:**

   $A = (f(m),$ I). The machine may consist of a group of Animated/Live components (ACs) working concurrently:

   $A = \{AC_1,$ ,$AC_n\}$. Each individual component can be represented using the information component abstraction as well: $ACi=(f(m),$ *I)*. The same mathematical concept is recursively applicable to the machine and all its components which may in turn consist of subcomponents.

b) **Information Machine without memory:**

   $A = (f(m))$. No information (I) is stored by the machine.

c) **Conceptual Machine:** machine able to process conceptual information (C). For processing purposes, messages $(M = (b1, , bn))$ are transformed into its equivalent (C) representation.

d) **Boole's Conceptual Machine:** conceptual machine capable of logical reasoning as defined by the deductive approach. It can be expressed as $A=(\beta(m), I.)$, where the function $\beta(m)$ represents logical processing of information, applied to incoming messages (m), as defined by Boole's Algebra of Logic (Laws of Thought!). It consists of a single main component, logical engine (LE), whose function $\beta$ $(m)$ has been substantially simplified (i.e. narrowed) in terms of its scope. Logical capabilities provide the foundation for other cognitive abilities including language learning/processing, decision making, and problem solving.

Information itself (I) can be classified into two categories: conceptual (C) and non-conceptual. The following definitions apply to conceptual information.

a) **Concept (C):** conceptual information expressed by a single language Construct, $C = \{a1, a2, , an\}$ where $a1, a2, , an$ are information associations.

b) **Information association (a):** $a_i$ is an association of the form (xi, yi), meaning that xi is equal or associated to yi (xi = yi) where xi and yi are defined as follows.
   - $xi = (b1, , bn)$; $b_i \in \sum$; $i = [1 .. n]$, or xi represents a concept as defined by C.
   - $yi = (b1, , bn)$; $b_i \in \sum$; $i = [1 .. n]$, or yi represents a concept as defined by C.

c) **Language (L):** Conceptual machines process messages that are constructed based on a Language (L) which consists of a set of symbols (i.e. words) and their associated definitions. L = {(symbol1, Definition (symbol1)), , (symboln, Definition (symboln))} where each symbol is an information chunk (or packet) as defined above: $symbol_i = (b1, , bn)$. The meaning (i.e. semantics) of each symbol is provided by its lexicographic definition: Definition (symbol) represents a function $f: \sum^* \rightarrow \sum^*$

d) **Sentence (S):** a sentence in the language (L) is a concept (C): S = {a1, a2 , an} where a1, a2, an are information associations.

e) **Procedure (P):**  a procedure is a concept (C) defined as a sequence of steps to be executed: $P = \{S1, , Sn\}$ where each step (or statement) is expressed in the form of a sentence (S) in the language (L).

f) **Conceptual Knowledge (K):** The conceptual portion of the information contained in the memory subcomponent can be expressed as $K = \{C1, , Cn\}$. Each chunk of conceptual information $(IC = (b1, ,bn))$ is transformed into its equivalent (C) representation. K consists of all the concepts known to the machine including procedures (P), and language information (L).

In summary, the model consists of following three (3) main concepts: machine (A), information (M,I) and processing of information as defined by a single mathematical function: *f(m)* or *processInformation (message)*. It should become obvious why information is the fundamental concept behind the model. A complex problem has been reduced, via conceptualization, to a complete and streamlined set of implementable concepts as part of a straightforward solution. Computer software based on traditional computing models is unnecessarily complex since nature's conceptual mind, as modeled here, is beautifully simple – which is consistent with Biomimetics principles and Occam's razor.

The concept of messaging is implicit and obviously tightly intertwined with the concepts of information (I) and message (M). Without messaging, information is unable to be transferred (i.e. travel) and the machine is unable to interact with its environment. Conceptual information introduces several additional entities: Language (L), Sentence (S), Procedure (P), Conceptual Knowledge (K), and Concept (C). Notice that all of them represent concepts themselves. For instance, language (L), procedures (P) and sentences (S) are concepts and can be represented using the (C) construct.

To visualize the natural concepts involved you may want to think about the human mind and the associated entities. Obviously, since the model attempts to mirror the mind, there is a realistic *one-to-one* correspondence. Notice that the mind serves a dual purpose and it is able to manipulate both non-conceptual and conceptual information. Non-conceptual information consists of entities like images, sounds, smells, flavors, and tactile sensations that do not carry conceptual information. For instance, the image or sounds associated to a familiar pet. On the other hand, images and sounds often carry concepts (C). For example, in the case of written/spoken sentences. In such case, the message (image/sound) needs to be transformed into its conceptual representation (C) during processing by the mind.

Obviously, the ability to process conceptual information is highly developed in human beings. It makes us unique since animals lack such level of cognitive abilities. As usual, nature is leading the way in terms of a paradigm for computing and information processing: conceptual paradigm. Due to its simplicity and expressiveness, the mathematical model is being introduced early to facilitate the explanation of the subsequent chapters. It is also very intuitive, based on abstractions that everyone can relate to and readily grasp.

# 5.    LIVE OR ANIMATED ENTITIES ($A = (f(m), I)$)

## 5.1    Intent

Live or Animated entities are able to process information and exhibit independent behavior – a "life of their own", so to speak. This abstraction encapsulates functionality, information, and processing (threading) mechanism required to provide the component with its independent behavior. In particular, it relies on its own independent processing mechanism or thread of execution.

Live/Animated entities improve decoupling, encapsulation, reusability and scalability while at the same time reducing overall complexity. Functionality, processing/treading mechanism, and messaging mechanism are decoupled entities, independent of one another. Messaging allows the interchange of information (i.e. messages) between the Live/Animated entity and other parts of the system. Although decoupled and independent of one another, processing/threading mechanism and component functionality are completely encapsulated within a single entity.

## 5.2    Applicability

This abstraction can be applied in a wide variety of scenarios. Live or Animated entities are all around us in the real world. Living beings, computers, automated systems, machines and subcomponents of these entities represent a few examples. All these entities are able to process information, exhibit an independent behavior, and therefore can be modeled as *Live* or *Animated* entities. Messaging is the mechanism of communication between Live/Animated entities and their external environment, including other entities, systems, and applications. This approach is not only realistic; it also handles many of the complexities associated with the implementation of traditional multithreaded and distributed applications.

From an information standpoint, Live/Animated entities represent 'information processors': information machines. In consequence, all these entities can be modeled using a common and straightforward mathematical foundation: $A = (f(m), I)$. From a mathematical and conceptual perspective, it can be said that both abstractions are equivalent. Notice also that the concept of Live/Animated entity has a precise mathematical definition – equivalent to the one given to information machines. For additional details, please refer to the chapter dealing with Information/Conceptual machines. Most of this section will be dedicated to Live/Animated *components* which represent the software/OO implementation of the information machine abstraction.

Because they share the same concepts, the Turing-complete mathematical model applies to all levels of organization: a component, a process, an application, a system, a computer, and arbitrary groups of these entities. It provides a complete mathematical foundation for every level. For instance, a component can be modeled using its precise mathematical definition (Live/Animated entity): $A = (f(m), I)$. So can a full-blown computer $(A = (f(m), I))$. A process/system/application can be mathematically modeled as a collection of these Live/Animated entities $(\{A_1, , A_n\}$ where $(A_i = (f_i(m), I)))$ working concurrently (or in parallel) and communicating via messaging.

## 5.3    Motivation

The implementation of traditional multithreaded and distributed applications is a complex undertaking which usually becomes costly, time consuming and prone to error. Quality defects related to multithreading are often encountered (thread management, synchronization, race conditions, deadlocks, etc). These software defects are difficult to avoid, reproduce and isolate.

Large multithreaded applications and/or implementation teams complicate the problem even further. The degree of complexity and risk considerably worsens as the number of threads and their interactions increases. When computers, smartphones, cars, and computerized systems in general, apparently experience random failures, it should not come as a surprise if the root causes are associated with complex multithreading defects. The quality issues become crucial when the software happens to be controlling mission critical applications.

Traditional Multithreading is widely employed as part of software applications. For instance, a banking application may need to model a teller component able to process multiple banking transactions concurrently. There will probably be several distributed teller components or threads running independently within the context of a banking application. Another real world example would be a highly interactive smartphone applications able to concurrently speak, recognize voice, play music, manage the graphical user interface while performing other operations (phone calls, text messages, notifications, alarms, GPS, etc). Multiple threads of execution are required. No single thread is allowed to monopolize the cpu for long periods of time, otherwise the offending thread may be forced to stop.

The conventional solution for general purpose applications, and in particular for the examples presented above, is based on multithreading. As mentioned earlier, multithreaded applications present a wide variety of challenges and problems including:

a) Complexity dealing with thread management, synchronization, race conditions, deadlocks, etc.

b) Strong coupling which ties the solution to a specific platform, multithreading technology and/or application language.

c) Lack of encapsulation since the threading mechanism is usually implemented as a separate object. A single thread may also be 'artificially' associated with multiple objects.

d) Lack of reusability which usually results from strong coupling, lack of encapsulation, and the inability to provide reusable threading functionality as part of a framework.

e) Complex quality issues brought about by the previous challenges which get compounded and harder to manage as the number of threads and/or team members increases. f) Scalability and interoperability limitations.

g) Quality/testing Issues.     Testing of traditional multithreaded applications can be a complex and challenging activity. It is fairly easy to introduce bugs. On the other hand, it can be fairly difficult and time consuming to avoid, reproduce, catch, and fix bugs within the context of traditional multithreaded applications. Large multithreaded applications complicate the problem further. Bugs may appear sporadically under very specific multithreading conditions that are hard to avoid and reproduce.

Object-oriented applications consist of a collection of components that interact with each other. In reality, some of these components should be modeled as Live/Animated components: they exhibit independent behavior, a "life of their own". Notice that the teller component should encapsulate the component functionality and the processing mechanism as two independent concerns within the component. On the other hand, they are both part of a single component (teller) and should not be artificially modeled as separate entities. In general, the implementation of a Live/Animated component calls for one single thread which provides the processing mechanism. Messaging provides the mechanism of communication.

A realistic software model capable of providing comparable functionality to arbitrary multithreaded applications would consist of several Live/Animated components communicating with each other via messaging. This solution avoids and solves many of the issues associated with comparable multithreaded applications including complexity, coupling, lack of encapsulation, limited reusability, scalability limitations, and overall implementation costs.

## 5.4    Participants

a) **Live/Animated component (receiver):** encapsulates functionality and independent processing/threading mechanism which provides the component with the ability to process information and its characteristic independent behavior (Fig. 1-3). Live/Animated components communicate with other components via messaging: components, message and messaging mechanism are decoupled, encapsulated and fully independent. All forms of messaging are modeled including synchronous (Fig. 3), asynchronous, streaming, distributed messaging, two-way messaging, secure messaging, and combinations of these forms

b) **Message Sender**: component that sends the message.

c) **Messenger:** intermediary that transfers the message from the sender to the Live/Animated component (Fig. 1). It is often the case that the messenger is not required (Fig. 2). The message can be sent directly to the Live/Animated component.

d) **Message:** any piece of information (i.e. data) that needs to be interchanged between sender and recipient. Two messages are usually involved: input message and output message (or reply message). The reply message is not required.

e) **Asynchronous Message Queue:** internal subcomponent used to enqueue the incoming messages (Fig. 1-2). The component relies on a queuing mechanism to store the incoming messages being sent asynchronously. The component's thread or processing mechanism dequeues the messages and processes them one at a time. A Conceptual framework usually implements the logic required to manage the component thread and the message queue. The component only needs to inherit this functionality from a framework superclass.

## 5.5    Structure

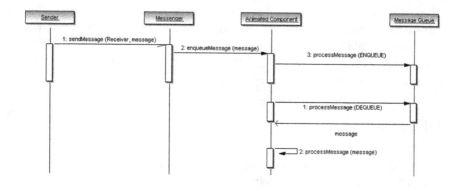

**Figure 1. Live or Animated component (with a messenger)**

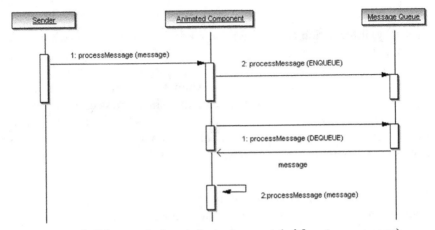

**Figure 2. Live or Animated component (without messenger).**

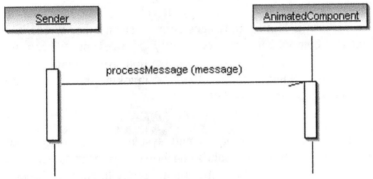

**Figure 3. Live/Animated component and synchronous messaging. All modalities of messaging are modeled.**

## 5.6 Collaboration

Live/Animated entities rely on messaging which is another concept that seeks to accurately mirror reality. Independent Live/Animated entities interact with each other and interchange information (i.e. messaging) within the context of predefined processes (Fig. 1-3). Live/Animated components rely on messaging as the realistic mechanism of communication with other components and applications. Sender, receiver, message, and messaging mechanism are decoupled entities, encapsulated and fully independent. Each of these aspects can be changed independently without impacting the others.

In reality, information (messages) can take many forms all of which can be modeled using computer software and the messaging concept: a number, an email message, a document, a spoken sentence, energy, biochemical message, and so on. Live/Animated components can also be incorporated into distributed applications, since messaging provides transparent access to distributed components as part of a complete distributed component model (Turing complete) – distributed components are treated as local ones.

In the case of asynchronous communication, Live/Animated components require a queuing mechanism to store incoming messages: enqueueMessage(message). A message is added to the asynchronous message queue directly or via a messenger (Fig. 1-2). The Live/Animated component processes incoming messages, one at a time, via its independent thread of execution. It relies on the information primitive to process incoming messages (Fig. 1-2). In other words, the Live/Animated component is constantly processing incoming information via its independent thread of execution, which mainly waits for incoming messages and processes them by invoking the information primitive (*processMessage (message)*).

Consider your short term memory, email system, postal mailbox or message recording machine. Messages can be sent asynchronously and placed in a message queue or pile until you are ready to "process" them. Animated/Live components are able to mimic this behavior and handle the complexities associated with asynchronous messaging, multithreading, distributed component access, security and so forth. A teller component, local or distributed, should be able to readily process messages associated to banking transactions (deposits, withdrawals, account balance, etc.)

## 5.7    Consequences

**Encapsulation.** The proposed abstraction improves encapsulation. Component functionality, information (I), and processing/threading mechanism are encapsulated into a single entity. They should not be artificially modeled as separate objects. It should be fairly obvious that the Live/Animated entity $(A = (f(m), I))$ is a fully encapsulated and independent entity.

**Coupling.** Decoupling is improved. Component functionality, processing/treading mechanism, and messaging mechanism are decoupled. Each one can be modified independently without impacting the others. Also, the processing or threading mechanism is decoupled from the calling component. The rest of the components in the system do not need to know how the processing mechanism of the Live/Animated component is implemented. There is no dependency between the calling component and this mechanism. The processing/threading mechanism can be changed freely without impacting the calling component. Decoupling is also improved as a direct consequence of using messaging as the communication mechanism and abstraction. Each component is a self-contained unit that can perform independently from the rest of the system. It should be obvious that the Live/Animated entity $(A = (f(m), I))$ is fully decoupled from its environment.

**Reusability.** Live/Animated entities improve reusability. The calling application is able to readily reuse a component that encapsulates functionality and threading/processing mechanism. It does not need to re-implement or become overly concerned as to how the threading/processing mechanism and asynchronous messaging are implemented. It also feasible to reuse components based on heterogeneous technologies and languages within the context of the same process. This is possible because Live/Animated components are fully encapsulated entities, decoupled and independent.

The processing/threading functionality should be implemented within the context of a Conceptual framework which also improves reusability. Live/Animated components can inherit and reuse the framework functionality. There is no need to re-implement it for each animated component to be involved, as opposed to traditional multithreaded applications.

**Abstraction level.** Live/Animated entities use a higher level or abstraction closer to the reality being represented: conceptual level. The proposed abstraction represents a living or an animated entity able to process information independently (information processor).

The Live/Animated entity ($A = (f(m), I)$) represents a single encapsulated entity from the point of view of the calling component, system, or application. The processing mechanism or thread of execution is inherently associated to the animated component.

**Traditional Multithreaded applications.** Live/Animated components constitute the building blocks required to assemble production quality applications, comparable in functionality to traditional multithreaded applications. On the hand, software processes are improved in terms of complexity, reusability, encapsulation, coupling, and so on. As a consequence, implementation time, quality, and cost are also improved.

**Component based frameworks and UML/BPM/BPEL tools.** Live/Animated components can be readily incorporated into UML/BPM/BPEL diagrams in order to design and implement complex applications. Notice that for components to be incorporated, in a straightforward fashion, they need to share the same interface. Messaging represents such interface.

**Distributed model and applications.** Live/Animated components can be used to assemble distributed applications. Conceptually, sending a message to a remote Live/Animated component is not different from sending a message to a local one.

**Conceptual Component Frameworks.** As mentioned earlier, the processing/threading mechanism should be implemented within the context of a Conceptual framework. This is feasible and recommended as a best practice. Management of the threading mechanism becomes responsibility of the framework. It involves thread creation, management, destruction, message queue synchronization, etc. Live/Animated components can inherit and reuse the framework functionality. There is no need to re-implement it for each component involved which is one of the reasons behind improvement in reusability, cost, quality, timeframes, and overall quality.

**Quality Assurance/Testing process.** Live/Animated components facilitate testing and debugging efforts. Components can be tested as independent units by sending messages to the component and verifying the expected reply messages (black-box testing). Because functionality and threading mechanisms are decoupled, the component functionality can be tested separately via synchronous messaging (single thread). Keep in mind that the main difference between synchronous and asynchronous messaging is the queuing mechanism required.

In general, functionality can be tested without using the asynchronous queuing mechanism, one message at a time. Threading capabilities and testing of such capabilities are usually ensured by the Conceptual frameworks that implements messaging. In general, only the component functionality, without multithreading considerations, needs to be thoroughly tested. A good Conceptual framework should ensure the quality of the threading and messaging implementation which are reused by the Live/Animated component.

**Race conditions and deadlocks.** By removing multithreading artifacts/APIs, race conditions and deadlocks are avoided. Keep in mind that the queuing mechanism ensures that messages are placed in the queue and processed sequentially by the Live/Animated component. The queuing mechanism also ensures that access to the shared resource (message queue) is properly controlled.

**Fault tolerance.** Live/Animated components ($A = f(m), I)$) can readily emulate state machines. Therefore, they can be extended to provide fault-tolerant capabilities in a very natural fashion by replicating components/messaging and coordinating their interaction via consensus algorithms [6,16]. Please refer to the chapter dealing with a Distributed Component/Service Model (fault-tolerant capabilities).

**Conceptual paradigm and learning curve.** In order to take advantage of the proposed concept, people need to think in terms of realistic abstractions when they model, design and build software applications. This may require learning time and training. Although a realistic model is natural, intuitive, and consistent with the real world, conventional multithreaded applications are based on method/procedure invocation and traditional multithreading capabilities.

Keep in mind that natural concepts have many qualities. Therefore it is challenging to find drawbacks associated with these entities, which is unexpected within the context of design patterns. A similar situation occurs when we look at other natural concepts that may be part of our software model, like Gravity and Force. Based on observation and faith, the Creator has a knack for perfection: "... the wondrous works of the One perfect in knowledge." The proposed abstraction is best studied and understood from the standpoint of Concepts where finding trade-offs is not as critical and perhaps unfeasible. Please see Comparison with Related Software Models.

**Overhead.** Transferring messages between components and handling a message queue introduces a small overhead when compared with traditional method/procedure invocation. As computers become faster this becomes less of an issue. Also, the benefits of the proposed abstraction and framework outweigh this performance cost.

**Pool of Live/Animated components**. Manipulating large numbers of concurrent Live/Animated components may prove to be computationally expensive since each component is associated with an independent thread. For this particular scenario, we may need to consider a design based on a pool of Live/Animated components in order to control the total number of threads running concurrently. Animated components can be created and destroyed as needed, in order to limit the total number of these entities running concurrently.

**Language limitations.** Not every computer language, especially an older one, implements concurrency or is able to deal with it efficiently. The proposed abstraction is best suited for modern technologies and object-oriented computer languages. Synchronous messaging, on the other hand, supports legacy technologies.

## 5.8    Known uses

**Design patterns:** Animated or Live components have been used to implement and/or facilitate the implementation of other well-known design patterns like Gang of Four design patterns (GoF), J2EE Design patterns, Master-Worker and MVC. Consider that Animated/Live entities are present in a variety of scenarios and that many pattern implementations may have to deal with concurrency and asynchronous messaging. For instance, a Command pattern implementation may need to process concurrent requests coming from several components within a traditional multithreaded application. The pattern implementation can use Live/Animated components as the basis for a realistic and comparable implementation. A MVC implementation may require model, view, and controller to be implemented as three separate Live/Animated components interchanging messaging asynchronously. Such scenario is common in the context of mobile applications running under Android.

**Component and Conceptual Frameworks:** The proposed abstraction can be used to build reusable component and conceptual frameworks. Again, consider that the Live/Animated entities are ubiquitous in the real world. Applications often require them for a realistic design and implementation. Once the abstraction is implemented (one time) as part of the framework, it can be reused over and over again to provide concurrency and asynchronous messaging capabilities. Such degree of reusability has a positive impact on overall complexity, cost, timeframe and quality.

**Distributed component and service model (SOA):** Live/Animated components are well suited for the implementation of a complete distributed component/services model and related distributed applications. Conceptually, communicating with a remote Live/Animated component is not very different from communicating with a local one since messaging is being leveraged. Actually, the Live/Animated component does not need to do anything special to support distributed access. The component is the same; no additional artifacts or logic are required. The Conceptual framework provides the communication infrastructure to convey distributed messages to remote components. The proposed abstraction helps deal with a whole set of problems associated with multithreading in the context of distributed applications.

**BPM/BPEL processes and technologies:** The proposed abstraction has been readily reused for the implementation of BPEL/BPM technologies, frameworks and processes. Actually, the set of abstractions provided by the information pattern family mirrors the set of entities found in processes of everyday life. They can be reused, in very natural ways, to implement complete BPEL/BPM technologies and processes. By doing so, the overall design and implementation are simplified.

Complicated process issues related to scalability, concurrency, distributed access, asynchronous messaging, security, and so on are handled by the proposed abstractions as part of a reusable and complete information infrastructure.

## 5.9    Related Patterns

As mentioned earlier, the implementation of several other design patterns may call for concurrency capabilities and asynchronous messaging. A robust model and implementation should include Live/Animated components to provide comparable functionality. In general, any design pattern participant can be potentially modeled using the live component abstraction by simply inheriting functionality from a Conceptual framework (AnimatedComponent superclass).   Command, Observer, Mediator, Decorator, Model View Controller (MVC) and J2EE Business Delegate are some examples of design patterns that can benefit from using the Live/Animated component abstraction since it accurately mirrors reality. Traditional approaches usually require that their participants reimplement multithreading and/or asynchronous messaging capabilities. A separate chapter includes a detailed comparison with related approaches.

## 5.10    Implementation

The Animated/Live entity ($A = (f(m), I)$) can be implemented using an OO component and the messaging interface (JtInterface). The interface consists of a single information primitive to process the input message and produce a reply message. It acts as a universal messaging interface that applies to remote and local components. It also applies to all modalities of messaging: synchronous, asynchronous, streaming, distributed messaging, two-way messaging, secure messaging, and combinations of these forms. The interface handles any type of message. It returns a reply (of any type).

The proposed implementation is mainly a reference implementation of the Animated/Live entity ($A = (f(m), I)$) and there are other potential implementations of the concept. In Java, the messaging interface can be declared as follows:

*public interface JtInterface { Object processMessage (Object message); }*

The generic type Object is used which is similar to the implementation of common design patterns (Iterator, for instance). In reality, the component may only be able to process and return specific types of message. In that case, appropriate types may be specified. For instance:

*public interface MyMessagingInterface {*
  *MyOutputType processMessage (MyInputType message); }*

The interface above is also a valid implementation of messaging. Advanced object-oriented technologies provide features like Java generics which allow the types to be parameterized:

*public interface JtInterface<Type, Type1> { Type1 processMessage (Type msg); }*

Notice that arbitrary computer languages can be used to implement messaging, including plain old java objects (POJOs):

*public  Object processMessage (Object message)*

Live/Animated components also require a mechanism to enqueue messages: *enqueueMessage(message)*. The Live/Animated component processes these messages using its own independent thread: messages are dequeued, one at a time, and processed using the information primitive *(processMessage(message))*. Notice that several execution threads have concurrent access to the messaging queue: the component is able to receive messaging from multiple components concurrently. Therefore, access to this shared resource needs to be controlled.

# 6.    MESSAGING

## 6.1    Also Known as

Messaging Design Pattern (MDP)

## 6.2    Intent

The concept of Messaging allows the interchange of information (i.e. messages) between entities: components, systems, and applications [2]. It improves decoupling, encapsulation, reusability and scalability by separating entities, message, and communication mechanism. In other words, entities, messages, and messaging mechanism are decoupled and fully independent.

## 6.3    Applicability

The concept of Messaging can be applied to solve a variety of problems in many diverse scenarios. Messages are interchanged all around us. Entities are constantly sending, receiving, and processing messages. Countless processes in nature and the real world rely on messaging: communities, organizations, families, human body processes, social networks, colonies of insects, your banking system, a collection of local and distributed components interchanging information and working cooperatively.

Human beings for instance:  when we watch TV, talk to a friend, talk over the phone, or send an email message. Right now, you are reading this written message which is possible because of messaging. Since computer applications seek to model the real world, it is only natural to design and write applications using a messaging approach. In order to fully understand messaging and its applicability, we need to think in terms of abstractions: messaging is about transferring or exchanging information. In the real world, information (messages) can take many forms all of which can be modeled using computer software: a number, a text/email message, a document, a spoken sentence, a letter, energy (light, sound, electric impulse, analog signal, etc.), biochemical message, and so on.

Messaging is ubiquitous. On the other hand, conventional software methodologies including object-oriented and distributed component technologies, tend to overlook it. The concept of Messaging addresses this problem by relying on a realistic information model. While designing and manufacturing software, we need to think not only in terms of software components but also in terms of the messaging being exchanged between these entities.

Components are one essential part of object-oriented methodologies. The interchange of information (i.e. messaging) between components is also an important and independent part of a complete and realistic information model. There seems to be a gap between conventional approaches and the reality that they seek to represent.

Depending on the application area, we may need to model other real-world concepts besides Messaging as part of a realistic information model. For instance, as part of a highly realistic computer game, the concepts of Messaging, Gravity, and Force may need to be modeled in order to provide a comprehensive representation and solution. Gravity and Force will be needed to model our solar system. However, none of these concepts are as prevalent as messaging within the context of typical software applications.

## 6.4    Motivation

OO applications consist of a collection of components that need to communicate with each other. As proposed hereafter, this interaction can be accomplished via a messaging approach. Conventional implementations, not based on the concept of Messaging, will present a variety of challenges and limitations including:

a) Strong coupling which ties the solution to a specific platform, technology, protocol, multithreading/distributed technology, and/or computer language.

b) Lack of encapsulation usually associated with not relying on the Messaging concept as the communication mechanism between participant components. A 'web' of tightly coupled component interdependencies gets created. Versioning of applications and APIs introduce unnecessary complexity. The threading mechanism is usually artificially implemented as a separate object. A single thread may also be artificially associated with multiple objects which hinders encapsulation.

c) Lack of reusability which usually results from strong coupling, lack of encapsulation, and the inability to provide reusable threading/distributed functionality as part of a framework.

d) Complexities dealing with distributed/SOA technologies based on distributed artifacts such stubs, IDLs, WSDLs, RPCs, descriptors, or similar. Distributed artifacts are also a source of interoperability limitations.

e) Complexity dealing with multithreaded technologies related to thread management, thread synchronization, race conditions, deadlocks, and so forth.

f) Complex quality issues brought about by the previous challenges which get compounded and harder to manage as the number of threads, remote interfaces and/or team members increases.

h) Scalability and interoperability limitations associated with several of the previous challenges.

i) Complexity incorporating remote and local components/services into BPM/BPEL processes derived from the lack of messaging as the communication mechanism and underlying realistic abstraction. This specific challenge applies when BPM/BPEL technologies are used as part of the implementation.

The challenges and limitations get compounded when additional real-world production aspects are considered such as security, access control, scalability, and fault tolerance. All the aspects outlined above have a

66

negative impact on software cost, overall complexity, maintainability, quality, timelines, and risk.

The concept of Messaging helps address the aforementioned shortcomings while at the same time reducing overall complexity. Actually, we can argue that messaging should be the principal mechanism of communication since components are independent entities. Therefore, they should be modeled and treated as such, in order to accurately mimic reality. A separate chapter demonstrates how design patterns based on Messaging are combined to implement access to distributed components/services (see Distributed Component and Service Model).

Alan Kay's comments should be carefully considered: "We can note in passing that one of the biggest problems in the development of object-oriented SW architectures, particularly in the last 25 years, has been an enormous over-focus on objects and an under-focus on **messaging** (most so-called object-oriented languages don't *really* use the looser coupling of messaging, but instead use the much *tighter gear meshing of procedure calls* – this hurts scalability and interoperability)." Alan Kay et al. Tighter gear meshing of procedure calls has also been characterized as "The complex machinery of procedure declarations" while discussing problems associated with traditional APIs [26].

The concepts of Animated/Live entity and Messaging are tightly intertwined. Messaging is the only realistic form of communication between an Animated/Live entity and its external environment – including the exchange of information with other Animated/Live entities as part of real-world processes. Gear meshing of procedure calls (artifact) must never be confused or mischaracterized as real Messaging. The natural concept and the artifact are *different*. Message, messaging mechanism, and communicating entities must be fully independent and decoupled from each other. Most traditional APIs do not rely on messaging. Since there is no realistic correspondence, it is not an uncommon misconception to think that the technology/application is relying on messaging when gear meshing of procedure calls is being employed.

Animated/Live entities represent information processors. They are equivalent to information machines mathematically defined as $A = (f(m), I)$. Information is transferred in the form of messages (m). Most of the forthcoming discussion will focus on the messaging being transferred between Animated/Live components which are the software implementation (OO) of the information machine abstraction.

## 6.5    Participants

a) **Message Sender**: Component that sends the message.

b) **Message Recipient (Receiver):** Component that receives the input message and may produce a reply (output message) after processing it. The input message, general in nature, may contain any type of information. The component may be instructed to perform computations based on the input message.

c) **Messenger:** Intermediary that transfers the message from the sender to the recipient. The sender and the recipient do not need to be concerned about how the message is transferred (communication protocol, message format, encryption/security mechanism, etc.) and the transformations performed on the message along the way. This is the messenger's purpose and responsibility. Similar to the real world, it is often the case that a messenger is not required. The message can be sent directly to the message recipient. All modes of communication are accommodated: synchronous, asynchronous, streaming, two-way messaging, and so on.

d) **Message:** any piece of information (i.e. data) that needs to be interchanged between sender and recipient. Two messages are usually involved: input message and output message (or reply message). The reply message is not required.

## 6.6    Structure

The concept of Messaging can be implemented using the messaging interface (JtInterface).

**Figure 1. Messaging Interface**

This interface consists of a single information primitive to process the input message and produce a reply message. It acts as a universal messaging interface that applies to remote and local components. The Messaging interface is straightforward, yet powerful. The simplicity of this interface can be deceiving. Actually, the information primitive is Turing complete. It also applies to all modalities of messaging: synchronous, asynchronous, streaming, distributed messaging, two-way messaging, secure messaging, and combinations of these forms. The interface handles any type of message. It returns a reply (of any type). In Java, the messaging interface can be declared as follows:

*public interface JtInterface*
       *{ Object processMessage (Object message); }*

*or*

*public interface JtInterface<Type, Type1>*
       *{ Type1 processMessage (Type msg); }*

The message receiver needs to implement this interface in order to receive and process incoming messages. Languages that do not use interfaces can simply declare a processMessage() function or method in order to implement Messaging.

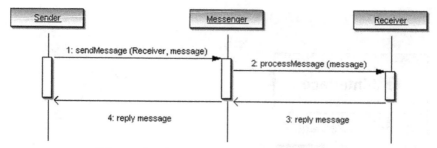

**Figure 2. Messaging (synchronous mode)**

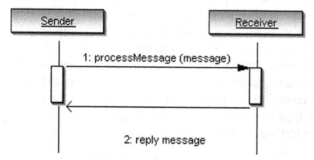

**Figure 3. Messaging (synchronous mode without messenger involved)**

## 6.7 Consequences

**Encapsulation:** The concept of Messaging improves encapsulation. Each component is a self-contained/independent unit: $A = (f(m), I)$: the only mechanism of communication with other components and applications is via messaging. Messages are also encapsulated.

**Decoupling:** Messaging improves coupling. Again, each component ($A = (f(m), I)$) is a self-contained unit that can perform independently from the rest of the system. The communication mechanism is decoupled from message and component functionality.

**Reusability:** Messaging improves reusability. Animated/Live components are similar to the building blocks in a "Lego" set. Very complex models can be built based on simple pieces that share a common way of interconnecting them (i.e. common interface). The power of the approach is derived from the number of combinations in which these toy pieces can be assembled. Components that use messaging ($A = (f(m), I)$) can be interchangeably plugged into complex applications.

Animated/Live components can be assembled in a limitless variety of configurations. The user of a component only needs to know the input/output messages that the component handles. Applications are also able to reuse components from other applications at the component level: a single component can be extracted from another application, provided that the Messaging is being used.

Live/Animated components do not need to share the same technology or computer language for reusability purposes: they can be reused and communicate via messaging even when heterogeneous technologies and/or computer languages are being used. Such characteristic behavior facilitates and fosters reusability.

**Scalability:** During the review process, it was proposed that the Messaging concept could be applied to improve scalability [2]. Because of tight coupling between client and server, conventional distributed/service technologies based on distributed artifacts require that client and server application be upgraded at the same time. This is usually not feasible and presents significant scalability limitations for infrastructures running 24/7 and/or expecting to handle a large number of computer nodes.

On the other hand, Messaging does not present this limitation because client component, server component, and communication mechanism are decoupled. Servers can be upgraded one by one without an impact on the client application and the rest of the infrastructure. Once all the servers have been gradually upgraded, clients can be upgraded to take advantage of the new software functionality. As a consequence, an infrastructure based on Messaging can scale well and handle an arbitrary number of servers and clients 24/7. This application of the Messaging concept assumes that the new software version is backward compatible.

**Quality/Testing process:** Messaging facilitates testing and debugging efforts. Components are tested as independent units by sending messages to the component and verifying the expected reply messages (black-box testing). Keep in mind that all the components share the same messaging interface. In general, unit testing can be performed via a testing harness. No need to include testing code inside the component code which can be time consuming and lead to the unexpected introduction of software defects.

**Design process:** Messaging improves and simplifies the design process. The bulk of the design work becomes defining the set of components, concepts, and input/output messages that each component needs to handle. There is a tight correspondence between UML design diagrams and the components needed for the implementation. Several UML diagrams are geared towards messaging (sequence and collaboration) although their implementation does not rely on it. The UML model and the implementation are disconnected when Messaging is not used. Since all components share the same messaging interface, they can also be readily added to BPM/BPEL diagrams and processes. As mentioned earlier, Live/Animated components are similar to independent building blocks that can be reused and connected in many different ways. Actually they can be reused at the component level.

**Development process:** Since each component that relies on messaging is self-contained, a large team of people can cooperate in the development effort without stepping on each other's work/code. In the ideal situation, responsibility for one component/package can be given to an individual. The rest of the team only needs to know the concepts and input/output messages that someone else's component is designed to handle. In general, there is no need to change someone else's code. The need for creating, maintaining and merging several versions of the code is also minimized or eliminated (see versioning). Testing/QA engineers can perform their testing independently via a testing harness. As a general rule, there is no need to add testing code to the component itself.

**Versioning:** Messaging supports backward compatibility. Consider an arbitrary modern human language. After evolving for a long period of time, human languages have become a very efficient, concise, flexible and versatile mechanism of exchanging information. New words and terms are being added constantly to the language. Take for instance, the new term 'smartphone'. Some words become archaic and progressively fade away, being replaced by newer words or concepts. A 'new version' of the language, so to speak, is being constantly created to meet changing information requirements.

The messages, part of the language, are constantly evolving without having an impact on the mechanism of communication itself (fully decoupled). Messages that use older 'revisions' of the language can still be understood and processed. The same principles apply to Live/Animated components based on messaging. As a consequence, the need to create, maintain, and merge several versions of the software – which quickly becomes time consuming, difficult, and error-prone – is reduced or eliminated.

**Logging and Debugging**: Since all the Live/Animated components use the same messaging interface, messages can be logged automatically. Such logging features minimize the need for print/logging statements inside the code which can be time consuming and error-prone. By taking a look at the messages being interchanged and automatically logged, the user is usually able to quickly track down the message/component that is causing the problem (with minimum or no extra effort).

**Security:** Well-known encryption and authentication mechanisms fit in well with the concept of messaging. Strong security can be provided by the conceptual framework that implements Messaging through the encryption and authentication of the messages being interchanged. The sender and the recipient do not need to be too concerned with how secure messaging is implemented. Strong security is provided by the framework while at the same time simplifying its implementation. If required, custom security mechanisms can also be incorporated: sender and receiver need to agree on and implement the message encryption/authentication mechanism to be used.

**Concurrency and Asynchronous Messaging:** The concept of Messaging is able to handle the complexities associated with concurrency and asynchronous messaging. Components that implement Messaging can execute in a separate/independent thread. This is a natural and realistic representation of the real world: each component (entity) is a self-contained unit and executes independently from the rest of the system.

Messages can be processed asynchronously using the component's own independent thread. The required abstractions are usually implemented in the context of a reusable Conceptual framework. The component itself does not need to add separate logic to handle concurrency which is time consuming, complex, and prone to error.

**Fault tolerance:** a Live/Animated entity (Turing Complete) can readily emulate a state machine. Therefore, it can be extended to provide fault-tolerant capabilities in a very natural fashion by replicating components/messages and coordinating their interaction via consensus algorithms. Adding fault-tolerant characteristics to a program that uses a traditional approach is, in general, a difficult undertaking. Please refer to the chapter dealing with the Distributed Component/Service Model (fault-tolerant capabilities).

**Speed of development and cost:** Because of all the reasons outlined above, the concepts of Messaging and Live/Animated entity are able to substantially improve the speed of development and reduce cost.

**Quality and software maintenance:** Quality and software maintenance efforts are also improved as a result of the all of the above.

**Conceptual paradigm and learning curve:** In order to take full advantage of the proposed abstraction, people need to think in terms of the messaging concept when they model, design and build software applications: independent entities (i.e. components) interchanging messages among each other. This may require learning time and training. Although a messaging approach is natural, intuitive, and consistent with the real world, traditional approaches are based on method/procedure invocation (both local and remote).

Keep in mind that messaging, as a concept, has many qualities which are inherited or absorbed by the proposed model. Therefore, it is challenging to find drawbacks associated with the concept of messaging which is unexpected within the context of design patterns. A similar situation occurs when we look at other real-world concepts that may be part of our software model, like Gravity, Energy, and Force. The proposed abstraction should be viewed from the standpoint of Concepts when it comes to trade-offs and drawbacks. There are several differences between design patterns and Concepts (see Comparison with Related Software Models).

**Overhead:** Transferring messages between components introduces a small overhead when compared with traditional method/procedure invocation. This is especially true when a messenger is used. As computers become faster and faster this becomes a non-issue. Also, the benefits of messaging outweigh this small performance cost. Notice that the messenger component is part of many real-world problems and applications in which an intermediary is necessary for message interchange.

**Disciplined approach:** the conceptual paradigm encourages a disciplined approach that may have a small impact on the initial development time of a component. Messaging should be the only channel of communication between components. External class methods may still be invoked using the traditional approach. On the other hand, this should be used sparingly in order to minimize coupling and maximize encapsulation.

A Live/Animated component *(A = (f(m), I)* is a self-contained unit that interacts with the other components only via messaging. The additional development time is again outweighed by the benefits introduced by messaging. Moreover, individual components based on messaging can be readily purchased or extracted from other applications.

## 6.8    Known uses

**Design patterns implementation:** Messaging has been used to implement and/or facilitate the reusable implementation of other well-known design patterns like Gang of Four design patterns (GoF), DAO, J2EE Design patterns, MVC, Master-Worker and so forth. Messaging provides a more natural, streamlined, and straightforward implementation.

Consider that the concept of messaging is ubiquitous. Therefore, most design patterns need to deal with the exchange of information (i.e. messaging) as part of their implementation. Messaging provides a natural and realistic match for such need. Not levering Messaging usually brings forth artificiality and limitations.

**Component and Conceptual Frameworks**: Messaging has been utilized for the implementation of complete component frameworks able to cope, in a very *natural* fashion, with complex challenges like concurrency, asynchronous communication, versioning, native interfaces, distributed component/service communication, interoperability, exception propagation, BPEL/BPM component integration and so on. Components that rely on Messaging can be interchangeably plugged into complex framework applications using the "Lego" approach mentioned earlier. Messaging is a fully implementable and reusable concept able to provide the communication framework required for building robust applications. Because it can be leveraged over and over again, a reusable Conceptual framework based on messaging improves maintainability, overall quality, cost, and timeframes.

**Distributed component and service model (SOA):** Messaging is particularly well suited for the implementation of a complete distributed component/service model (Turing complete). It is able to provide seamless access to remote components regardless of the protocol, technology and communication mechanism being used. The concept of Messaging is able to gracefully cope with real-world complex considerations including parallelism, fault tolerance, interoperability, distributed components/services, and so on.

Messages can be transferred via web services, REST, EJBs, HTTP, sockets, SSL or any comparable communication interface. Design patterns implemented using Messaging (adapters, remote proxies and facades) make this possible by hiding the complexities associated with distributed APIs. Messaging solves a whole set of problems dealing with remote application interfaces and access to distributed components/services. Because of Messaging, sender and recipient do not need to be concerned about the implementation of the messaging mechanism and infrastructure.

Messaging has been utilized to implement SOA technologies including REST. A Web service basically provides a mechanism of communication (i.e. messaging) between heterogeneous applications. Such need represents a good match for Messaging. Notice that it does not place any restrictions on message sender and recipient. These components can be running on multiple computers and operating systems. They can also be implemented using multiple computer languages and technologies.

Messaging has been used to implement ESB technologies and frameworks. Once all the building blocks are present (remote proxies, adapters, facades, etc), they can be assembled to create complete ESB solutions.

**BPM/BPEL processes and technologies:** Messaging has been employed for the implementation of BPEL/BPM technologies, frameworks and processes. Consider that the information pattern family represents a group that is Turing complete. Arbitrary technologies can be implemented using these concepts. Components that rely on Messaging can also be readily incorporated into BPEL/BPM processes. Notice that for components to be incorporated interchangeably, they need to share the same interface. The concept of Messaging provides a common and realistic interface. In consequence, a realistic and natural implementation of BPEL/BPM technologies can be achieved: a process usually consists of components interchanging information via messaging.

## 6.9    Implementation

Messaging is about transferring or exchanging information between entities. It is a ubiquitous concept with a straightforward implementation and wide applicability. It is unlikely to find an application or problem area where interchange of information (i.e. messaging) is not present: from business applications, all the way to distributed component/service technologies, and speech/vision processing systems.

Similar to the software model, the implementation of Messaging should also mimic the reality being modeled. There will probably be some implementation differences depending on the specific application. There are many factors to consider based on the type of messaging being implemented and the technology/language in use: messaging delivery characteristics, streaming, messaging reliability, asynchronous messaging, security, and so forth.

The Messaging interface (JtInterface) is mainly a reference implementation and there are other potential implementations of the messaging abstraction:

*public interface JtInterface { Object processMessage (Object message); }*

The generic type object is used. This is similar to the implementation of several design patterns (Iterator, for instance). In reality, the component may only be able to process and return specific types of message. In that case, appropriate types may be specified. For instance:

*public interface MyMessagingInterface {*
*MyOutputType processMessage (MyInputType message); }*

The interface above is also a valid implementation of messaging. Advanced object-oriented technologies provide features like Java generics which allow the types to be parameterized:

*public interface JtInterface<Type, Type1> { Type1 processMessage (Type msg); }*

Notice that arbitrary computer languages or technologies can be used to implement Messaging, including plain old java objects (POJOs):

*public Object processMessage (Object message)*

Depending on the application, another messaging primitive may be needed:

*public Object sendMessage (Object component, Object message);*

The sendMessage() primitive sends a message to a local or remote component. Although Messaging features a straightforward implementation, based on basic primitives, it is able to transparently handle complex real-world scenarios: distributed components, all modalities of messaging including two-way asynchronous communication, component interoperability, concurrency, streaming, authentication, encryption, exception handling and propagation mechanism, reliable messaging, fault tolerance, and so on. By including messaging, software model and implementation absorb its inherent qualities including versatility, reliability, efficiency and robustness.

78

## 6.10   Related Work

Related literature [9] has been published describing messaging patterns in the specific realm of Enterprise Application Integration (EAI) and SOA. This work focuses on the communication between multiple applications. The proposed approach is distinctively different in terms of realistic information model based on natural concepts, mathematical formulation, Turing-complete information machine $(A = (f(m), I))$, single information primitive, applications domains, realistic implementation, and so on. Since the concept of messaging is ubiquitous, so is its applicability which includes pattern design/implementation, Conceptual frameworks, distributed component/service model, fault tolerance, communication between local components, concurrency, asynchronous messaging, BPM/BPEL technologies, and software modeling/design.

The concept of Messaging may be confused with message-oriented middleware (MOM) technologies like the Java Messaging Service (JMS). Although MOM *technologies* rely on the *concept* of messaging, they are not the same. MOM is one of the many technologies that utilize messaging. Your e-mail application also relies on messaging. Concept and technology are two different entities. The concept can be applied to a wide variety of problems and technologies. It is not limited to MOM or EAI applications. On the other hand, MOM technologies cannot be used to handle the wide range of technologies and applications mentioned above. In general, technologies are more concrete than Concepts, and target specific problems. A separate chapter includes detailed comparison aspects and overall comparison criteria.

# 7.    CONCEPTUAL INTERFACE (CI)

Software systems should tackle problems at the conceptual level, in order to mirror the mind which is a conceptual engine. As a consequence, I should introduce the idea of a conceptual interface (CI).

In simple terms, a conceptual interface is one that transfers information using concepts in order to accomplish specific functionality. You happen to be using a conceptual interface right at this moment, while you read this document. Information is being communicated using concepts. Actually all forms of human communication (verbal and written) are based on a conceptual interface which consists of information in the form of messages. However, such messages are employed to transfer concepts – a higher level of abstraction. Human languages constitute examples of conceptual interfaces. Notice that without the concept of messaging, information is unable travel so to speak. A conceptual interface is also a messaging interface defined by the information primitive. Not every messaging interface is a conceptual interface. In general, graphical user interfaces and man-machine interfaces (elevator buttons, car controls) allow the transference of information via messaging. On the other hand, the messages do not convey concepts like natural languages do. The mind communicates with other components of the body via messaging; however, no conceptual information is exchanged.

From the information standpoint, the following aspects need to be specified as part of an arbitrary conceptual interface (CI):

1) Concepts/Components: Specify the entities relevant to the problem in the real world. The entities involved can be divided into two categories: a) entities that can process information (Components) and b) Entities that cannot (Concepts).
2) Messages: Specify the messages that need to be exchanged in order to achieve the required functionality. A message is a Concept. As demonstrated in this section, there are seven types of operation (message) applicable to every conceptual interface: Create, Read, Update, Delete, Send, Decision, and Action.

Conceptual interfaces are based on the information primitive:

*processInformation (Message)*

Entities able to process information, like our minds, do it based on the following operations.

1) Create (manufacture) information
2) Read (retrieve) information
3) Update information
4) Delete (discard) information
5) Send (transfer information using the messaging abstraction)
6) Decision (if – make decisions based on information).
7) Action (take actions based on information). This type of message only applies to entities able to interact with the physical world like a robotic arm.

The operations above can be translated into seven categories of messages. These messages apply to every conceptual interface regardless of the type of information been processed. The shared information concept results in a simplified set of common messages independent of the type of information. For convenience purposes other message types may be added. However, equivalent functionality can be accomplished by combining the messages above. A 'Search' message is convenient while looking for information. However, the same results can also be accomplished by repetitive uses of the 'Read' message. As mentioned earlier, few computer components interact with the physical world. For instance, a component able to produce voice (speak) or move (robotic arm).

In order to design a conceptual interface, imagine yourself solving the problem at hand with another person instead of a computer. In other words, think about the concepts and messages that need to be shared with another person if you want him/her to perform specific tasks required by an arbitrary application. We can come up with a complete solution for the problem at hand based on a conceptual interface. Human languages already provide the concepts and messages that are required.

For our specific mobile application, the following are some examples of the messages that you would share:

1) "Please read *page* one of the document"
2) "Update *paragraph* three of page five to read I get the concept"
3) "Update *font* of *page* 3 to Times Romans size 10"

The natural language provides the concepts of document, page, paragraph, sentence, font, header, footer, margin, and so on. It also determines the interrelationships, or information associations that exist between these concepts. For instance, a document is associated to a group of pages. Each page is associated to a group of paragraphs, a header, footer and margins. Each paragraph is associated to a group of sentences, and so forth.

Since computers are basically information processors, like our minds, the same concepts and conceptual interface apply. In other words, a complete conceptual interface can be implemented, in the form of software, by using the same concepts and messages utilized by the mind. Information exchange between humans and between components represent the same concept (Conceptually equivalent). Therefore, we can apply the same principles and solution to both scenarios.

A complex problem has been reduced to a very manageable set of concepts and messages (perhaps optimal). Nature is ahead of us, as usual. The conceptual approach operates at a higher level of abstraction. Efficiency, conciseness, completeness, 'fluency', and realism are achieved, among other natural qualities, while at the same time eliminating redundant unrealistic artifacts and primitives. The approach can be generalized to arbitrary problems. Obviously, the set of concepts will change depending on the problem at hand. The concepts part of the information pattern family will be applicable regardless of the real problem being solved. Again, information is a concept, therefore a highly reusable entity. It is probably impossible to think of any problem, in reality, where information is not involved.

In the case of the proposed problem, the same concepts apply regardless of the technology, language, document format, and hardware device being used. Traditional O-O APIs that do not rely on concepts present

82

many limitations: coupling, language dependencies, lack of encapsulation, hardware dependencies, and so on. Based on Biomimetics principles and concepts, there is no point in arguing with nature when it comes to information processing. As usual, nature has spoken and set the golden standard in terms of information processing: conceptual mind! Let us attempt to understand it and mirror it as our best bet. Based on the concepts presented, it should become clear that software should *evolve* and mimic the thinking patterns of the mind in order to gain substantial improvements.

# 8. INFORMATION PROCESS

## 8.1 Intent

This pattern models an information process. In order to provide a complete and accurate representation of the real world, the information process pattern consists of abstractions that mirror reality: a collection of independent entities or individuals, some of which are *Live or Animated,* interacting with each other and/or interchanging information via *Messaging* within the context of the information *Process. Live* or *Animated* entities are able to process information and exhibit independent behavior (a "life of their own" so to speak). The process pattern also separates the critical information aspect from how such information is stored, represented, transferred, secured, and processed.

## 8.2 Applicability

The information process abstraction has wide applicability. It can be used to model and solve a variety of problems. Obviously, countless processes in nature and the real world follow the same pattern: communities, organizations, families, human body processes, social networks, colonies of insects, your banking system, BPM/BPEL processes, a collection of local and distributed components interchanging information and working cooperatively within the context of a process, etc. These are just some examples of the scenarios that can be modeled using the information process abstractions. All these scenarios share common patterns, abstractions, challenges, and problems: reliable and secure communication between entities, redundancy, fault-tolerant considerations, process reliability, concurrency, interoperability, scalability, and the need for an accurate and complete model.

## 8.3 Motivation

The implementation of traditional multithreaded and distributed applications/processes is a complex endeavor, expensive and prone to error. Complexity, cost overruns and quality issues are usual in the context of these software development projects. Challenges include communication, reliability, fault-tolerance, redundancy, monitoring, interoperability, quality, scalability, and so on. The same set of problems applies to processes implemented using BPEL/BPM technologies (Business Process Execution Language/ Business Process Modeling).

Consider an organization or any of the processes described above where multiple entities, or groups of entities, work cooperatively to achieve specific common goals. The survival and development of these organizations have depended on finding solutions for the information and process challenges listed earlier. For instance, communities of individuals have developed sophisticated ways of communication (i.e. messaging). Human speech, and in general communication between members of the same species, would be an example.

The interchange of information is vital to every organization or community. Societies have built sophisticated information infrastructures and frameworks to carry the messaging required for communication and decision making purposes. Communities and organizations have been able to deal with fault tolerance challenges by providing individual and message redundancy. In summary, nature and its natural selection processes have already addressed and solved, in very robust and simple ways, the main challenges faced by distributed systems and models. Therefore, there is no need to reinvent the wheel so to speak. We just need to mimic the models, processes and solutions found in nature and the real world.

Now consider for example, the design and implementation of the Master-Worker design pattern using BPEL/BPM and traditional multithreaded/distributed technologies. The Master-Worker pattern, also known as divide-and-conquer, is usually applied in the context of distributed/parallel applications. In simple terms, the pattern divides a complex task into smaller subtasks that are assigned to individual workers to be completed in parallel. The conventional solution for general purpose business process applications, and in particular for this particular example presented, will present a variety of challenges and limitations including:

a) Complexity dealing with multithreaded and distributed technologies related to thread management, thread synchronization, race conditions, deadlocks, etc.

b) Complexities dealing with distributed/SOA technologies which require the manipulation of distributed artifacts such as stubs, IDLs, WSDLs, RPCs, descriptors, or similar. This is also a source of interoperability limitations.

c) Complexity incorporating remote and local components/services into BPM/BPEL diagrams derived from the lack of messaging as the communication mechanism and underlying realistic abstraction.

d) Strong coupling which ties the solution to a specific platform, BPM/BPEL technology, protocol, multithreading/distributed technology and/or computer language.

e) Lack of encapsulation usually associated with not using the messaging abstraction as the communication mechanism between participant components. The threading mechanism is usually implemented as a separate object. A single thread may also be artificially associated with multiple components.

f) Lack of reusability which usually results from strong coupling, lack of encapsulation and the inability to provide reusable threading/distributed functionality as part of a framework.

g) Complex quality issues brought about by the previous challenges which get compounded and harder to manage as the number of threads, remote interfaces and/or team members increases.

h) Scalability and interoperability limitations associated with several of the previous challenges.

The challenges and limitations get compounded when additional real-world production aspects are considered such as security, access control, scalability, and fault tolerance. The appendix contains a detailed comparison between the proposed pattern and traditional technologies based on multithreading and distributed artifacts. All the scenarios presented share the same patterns. They can be modeled using the same group of information abstractions taken from reality. A complete model and solution, applicable to arbitrary information processes, should include the following ubiquitous concepts: a collection of *independent individuals or entities* interacting with each other and interchanging information (i.e. *messaging*) within the context of predefined *processes*. Some of these independent entities exhibit a life of their own: *Live* or *Animated* entities.

As discussed earlier, the problems and challenges found in a distributed component/service model mimic the ones face by most organizations, communities and natural processes. We can find solutions to complex problems associated with software engineering processes, and specifically distributed/multithreaded processes, by extracting them from nature.

The information process abstractions can provide comparable capabilities to the ones provided by multithreaded and distributed applications/processes, while at the same time improving overall complexity, decoupling, encapsulation, reusability and scalability. As a consequence, software engineering processes are also improved in terms of reliability, cost, implementation timeframes and so forth. Comprehensive security, redundancy and fault-tolerant considerations can also be accommodated as part of a complete distributed component/service model based on the proposed information abstractions.

## 8.4    Participants

a) Concrete process components: Collection of independent entities that participate in the process. Notice that many of the objects can be modeled as Live or Animated components. They are able to behave and process information (messaging) independently from the rest of the system, which means that the component uses its own independent processing mechanism or thread.

b) Messaging: The interchange of information between participants is achieved via the concept of Messaging: sender, receiver, message and messaging mechanism are decoupled, encapsulated and fully independent.

In the context of a realistic model, messages can take many forms all of which can be modeled using computer software: a number, a text/email message, a document, a spoken sentence, a letter, energy (light, sound, electric impulse, analog signal, etc.), biochemical message, and so on. All forms of messaging are modeled: synchronous, asynchronous, streaming, distributed messaging, two-way messaging, secure messaging, and combinations of these forms.

c) Design Patterns and other abstractions: Besides objects (animated and unanimated) and Messaging, real-world processes consist of other concepts or abstractions. Many of these abstractions have been documented as design patterns (Proxy, Strategy, Adapter, Messaging, etc). Notice that an information process is a specific type of process, part of the more general process category.

As the name implies, information processes mainly deal with information. Other abstractions like Gravity, Force, Reflection, Refraction, and comparable natural laws may also need to be modeled as part of a complete model. For instance, the concepts of gravity and force may need to be part of a model of the solar system or a realistic computer game. It should be noted that none of these concepts are as ubiquitous as object (animated or unanimated), messaging, and process within the context of typical software applications.

## 8.5    Structure

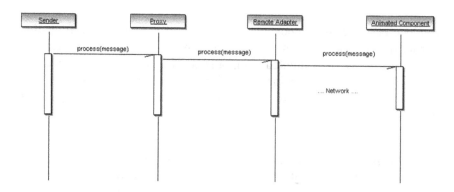

**Figure 1. Messaging and remote Animated/Live component within the context of an information process.**

## 8.6    Collaboration

The information process abstraction and its implementation are based on other abstractions that seek to accurately mirror reality: a) Messaging Concept. Sender, receiver, message, and messaging mechanism are decoupled entities, encapsulated and fully independent. b) Live or Animated components $(A = (f(m), I)$ that interact with each other and interchange information (i.e. *messaging*) within the context of predefined information processes. Animated components rely on messaging as the mechanism of communication with other components and applications.

Live/Animated components can be readily incorporated into distributed BPM/BPEL processes and applications since messaging provides transparent access to distributed components as part of a complete distributed service/component model: distributed components are treated as local ones. Animated or Live objects are able to engage in elaborated patterns of collaboration and dialog with other animated components, in order to exchange information as part of complex processes.

The proposed abstractions are capable of modeling all forms of messaging: synchronous, asynchronous, streaming, distributed messaging, two-way messaging, secure messaging, and combinations of these forms. Information itself, encapsulated as a message, can assume many forms as well. In the case of asynchronous communication, Live or Animated components require a queuing mechanism to store incoming messages: *enqueueMessage(message)*. A message is added to the asynchronous message queue directly or via a messenger. The Animated component processes incoming messages, on at a time, via its independent thread of execution. It relies on the information primitive to process incoming messages. In other words, the Live/Animated component is constantly processing incoming information via its independent thread of execution, which mainly waits for incoming messages and processes them by invoking the information primitive (*processMessage(message)*).

Living beings and automated systems are constantly processing and making decisions based on the stream of messaging received through their senses. Messaging is the only channel of *communication* with their external environment. The proposed information process abstractions are able to mirror these behaviors and handle the complexities associated with asynchronous messaging, multithreading, distributed component access, security and so forth. Notice that all the proposed abstractions have to do, in one way or another, with one fundamental aspect: *information*. Probably as it should be expected, since information is a cornerstone of real-world processes.

## 8.7    Consequences

**Decoupling:**    The proposed abstraction helps maximize decoupling. Process entities $(A = (f(m), I)$ are completely independent (decoupled) within the context of the process pattern. Messaging is the only channel of communication between components which accurately mirrors reality.

**Encapsulation:** The proposed pattern helps maximize encapsulation. Process participants are totally encapsulated. Each component, message and concept is a self-contained/independent unit. Again, messaging is the only channel of communication.

**Reusability:** The proposed pattern helps improve reusability. Most of the functionality required to implement the process abstractions can be reused. A generic implementation can be achieved. The reusable functionality is usually provided by the conceptual framework that implements Messaging. The information process pattern also improves and encourages reuse because components can be integrated from multiple platforms, computer languages, communication protocols and technologies. In other words, technologies, languages, protocols can be freely mixed and matched within the context of the process pattern.

Obviously, reuse is made easier if the messaging abstraction is being utilized. Processes implemented based on the proposed abstractions can be reused as part of more complicated processes. The proposed abstractions can also be leveraged to provide reusable implementations of design patterns[4,5,2]. For instance, the reusable implementation of Master-Worker is feasible.

90

**Scalability:** Traditional approaches and processes present scalability limitations [2, 14]. Because of coupling, client and server software need to be upgraded at the same time which is usually not feasible for large installations and/or operations running 24/7. Under the proposed approach, client, server and communication mechanism are fully decoupled. Client and server software can be upgraded independently. Processes based on the proposed approach are able to transparently scale and handle arbitrary large infrastructures running 24/7. Gradual upgrade of servers and clients is feasible without disrupting the rest of the infrastructure. Once all the servers have been gradually upgraded, client nodes can be upgraded to take advantage of the new software functionality. It is assumed that the new software version is backward compatible.

**Distributed Component/Service Model:** This pattern consists of a set of information abstractions required for the specification and implementation of a complete distributed component/service model. Remote animated components are treated as local ones. Actually, there is no *artificial* difference between local and remote components. They are both exactly the same component. Stubs, IDLs, RPCs, WSDLs or similar artifacts add complexity and are not required. The process abstractions provide transparent access to distributed components. As a best practice, it is the responsibility of a conceptual framework based on Messaging to provide the infrastructure required for communication between distributed components and/or services.

**Multithreaded applications**: Traditional multithreading has been replaced by the realistic process abstractions. In reality, object functionality and threading/processing mechanism are inherently linked and part of a single encapsulated unit: Live or Animated Entity. They should not be artificially modeled and implemented as separate entities. Animated components minimize the complexity and issues associated with traditional multithreaded implementations. Race conditions and deadlock are minimized. Keep in mind that the queuing mechanism ensures that messages are placed in the queue and processed sequentially by the animated component. The queuing mechanism, usually implemented by a framework, ensures that access to the shared resource (message queue) is properly controlled.

**Interoperability**: The process abstraction can incorporate components and applications that use multiple technologies, languages, platforms, and protocols. As stated earlier, this pattern separates the critical information aspect from how such information is stored, represented, transferred and processed. All these aspects can be altered independently without impacting the actual information. The information primitive is independent from a specific computer language, technology and/or protocol. Platforms, languages, technologies and protocols can be freely mixed and matched within the context of a process. For instance, the information remains the same (semantics) regardless of what communication technology or protocol is being used: sockets, .Net, HTTP, RMI, REST, SSL, EJBs, etc. All these technologies and protocols can be transparently incorporated as part of an integrated information process.

**UML/BPM/BPEL diagrams and applications**: The abstractions that are part of the process pattern can be readily incorporated into UML/BPM/BPEL diagrams and production quality BPEL/BPM applications. The overall design and UML diagrams are also simplified and streamlined making them easier to understand and implement.

**Conceptual Framework**: As a best practice, the process abstractions should be implemented via a conceptual framework able to accommodate the reusable information infrastructure required. Component implementation is able to focus on the business logic. In general, under the traditional models, users need to re-implement the communication and multithreading mechanisms for each component which is the source of implementation complexity, cost, timelines delays, and quality defects.

**Conceptual paradigm and learning curve**: In order to grasp the ideas associated with the process abstractions, people need to think in terms of concepts and a conceptual paradigm which may require time and training. The proposed abstractions are natural, intuitive and mirror reality: a collection of *independent entities (animated and unanimated)* interacting with each other and/or interchanging information (i.e. *messaging*) within the context of predefined *processes*.

On the other hand, it is challenging to find drawbacks or trade-offs, which is unexpected within the context of design patterns. A similar situation occurs when we look at other real-world concepts that may be part of our software model, like gravity, energy, and force. It is probably best to study and model the process abstractions from the standpoint of concepts where finding trade-offs is not really critical and perhaps unfeasible.

**Fault tolerance considerations:** Processes and groups of living beings in nature employ sophisticated fault-tolerant mechanisms as a way of adaptation and survival. The proposed process abstractions, mimicked from nature, can be employed to accurately mirror such mechanisms. *Live/Animated* entities can readily emulate state machines. Therefore, they can be extended to provide fault-tolerant capabilities in a very natural fashion by replicating components (or messages/processes) and coordinating their interaction via consensus algorithms [6,16]. Please refer to the chapter dealing with a Distributed Component/Service Model (fault-tolerant capabilities).

**Pool (or *team*) of Animated/Live components:** Manipulating large numbers of concurrent Animated/Live components within the context of a process may prove to be computationally expensive since each component is associated with an independent thread of execution. For this particular scenario, we may need to consider a design based on a pool of Animated/Live components, in order to control the total number of threads running concurrently. Components can be created and destroyed as needed in order to limit the total number of Animated/Live components running concurrently. Obviously, additional computer nodes should help improve capacity when dealing with these implementations issues.

**Overhead:** Transferring messages between components introduces a small overhead when compared with traditional method/procedure invocation. As computers become faster and faster this becomes a non-issue. Also, the benefits of messaging outweigh the small performance cost.

## 8.8    Known Uses

**UML/BPM/BPEL frameworks and technologies.** The proposed process abstractions have been used for the comprehensive implementation of business process technologies (BPEL/BPM), frameworks, and applications. They can also be readily reused as part of UML/BPM/BPEL diagrams (and processes) in order to design and implement applications with comparable functionality to traditional business process applications. The proposed abstractions provide a reusable set of components able to deal with process related considerations such as distributed component/services access, concurrency, asynchronous messaging, interoperability, redundancy and scalability. By reusing the process abstractions, improvements can be realized in terms of cost, quality, overall risk, realism, overall reusability, and timelines.

BPM/BPEL processes based on the proposed patterns can invoke local and distributed components seamlessly. Distributed access to Live/Animated components does not require additional artifacts and unnecessary complexity.

**Design patterns.** The proposed abstractions have been used to implement and/or facilitate the implementation (i.e. reusable implementation) of other well-known design patterns like Gang of Four design patterns (GoF), DAO, J2EE Design patterns and Master-Worker[2]. Consider that the proposed process abstractions represent a Turing complete group and are fully implementable. They can be reused for the implementation of arbitrary computing technologies including design pattern. Actually they can be used for a realistic and natural implementation of design patterns while at the same time improving complexity, reusability, quality, encapsulation, cost, and so on.

**Distributed component and service model.** The process abstractions are well suited for the implementation of a complete distributed component/service model able to realistically handle complex real-world considerations such as security, redundancy, fault tolerance, concurrency, scalability, and so forth. The information machine is Turing complete. The proposed abstractions also provide a complete

94

information infrastructure able to support and implement, in natural ways, arbitrary technologies including Enterprise Service Bus (ESB). Once a conceptual framework has been implemented (one time), it becomes a matter of reusing its components to implement other technologies and processes. The additional effort that is required becomes minimal.

## 8.9    Implementation

As stated earlier, any technology can be used to implement the information primitive required by the proposed information abstractions and model:

*public interface JtInterface { Object processMessage (Object message); }*

Advanced object oriented technologies provide features like Java generics which allow the types to be parameterized:

*public interface JtInterface<Type, Type1>  {  Type1 processMessage (Type msg);  }*

In particular, BPEL/BPM tools can be extended to implement it. The examples provided use the Jt Framework implementation which extends the BPEL specification to implement the information primitive. The Jt Framework also implements BPEL extensions to manage local and distributed Live/Animated components within the context of BPEL/BPM processes. A total of seven information "primitives" were required: createInformation, readInformation, updateInformation, deleteInformation, lookupInformation, sendMessage, and processMessage. The first six information "primitives" are derived from the one above, and mainly provided for clarity and convenience purposes. Several authors have proposed extensions to the BPEL specification in order to accommodate specific requirements and make the specification suitable for particular applications [17].

Secure messaging and access control can be implemented by adding appropriate components to the Messaging pipeline. These security and access control components are usually provided by the conceptual framework that implements the information/messaging infrastructure.

## 8.10    Related Patterns

The reusable implementation of several other design patterns may call for concurrency, asynchronous messaging and distributed capabilities within the context of a process. A complete model and implementation should include the process abstractions to provide realistic functionality. Command, Observer, Master-Worker, Mediator, Decorator, Model View Controller (MVC) and J2EE Business Delegate are some examples of design patterns that can benefit from using the process abstractions since they accurately mirror real-world processes.

The term "process pattern" has been used to describe a collection of general techniques, actions, and/or tasks (activities) for developing object-oriented software [19]. This term should not be confused with the proposed design pattern: information process design pattern.

# 9. INFORMATION OR CONCEPT ASSOCIATION

*Concepts* were discussed before information associations on purpose. For better understanding, I figured it would be better to cover this abstraction afterwards.

## 9.1    Intent

Information associations are the building blocks or basic units of information. A concept consists of a group of information associations. Concepts are also associated or interrelated to other concepts via information associations.

## 9.2    Applicability

Every single aspect of reality can be expressed as a concept. By the same token, every concept is expressed as a group of information associations. Concepts are also associated or interrelated to other concepts via information associations. Our minds use these entities to understand, interconnect, communicate and process every aspect of reality. They constitute the fundamental building blocks as far as conceptual information is concerned.

As a matter of speech, concepts are very sociable entities. They have a real tendency to become associated with other concepts, via information associations, to form new concepts or ideas. Consider the concept of a reservation and the sentence:"I 'd like to make a reservation". A concept can easily become associated to countless other concepts to form new concepts or ideas. Take the following sentence for instance:

"I'd like to make an airplane reservation for Seattle departing next week".

A new concept has been created, based on information associations. The specific example above includes additional associations to the concepts of time and place.

Consider for example a young child. Her first word is based on the creation of an information association. When she speaks it: for instance, Mom or Dad. An association has been made. The association between a word and a person. Her young mind has made a leap and learnt a new information association ,and her first word. It is also one of the early signs of *intelligence*. Moreover, conceptually the learning process followed by the mind consists of making information associations: starting with colors, numbers, people, animals, and so on. It develops into a sophisticated web of conceptual knowledge interconnected by information associations.

As the building blocks of conceptual information, associations are ubiquitous and applicable to every possible context and solution. The same principle applies to computer technologies and software which should mirror the mind and its information patterns. In particular, information associations, the fundamental building blocks of information. They are applied as part of every single concept and message employed in applications based on a conceptual paradigm and solution.

## 9.3    Motivation

Consider the mobile application proposed earlier: a document manager for mobile devices. Due to changing requirements the proposed mobile application is now required to provide voice recognition capabilities (IVR). Additionally, the application should interact with the user and provide personal assistant capabilities: voice activated call, directions, reservations, weather reports, traffic alerts and so on.

In order to improve service, increase efficiency and reduce delays, modern computer systems are being required to provide voice recognition and AI capabilities. Examples are everywhere these days: banking system, car systems, reservation systems, and so on. The proposed model based on concepts and associations are ideal when dealing deal with such emerging challenges.

Most of the challenges described in regards to traditional O-O multithreaded and distributed applications/services still apply: complexity, reusability, coupling, encapsulation, versioning, scalability, interoperability, and so forth. Keep in mind that Concepts and information associations are tightly intertwined. For brevity sake, I will not list them again as part of this section. Traditional APIs are also ill-equipped to handle new challenges related to the processing of natural language which are based purely on a conceptual approach.

The new set of requirements introduces new complications. The general problem of extracting meaning from natural language is a complex one. Such general problem is outside the target scope. On the other hand, most computer systems are limited to a specific information domain which reduces the scope and complexity of the problem: banking, reservations, etc. Our specific problem domain is related to this type of system. For the purpose of the discussion, the mobile application will be dealing with personal assistant capabilities.

Consider the question who was Mr. Jefferson's wife? It is a vague question, on purpose. As you can see, there is no enough information (i.e. information associations) to precisely define what is being asked. Additional information needs to be given so that your mind is able to make the right associations. For instance, the following: the question is referring to Mr. Thomas Jefferson, principal author of the U.S. Declaration of Independence.

You may not know the answer to the question, which is fine, because it helps illustrate how the mind process information associations. The same principles apply to any other questions for which you do not know the answer. It also applies to applications like the mobile application being discussed. To answer the proposed question, you will need to find sources of information related to the subject. In particular, you may need to use the internet and read Mr. Jefferson's biography.

From the question itself, several associations can be derived that will help resolve the proposed problem. Specifically, the question is asking for the identity of his wife (X). From the question you can deduct the following information associations:

X is a Person

X is a Woman


X represents Mrs. Jefferson (unknown piece of information). You can find the solution by reading his biography and looking for people related to Mr. Jefferson. At some point during the search, you should find a sentence like: "… Jefferson married Martha …". This sentence gives enough information to answer the question. However, there are two additional information associations that need to be made in order to arrive to the answer. Since Mr. Jefferson married Martha, they became husband and wife.


The proposed problem can be specified using the following concepts and associations. C represents Mr. Jefferson:


C = {(name, Mr. Jefferson), (wife, X), (principal author, Declaration of Independence)}


X= {(Person, true) , (Woman, true)}


After reading the sentence S = {(Mr. Jefferson), (married), (Martha) } the following associations can be drawn. If two people (X, Y) get married, it can be logically deducted that Y becomes the wife of X and X becomes the husband of Y. Using the conceptual notation:


{(X), (marries), (Y)} ➜ (X->wife = Y) and (Y->husband=X)


The same associations can be found by retrieving the definition of 'wife' from the dictionary. Therefore, the answer is found: Martha


Martha = X= {(Person, true), (Woman, true)}


If there is a logical answer to the question, the mind will find it, provided that the question contains enough information (i.e. information associations). As a later section demonstrates, the proposed deductive

100

approach based on information associations can be generalized and applied to arbitrary information domains.

For the specific mobile virtual assistant, consider the following question: Can I make a flight reservation to Hawaii for next Tuesday? For this specific question, the mobile assistant will need to handle the concept of reservation and its associations in order to proceed: city of departure, city of destination, time, date, airline, ticket class, etc.

The concept of reservation (R) can be expressed as follows:

R = {(passenger, me), (city of departure, my home city), (city of destination, Hawaii), (airline, X), (date, next Tuesday), (ticket class, $X_1$)}

As shown, the question itself will contain some of the required associations. Some other associations can be implicit (city of departure, passenger). The application needs to inquire about the unknown associations before searching for potential flights.

The application may need to handle other concepts and associations. For instance, the user may use concepts like 'next Monday', Today, Tomorrow, and so forth while communicating information about a specific task. A realistic implementation should be able to handle these concepts. A more advanced system should be able to handle concepts like: "same flight as last time", "tickets for the whole family", and so on. The mind is able to handle all these concepts and associations. A computer system, based on a conceptual approach, can do it too.

Many concepts and associations may already be known by the mobile application, based on previous interactions, like personal information, family members, previous itineraries, preferences, and so forth. Such personal information can be conveniently and securely stored by the mobile device. Notice that with an optimal amount of additional information, the specified task can be accomplished via a conceptual interface. Systems based on traditional O-O APIs, on the other hand, present a variety of challenges including: tight coupling, lack of encapsulation, interoperability, versioning, reusability limitations, overall complexity, and lack of conceptual communication.

## 9.4    Consequences

Since concepts and associations are tightly intertwined, most of the consequences related to Concepts apply to information associations. They will not be listed again as part of the current section. The discussion will be limited to the consequences related to AI systems.

**AI Systems**: since the proposed model, based on concepts and associations, attempts to mimic how the mind processes information, they can be utilized to model, study, and implement such systems. Specifically computer systems limited to a specific domain of information like automated reservation and banking systems. On the other hand, the proposed conceptual model is complete and versatile enough to frame, conceptualize and study more general problems like the ones associated with general natural language processing.

The conceptual deductive process described in the earlier section can be generalized. The question itself provides a group of concepts and related information associations. Other relevant concepts and associations may already be known (previous acquired knowledge). The whole group of concepts (I) can be expressed as:

$$C1 = \{(x11, y11), , (x1n, y1n)\}$$
$$C2 = \{(x21, y21), , (x2n, y2n)\}$$
$$...$$
$$...$$
$$X = Cn = \{(xn1, yn1), , (xnn, ynn)\}$$

In order to resolve the unknown association Ci->xij = X, additional information associations are required. New associations (xi, yi) and Concepts can be logically deducted from the existing associations or gathered from the new information being acquired (learnt). Such information can be searched for, read and/or requested from the user. It comes in the form of sentences expressed using the conceptual notation, S= {(x1, y1) ... (xn, yn) }. The process can be repeated until an answer is found or until the information sources and clues are exhausted. Notice that C1, , Cn can be represented as a graph, where the nodes represent

102

the concepts (C1, , Cn). The edges represent the information associations.

By using concepts and information associations, a computer system can realistically mirror the procedure described above and find in deterministic ways the solution to proposed questions or tasks. Obviously there are several obstacles and challenges that need to be addressed in order to mimic the mind when dealing with information associations. These challenges are mitigated by limiting the scope of the problem to a specific information domain.

The section dealing with implementation considerations includes a brief discussion of such challenges. In any case, based on the Biomimetics principles, it should be clear that the thinking patterns of the mind must be studied and mimicked as part of computer systems. After all, computers systems are conceptually information processors and the mind is the ultimate information processor currently known. As a consequence, natural languages should also be emulated as highly evolved messaging mechanisms of communicating conceptual information.

I hope you had the chance to browse through Mr. Jefferson's biography. You may have come across his ideas and writings. In any case, I would like to leave you with enlightened concepts grasped by a timeless and inspired mind:

*"We hold these truths to be self-evident, that all people are created equal, that they are endowed by their Creator with certain unalienable Rights, that among these are Life, Liberty and the pursuit of Happiness."*

Note: Mr. Jefferson would not mind the minor edition.

## 9.5     Conceptual Deductive Approach (demonstration)

In order to demonstrate the conceptual deductive approach, a graph representation can be used. C1, , Cn can be represented as the nodes of the graph. Associations of the form (xi, yj) represent the edges of the graph. The answer to the question is represented by one of the edges: Ci->xij = X

It is necessary to prove that the conceptual approach can find the correct answer (X) based on the known information (provided and acquired): I = {C1, , Cn}

There are three possible cases that need to be proved:

a)  X does not exist according the known information I ={C1, ,Cn}. Therefore no such association exists. The correct answer is found: no such association exists.

b) Explicit information association. The association is made explicit as part of {C1, , Cn}. In other words, Ci->xij=Ck is part of {C1, ,Cn}. Therefore the correct answer is found: X = Ck.

c) Logical deduction. The association can be logically deducted from the known information {C1, , Cn}. To prove this case, the pertinent inference rules {Pe,1, ,Pe,n} need to be looked at. Consider the predicate P that represents the association between C and X:

$$P(C, X) = (Ci\text{->}xij = X)$$

And all the rules related to the creation of the information association (edge) between C and X:

   Pe,1 → P (C, X)
   Pe,2 → P (C, X)

   .....

   Pe,n → P (C, X)

The cause and effect principle applies. If there is an association between C and X (predicate P), a least one predecessor predicate (Pe,k) needs to be true for the association to exist. In other words, for P(C,X) to be true, at least one predecessor predicate (Pe,k) needs to be true so that P(C,X) can be logically deducted.

If the predicate Pe,k is true, we prove P(C,X): Ci->xij=X. To directly prove Pe, k, explicit information needs to exist (step b). If Pe,k is part of {C1, ,Cn}, Pe,k is true. Therefore the answer is found. If Pe,k cannot be proved using {C1, , Cn}, logical deduction (step c) needs to attempted to prove Pe,k. The process is repeated until finding explicit information to prove Pe,k or until the inference rules are exhausted. In which case, the correct answer cannot be found using logical deduction and the known information I = {C1, , Cn}. In summary, for each predicate P there is a group of predecessor predicates (Pe,k) that needs to be checked (zero or more):

Pe,1 v Pe,2 ....v Pe,n → P (C,X) where n>=0

It has been demonstrated that for all the possible scenarios, the correct answer is found, either explicitly or by logical deduction. The process is also able to offer a detailed and rational explanation (i.e. logical) of how the answer was derived based on information associations.

Consider the example provided. According to the demonstration, there are three possible scenarios:

a) X does not exist. If the sentence S = {Mr. Jefferson did not have a wife} is part of {C1, ,Cn}. The current answer is found: no such association exists.

b) Explicit association. If, for instance, the sentence S = {Martha was Mr. Jefferson's wife} is part of {C1, , Cn}. The correct answer is found: X = C->wife = Mrs. Martha Jefferson

c) Logical deduction. While applying logical deduction to find a wife association (C->wife=X) the pertinent inference rules need to be checked:

X married Y → X->wife = Y ^ Y->husband=X

The predicates involved are P: Y is the wife of X, and Pe,1(X,Y): X married Y. The information provided {C1, , Cn} is checked looking for explicit information to prove Pe,1 (X married Y). If such association is explicitly found S= {(Mr. Jefferson) (married) (Martha)}, the correct answer can be given. In other words, Pe,1 (X,Y) is true, therefore P is true by logical deduction. Otherwise the answer cannot be logically deducted since the inference rules have been exhausted. Unless, there are additional inference rules like the one associated with the concept of 'Honeymoom':

X went on a Honeymoon with Y → X married Y →
X->wife=Y ^ Y->husband=X

If so, such inference rule (deeper level) needs to be checked against the known information (step c).

If incomplete information is provided, the deductive process is unable to produce comprehensive results. Consider the sentence S = {Our friend, Mr. Jefferson, married this year}. It does not give enough information to determine a specific answer (name). Obviously, in terms of implementation considerations, it is necessary to provide the system with a complete set of conceptual information (I) and inference rules, in order to expect comprehensive answers. This is feasible, especially for information domains of limited scope. Notice that the known information I = {C1, , Cn} can be *massaged* (or preprocessed) to avoid deep levels of inference as a way of producing better performance. Inference rules may not have to be given explicitly.

An advanced AI system may be able to generate inference rules automatically based on the meaning or definition of the concepts involved. For example, the inference rules above can be automatically

106

derived from the definitions (meaning) of 'wife', 'husband', 'married' and 'honeymoon'.

There is another way in which the conceptual deductive process can be demonstrated. Let us assume that the correct answer is $Y \neq X$. The answer given (X) is incorrect:

$P(C,Y)$ is true. Ci->xij=Y, where $Y \neq X$

If there is an explicit association, the answer Y needs to be consistent with the known information $\{C1, , Cn\}$. However, this would be a contradiction: Y would have been the answer given, by applying the conceptual process, not X. Therefore inference had to be used in order to derive the answer Y:

Pe,1 v Pe,2 ....v Pe,n $\rightarrow$  P(C,Y)

Based on the assumption, $\sim P(C,X)$ is true. Therefore the following can be inferred:

$\sim P(C,X) \rightarrow \sim( Pe,1 \text{ v } Pe,2 ....v Pe,n)$
$\sim P(C,X) \rightarrow \sim Pe,1 \wedge \sim Pe,2 ....\wedge \sim Pe,n$

This represents a contradiction because X was given as the correct answer: at least one predicate Pe,k had to be true. Therefore $Y = X$, the correct answer.

## 9.6    Implementation

The proposed conceptual approach works well for information domains of limited scope. The information domain (D) is restricted to a set of concepts and associations which makes it more manageable:

$D = \{C1, ,Cj\}$   where C1, , Cj are concepts within the specified information domain (D)

For example, the concepts of 'Airline', 'Departure city', 'Ticket', 'Next Monday' have very specific meaning within the context of a reservation application. The degree the ambiguity the application has to deal with is therefore limited. The context of the communication is also very specific.

On the other hand, the more concepts a system is able to handle, the more complex it becomes. A rich an expressive language allows the same concept or idea to be expressed in many different ways. Versatility comes at a cost in terms of system implementation. There are many ways to express "Thomas married Martha". For instance:

A) Thomas and Martha got married

B) Thomas wed Martha

C) Thomas and Martha were joined in marriage

In terms of voice recognition functionality, the system may need to limit the number of ways in which the information is asked. Obviously the more flexibility the system provides, in terms of acceptable concepts and sentences, the more realistic the system becomes.

The general challenge can be specified as follows. Two concepts ($C1 = C2$) are said to be equivalent if they have the same meaning. A, B, C above are equivalent concepts. The computer system needs to be able to process all these sentences and make the associations of equivalence.

Definition (C) = Definition (C1) $\rightarrow$ C = C1

Sentences need to be 'normalized'. Under the current context, it means simplifying their grammatical structure so they can be readily compared. For example, B, C and D can normalized as A because they have the same meaning.

The proposed conceptual approach is flexible and versatile enough to be extended to more general problems related to natural language processing. A detail discussion is beyond the scope of the current effort.

It is also work in progress. However, a brief discussion is provided hereafter.

Such extension is based on a divide-and-conquer approach. Most general natural language processing problems have to deal with many information domains simultaneously. On the other hand, since the proposed approach works well for arbitrary information domains of limited scope, the more general information domain can be divided into restricted information domains $\{D1, ,Dn\}$. The proposed approach can then be applied to such restricted information domains (Dj). One main challenge becomes the identification of the specific domain. Also, it is necessary to find ways of classifying the information into suitable information domains.

For instance, a restricted domain can deal with time related concepts (*when*): 'next Tuesday', 'tomorrow', 'today', and so forth. Another information domain can deal with location related concepts (*where*): 'Hawaii', 'Orlando', 'Seattle', 'home' and so forth. Yet another information domain may deal with concepts related to people (*who*): 'friends', 'family', 'wife', 'daughter', 'son', 'me' and so on. Actually, these three information domains are very reusable and relevant to many applications. This is just an example since there are many ways in which information can be classified.

Consider another example. The mobile personal assistant may have to deal with many types of reservations. The request "I'd like to make a reservation" is ambiguous. In order to prevent ambiguity, the application must request information about the type of reservation being requested. Such piece of information clearly indentifies the subject being discussed and the information domain to be used.

In general, a concept C may have several meanings based on the context (Ctx) which is a concept that needs be taken into account: $Ctx = \{(x1, y1), , (xn, yn)\}$. In particular the context will contain an information association related to the *subject* or *topic* being discussed.

The definition of a specific concept may be dependent on the context being used. In other words, the same concept may have associated several meanings depending on a specific information context.

C = Definition (C, Ctx)

A highly interactive application like the mobile application, the software may request additional information in order to avoid ambiguity: What type of reservation would you like to make? After hearing the question, who is Mr. Jefferson's wife? , the first thing that comes through your mind probably is: Who is Mr. Jefferson? Who is he referring to? The answer to this question clearly identifies the subject of the discussion and deals with ambiguity. I could be speaking about Mr. Jefferson in several contexts including friends, co-workers, and so forth. The meaning of the name will depend on the specific context. Once the context is identified, the ambiguity is resolved. Notice that for systems restricted to specific information domains, the meaning of each concept is usually well-defined. There is a unique definition for each concept being employed.

Other applications may not be as interactive and require autonomous or semi-autonomous processing of information. Such applications need to deal with ambiguity in different ways. Obviously the mind can process what-if scenarios. The proposed conceptual approach can mimic such behavior. Since one or more concepts may have several meanings, depending on the specific context, the application needs to apply heuristic approaches and work with several what-if scenarios concurrently. Such scenarios need to be created and exhaustibly evaluated in order to cope with ambiguity during autonomous or semi-autonomous processing

## 9.7    Related Work

To fully grasp the expressed concepts, you may want to rely on disciplines like philosophy [30], natural language processing [27, 35], knowledge representation [27, 24, 35], cognition [29, 30, 32, 33, 34], and artificial intelligence [25, 28]. Concepts and information associations can be applied to multiple areas in the realm of software engineering. Their applicability is not limited to natural language processing, knowledge representation, and related disciplines. It extends beyond the domain of these disciplines.

The proposed conceptual approach, based on concepts and information associations, is different in several areas including overall realistic approach, application domains, mathematical model, primitive, and information/concept representation. In particular, it attempts to mirror how concepts and information associations are represented by typical natural languages and the mind. Consider that our thinking patterns are based on the same messaging (syntax and semantics) used for human communication. In a sense, we think by 'talking' to ourselves in the confines of the mind by using concepts to achieve understanding.

Several natural language representations have been proposed including the well-known grammatical tree representation. Conceptual graphs [27] are also well-known and rely on first-order logic (predicate calculus). Although the conceptual model does not tackle the general NLP problem, the proposed approach can incrementally scale to address it by using a divide-and-conquer methodology. The topics of ambiguity and the division of information into manageable information domains are also discussed. The deductive approach is based on well-known backward chaining methods of reasoning employed by AI systems which have their mathematical foundation on Boole's Algebra of Logic [1, 22].

## 10.   GROUP

### 10.1   Intent

A group is a concept. As stated before, a concept consists of information about specific aspects of reality. Concepts allow the conceptualization, communication, and processing of information. A group is basically a collection of concepts. Groups serve to organize information (concepts) into more complex information structures. The group abstraction improves reusability, decoupling, encapsulation, interoperability by separating the fundamental information aspect from all other aspects such as how the group is stored, represented, transferred, secured, processed and so forth. Groups are also fully decoupled from the entities that process them.

Entities (sender/receiver), concepts and processing mechanism are decoupled entities, fully independent Consider that there is clear separation between a concept and the mind (or entity) that communicates and processes it. Notice that in many cases, there is not physical connection between the entities in a group. For instance, a group of individuals: there is no physical connection between the individuals themselves. The concept of a group becomes a pure mental abstraction utilized to organize information.

### 10.2   Motivation

The implementation of traditional O-O APIs   applications/services present a variety of challenges including coupling, reusability, versioning, interoperability, lack of encapsulation, scalability, and so on. Consider for example, the design and implementation of a typical mobile application using traditional O-O APIs. This application needs to provide capabilities for accessing, displaying, and updating information stored locally on a database or remotely via web services. The conventional solution for general purpose O-O applications, and in particular for the proposed mobile application, will present a variety of challenges and limitations including:

a) Traditional APIs that deal with collections of entities present strong coupling which ties the solution to a specific platform, technology, data

112

format, and/or computer language. Also, information and processing mechanism are tightly coupled.

b) Traditional collection APIs present reusability limitations which usually results from strong coupling and lack of encapsulation. Such APIs are limited to a specific platform, technology, data format, and/or computer language.

c) Lack of encapsulation usually associated with not using the messaging concept as the communication mechanism.

d) Traditional collection APIs cannot be readily incorporated into components able to handle concurrent processing.

e) Complexities dealing with distributed/SOA technologies which require the manipulation of complicated artifacts such as stubs, IDLs, WSDLs, RPCs, descriptors, or similar. This is also a source of interoperability limitations. Traditional APIs cannot be readily exposed as distributed components or services without a fair amount of effort.

f) Traditional APIs cannot be readily incorporated as part of BPEL/BPM processes.

g) Strong coupling is also the source of complexity, represented as a web of component/module interdependencies and the associated versioning challenges.

Consider any arbitrary traditional object oriented API that interfaces with a database to retrieve a group of entries. For instance, the API used for accessing databases from the Java architecture (JDBC). JDBC components cannot be shared across heterogeneous applications. They are tied to the Java platform. The JDBC API cannot be readily used outside Java. Information and Information processing methods are tightly coupled within JDBC components.

## 10.3 Participants

A group is a concept that can be expressed using the proposed notation:

$$G = \{a1, , an\}$$

Expressed in plain terms, a group is an ordered set of concepts:

$$G = \{C1, C2, .. , Cn\}$$

A concept is defined as a group of information associations:

$$C = \{a1, a2, ..., an\}$$

$ai$ is an information association of the form $(xi, yi)$, meaning that $xi$ is equal or associated to $yi$ ($xi = yi$). A Concept ($C$) can be recursively expressed as:

$$C = \{(x1, y1), (x2, y2), , (xn, yn)\}$$

- xi/yi represents a valid sequence of symbols (word or number) in any arbitrary language.
- Or, xi/yi represents a concept as defined by C.

A group can be expressed as:

$$G = \{(1, C1), (2, C2), , (n, Cn)\}$$

Each association $(xi, yi)$ consists of a concept $(Ci)$ and the position of the concept $(i)$ in the group $(i, Ci)$. For simplicity and readability sake, groups will be expressed implicitly as:

$$G = \{C1, , Cn\}$$

114

For instance, the result of an arbitrary database query can be expressed as a *group* of concepts. Each individual concept represents a row in the database. Consider a query that returns a group of entries from a database:

$$G = \{C1, C2, \quad , Cn\}$$

$$C1 = \{(name, Danny), (age, 20)\}$$
$$C2 = \{(name, Jenny), (age, 19)\}$$

....

$$Cn = \{(name, Paul), (age, 50)\}$$

## 10.4   Consequences

**Reusability:** Concepts, and groups in particular, improve reusability. Actually they are highly reusable entities. The mind is able to reuse concepts to understand, frame, communicate and solve diverse problems. Groups can be used to convey information in a variety of scenarios. A few examples include:

- A collection of entities is a *group* of entities.

- A list of entities consists of a *group* of entities.

- The entries contained in a hash table, array, vector and so on, constitute a *group*. Complex structures can be represented as *groups* of entities.

- A document consists of a *group* of pages which in turn consist of *groups* of paragraphs composed of *groups* of sentences and so forth.

- Information consists of a *group* of concepts: $I = \{C1, , Cn\}$

- Conceptually, a database is a *group* of interrelated entries. All the information (I) contained in the database can be expressed as a *group* of concepts. The same principle applies to a *group* of entries retrieved using an arbitrary database query.

As a consequence, groups can be reused for the implementation of a variety of technologies. Notice that a single abstraction can be reused to represent arbitrary data structures.

**Decoupling:** Groups improve decoupling. There is separation between the concept itself (group) and the entity that process it. Both concerns can be altered independently. Groups also separate the fundamental information aspect from other aspects such as how the group information is stored, represented, transferred, secured, processed and so forth. Groups, like all other concepts, are passive entities that only serve the purpose of conveying information.

**Distributed Component/Service Model:** The information pattern family consists of a set of abstractions required for the specification and implementation of a complete distributed component/service model (Turing Complete). Remote animated components are treated as local ones. Actually, there is no *artificial* difference between local and remote components. They are both exactly the same component. Stubs, IDLs, WSDLs or similar artificial abstractions add complexity and are not required. The information patterns provide transparent access to remote components. Conceptual information, represented as groups ($G = \{C1, ,Cn\}$), can be freely transferred between distributed components and systems regardless of platform, technologies, languages, protocols, data representation, and so on.

**Interoperability**: Groups help improve interoperability. As discussed earlier, groups of the form $G = \{C1, , Cn\}$ can be freely interchanged between systems and components regardless of technologies, computer languages, protocols, data representation, and so on. The same principle applies to any arbitrary group ($G$). In a sense, concepts are fluid abstractions that can be interchanged between systems, components and applications.

An information process, based on the family of information patterns, can incorporate components and applications that use multiple technologies, languages, platforms, protocols, and so forth.

**BPM/BPEL/ESB processes**: Groups can be readily incorporated into BPM/BPEL/ESB processes because of their interoperability and platform agnostic characteristics. Group information can be transparently shared between heterogeneous components and applications.

## 10.5 Known Uses

**Design patterns.** Concepts including groups have been used to implement and/or facilitate the implementation (i.e. reusable implementation) of well-known design patterns like Gang of Four design patterns (GoF), DAO, MVC, J2EE Design patterns, Master-Worker, and so forth [2]. Consider that many design pattern implementations need to deal with information in the form of groups of objects or concepts. The concept of group can be applied each time a collection of entities is required.

The reusable group abstraction is a perfect match for those situations. By using it, you also avoid coupling, reusability, data representation, and interoperability limitations. Consider that groups and concepts in general, can be freely interchanged between local and distributed components part of heterogeneous architectures and processes. For instance, a DAO implementation often requires that groups of data source entries be returned as part of data queries. Such information may need to be sent to a distributed application based on a different architecture which is readily accomplished by relying on the group concept.

**Distributed Component and Service Model.** As mentioned earlier, concepts including groups, are well suited for the implementation of a complete distributed component/service model (Turing complete) able to handle complex real-world considerations such as security, redundancy, interoperability, fault tolerance, concurrency, scalability, and so on. The group abstraction contributes to achieving such seamless distributed model and implementation because it allows the transparent interchange of information, in the form of groups of concepts, between application using heterogeneous technologies, data representations, computer languages and protocols.

**BPM/BPEL frameworks and technologies.** The group abstraction is part of the conceptual framework required for the implementation of reusable business process technologies (BPEL/BPM), frameworks, and applications. Groups can be readily reused as part of UML/BPM/BPEL diagrams (and processes) in order to design and implement applications with comparable functionality to traditional business process applications.

The group abstraction contributes to the seamless interchange of information between local and distributed components, part of heterogeneous business processes (BPEL/BPM): groups of concepts can be freely exchanged across the board. Groups and concepts in general, minimize coupling, interoperability, and data representation limitations. They represent a key aspect of a communication framework able to support fluid exchange of information between process participants (both local and distributed).

## 10.6    Implementation

Concepts, including groups, can be implemented using arbitrary computer technologies. The object abstraction is implemented via the language compiler or interpreter. Groups can be implemented using similar capabilities. Consider the concepts C1, , Cn and the group G:

C1 = {(name,Danny), (age,20)}
C2 = {(name, Jenny), (age,19)}


....


Cn= {(name, Paul), (age, 50)}

G = {C1, ,Cn}

These concepts can be constructed and managed using a hypothetical conceptual computer language as follows:

118

Concept Person1 = new Concept ();
Concept Person2 = new Concept ();
Group G = new Group ();

Person1->name = "Danny";
Person1->age = 20;

Person2->name = "Jenny";
Person2->age = 19;

Person3->name = "Paul";
Person3->age = 50;

G = {Person, Person1}; // Initialize the group

G += Person3;           // Add a member to the group

The semantics of "->" is similar to "." for O-O objects. It expresses the information association (or attribute). For instance, C->name is the name associated to the Person (C). "+" and "-" represent the usual set operations.

A conceptual interface (CI) can be defined to manage the group abstraction. The following are the main messages needed:

1) Create information (CREATE).
   1.1) Create group: $G = \{M1, , Mn\}$ where M1, , Mn are concepts
   1.2) Members can be added to the group: $G + M$
2) Read information (READ).
   2.1) First member of the group: $G$->*first*

   2.2) Last member: $G$->*last*

   2.3) Next member: $G$->*next*

   2.4) Previous member: $G$->*previous*

119

3) Update information (UPDATE). CREATE and REMOVE cover the functionality required to update the group.

4) Remove information (REMOVE).

4.1) Remove group

4.2) Remove member from the group: $G - M$

5) Send information (SEND). This message is implemented by the messaging abstraction.

## 10.7 Related Patterns

The group abstraction is related to the Composite design pattern in terms of functionality. The main difference is that groups, like all other concepts, do not have information processing capabilities. The concept, a passive entity, only conveys information. There is complete separation between the group abstraction and the component handling it. Both concerns are fully decoupled. A third party, like a Factory or conceptual computer language, is responsible for handling and maintaining the group abstraction. Groups are also handled via a conceptual interface based on Messaging and a well defined set of information related messages. As a consequence, the group abstraction may be leveraged for the reusable implementation of the Composite design pattern. Like the other patterns, part of the information pattern family, groups can also be used for the reusable implementation of design patterns dealing with collections of entities.

# 11.  MEMORY OR INFORMATION REPOSITORY

## 11.1  Intent

The concept of memory or information repository represents the ability to store persistent information for later retrieval and use. Animated or Live entities are able to independently process information and usually rely on a memory component or subsystem to provide information storage capabilities. The memory abstraction improves decoupling, encapsulation and reusability. It also separates the information aspect from other aspects such as representation, storage technology, and computer language. Information is usually stored in the forms of concepts: conceptual information.

## 11.2  Applicability

The memory or information repository abstraction can be applied in several situations. Specifically, it can be applied in the context of persistent information. Information processors are able to store persistent information via its memory capabilities. Consider the human memory. It is able to store many types of information in the form of concepts. It also allows individuals to learn new concepts and apply learned ones. As a consequence, individuals can better cope and adapt to their environment. Many of their information processing capabilities rely heavily on having a way to store and remember persistent information.

Obviously the same concepts and principles apply to computer systems and software since they are also information processors. Persistent information can be stored using many electronic representations, technologies and APIs including XML, binary files, relational databases, noSQL, object databases, WWW (html), flat files and so on. A conceptual interface (CI) is well suited for arbitrary problems in reality since it deals with information, and conceptual information, in particular. The memory abstraction is about storing and managing persistent information.

In terms of functionality, the conceptual interface associated to the memory abstraction, is straightforward. Conceptual information, consisting of information associations and concepts, can be either stored or updated regardless of the type of information. On the other hand, it cannot be selectively removed from memory. However, there are mechanisms by which information is forgotten, perhaps as an efficient way of removing it and making room for new information.

As discussed earlier, computer systems, smartphones, and automated systems in general, consist of memory components. However, a lot of information contained in the human memory is stored in the form of concepts (conceptual information). Based on the understanding of the concepts and principles behind Biomimetics, it should become clear that such characteristic behavior should be mirrored by computer systems and software.

The proposed conceptual interface is applicable regardless of representation, storage technology, and computer language. In terms of simplicity, which is a valuable software characteristic, the natural conceptual interface is probably the simplest interface available. Then again, nature sets the golden standard to be mirrored when it comes to efficiency, completeness and streamlined design.

Memory is an internal information repository limited to be used by a single entity. On the other hand, a general information repository is not limited to be accessed by a single Animated/Live component or entity. Consider the case of a database which is a typical information repository. It can handle concurrent and distributed access requests coming from a diverse set of components and/or applications. A similar situation applies to the World Wide Web which is also an external information repository. Human beings rely on many sources of information, or information repositories, as the basis for decision making: WWW, databases, and so forth.

A general information repository usually needs to handle additional considerations such as transactions, locking, authentication, authorization permissions and so on. The information (I) contained in a database, or any other information repository for that matter, can be represented as a group of concepts: $I = \{C1, C2, ,Cn\}$

As a lesson learned from nature and the mind, we should observe that information processing (computing) can be achieved without consideration of the specific storage mechanism and/or representation being employed. Again, consider the human memory, people are able to use the information stored in memory without knowing how the actual information is represented and stored. Scientists have limited knowledge in terms of the actual mechanism being employed. From the standpoint of our information processing capabilities, such lack of knowledge have no impact on how effectively we process information.

The same concept applies to software. Systems and applications should be able to operate independently of how the information is being represented and/or stored: storage technology, computer language, data format, etc. After observing the human mind, it should be clear that such considerations are of secondary nature. Information content represented by semantics (i.e. meaning) rules over representation: content over form as expected.

All the conceptual information contained in the mind, or any information repository for that matter, can be expressed as a group of concepts: $I = \{C1, C2, , Cn\}$. On the other hand, the group of concepts (I) can be expressed using arbitrary data representations and technologies. Consider the XML representation where each concept (Ci) is represented as an XML element. The information associations $Ci = \{a1, a2, , an\}$ can be represented using XML subelements. A similar procedure and argument can be utilized for any data representation or technology including relational databases.

Mathematically speaking, all possible representations of information are equivalent regardless of storage technology, computer language, and/or data representation. Such representations carry exactly the same information. Expressed in mathematical terms all possible representations are equivalently expressed as $I = \{C1, C2, , Cn\}$. All possible representations also have the same *amount* of information and content (semantics). Semantically speaking they all share exactly the same meaning.

Having a multitude of representations, technologies and traditional APIs does not always have a positive impact on software. It brings forth the issues of lack of efficiency, redundancy, software cost and the 'Tower of Babel syndrome' which hinders interoperability between heterogeneous technologies, APIs, computer languages and data sources.

By using a common conceptual interface based on realistic abstractions and messaging such challenges are either mitigated or eliminated. Notice also that besides its memory, the mind does not require any additional information storage capabilities. Obviously there are implementation considerations that need to be taken into account: data volume, speed/performance, response time, and so forth. However, such considerations can be hidden from software components and applications, by the information repository abstraction and its conceptual interface.

## 11.3   Motivation

The implementation of the information repository abstraction based on traditional O-O APIs present a variety of challenges including coupling, reusability, versioning, interoperability, lack of encapsulation, scalability, and so on.   Consider for example, the design and implementation of the proposed mobile application using traditional O-O APIs. The application needs to provide capabilities for accessing, displaying, and updating arbitrary information stored locally on a database or remotely via web services.

Consider also any arbitrary traditional object oriented API that interfaces with a database or information repository. For instance, the API used for accessing databases from the Java architecture (JDBC). JDBC components and API cannot be shared across heterogeneous applications. They are tied to the Java platform. The JDBC API cannot be readily used outside the Java platform. The conventional O-O API will present a variety of challenges and limitations including:

a) Strong coupling which ties the solution and API to a specific platform, technology, data representation, and/or computer language. Information and processing mechanism are also tightly coupled.

b) Lack of encapsulation usually associated with not using messaging as the communication abstraction and mechanism.

c) Lack of reusability which usually results from strong coupling and lack of encapsulation. The solution and API are tied to specific platform, data representation and/or computer technology which hinders reusability.

d) Complexities dealing with SOA and distributed component access. Traditional O-O APIs do not rely on a conceptual/messaging interface and cannot be readily exposed as web services and/or distributed components. They present the complexities associated with distributed artifacts required for remote invocation.

e) Interoperability limitations brought about by strong coupling in the form of platform, technology, language and/or data representation dependencies.

f) Traditional O-O APIs cannot be readily reused as part of BPEL/BPL processes and technologies.

g) The lack of a realistic conceptual interface introduces a higher level of unnecessary complexity, versioning challenges, artificiality, and lack of reusability/portability.

By the way, if the proposed mobile application needs to be ported from pure Java to the Android platform, you will quickly realize that Android does not provide support for the standard JDBC API. A new Android API needs to be learned. Most of the database functionality will need to be discarded and re-implemented using a non-standard Android API with the associated impact in terms of reusability, portability, cost, quality, timelines, learning curve, and so on. Two separate incompatible APIs need to be supported. Substantial changes to the existing software will probably be required in order to replace the existing API calls. The described challenges help illustrate some of the limitations shown by traditional O-O APIs.

By using a conceptual paradigm and API such challenges can be significantly mitigated or minimized. A new Adapter can be implemented and incorporated to interface with the Android API, without having to make any changes to the existing software. The needed Android adapter may already be available for reuse or purchase. Live/Animated components $(A = (f(m), I))$ are fully encapsulated and can be independently reused at the component level.

## 11.4   Participants

In the real world, and as part of a realistic information model, participant components can be divided into two main categories: a) entities that can process information (Components) and b) Entities that cannot (Concepts).

a)   Memory component. Single component responsible for implementing the memory abstraction and the associated conceptual interface.

b)   Concepts. All the information (I) contained in the data source can be represented as a group of concepts regardless of the type and complexity of the information being stored: $I = \{C1, C2, , Cn\}$ A representation based on concepts completely separates the information itself from the component(s) processing the information.

c)   Data Source Adapter. Component responsible for interfacing with the data source. It transforms the messages used by the conceptual interface to the appropriate API calls needed to interface with the data source. An independent adapter is needed for each technology, API and data representation being employed by the application. For instance, the particular application being implemented may need adapters for JDBC, Android, XML, and so on.

## 11.5　Diagram

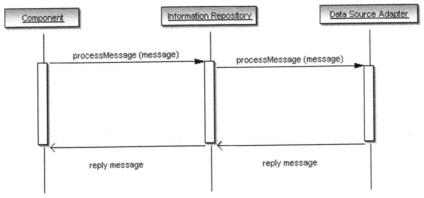

**Fig. 1 Memory or Information Repository**

## 11.6　Collaboration

Other components and applications interact with the memory component via a conceptual interface (CI). There are four messages applicable to the memory abstraction:

> Create (manufacture) conceptual information
> Read (retrieve) conceptual information
> Update conceptual information
> Delete (discard) conceptual information

These messages mimic the capabilities exhibited by the human memory. They also represent a straightforward and complete set based on the fundamental concept of information. Messages received by the memory component are forwarded to the preconfigured Data Source Adapter required by the application. In turn, the Adapter interfaces with the data source using an appropriate API in order to retrieve and maintain the stored information. For instance, Adapters may be needed for JDBC, Android, relational database APIs, object database APIs, XML, binary representation, flat file and so on.

## 11.7    Consequences

**Decoupling:**    The memory abstraction improves decoupling.    The component responsible for its implementation is completely independent (decoupled). Messaging is the only mechanism of communication between the memory component and other components and applications. The abstraction also separates the information aspect from how such information is stored and represented.

**Encapsulation:** The memory abstraction helps maximize encapsulation. The memory component and the concepts being stored are totally encapsulated entities.    Messaging   is   the   only   mechanism   of communication.

**Reusability:** As stated earlier, information is a highly reusable concept which applies to every aspect of reality. The conceptual information stored by the memory or information repository can be expressed as a group of concepts regardless of the type and characteristics of the information being managed: $I = \{C1, C2, ,Cn\}$. The same straightforward conceptual API, mirrored from nature, can be reused regardless of technology, language, data representation and so on.

A reusable implementation of the information repository abstraction is feasible and recommended. Such implementation can be reused independently of the specific information being store. The proposed abstraction also improves reusability because its implementation can be readily reused as part of heterogeneous processes in the form of SOA service or distributed component.

Because of the complete separation of information (concept) and the component processing the information, the memory abstraction improves information reusability. An application can make use of information repositories or data sources intended for other applications. For instance, the proposed mobile application can communicate with external information repositories while looking for conceptual information related to hotel or airline reservations. Using a common conceptual interface significantly facilitates the reuse and sharing of information. The concept of reuse is not limited to computer software and components; it can be

128

extended to information repositories and data sources. A conceptual paradigm fosters information reuse as well.

**Scalability:** Since it is not based on distributed artifacts, the conceptual interface associated to the information repository abstraction, do not present scalability limitations. Client and Server software can be transparently and methodologically upgraded avoiding service interruptions. Conceptual interfaces are able to gracefully scale and support large installations running 24/7. Messages can be updated and new messages can be added without having any impact on the messaging infrastructure and mechanism.

**Distributed Component/Service Model:** As mentioned before, the conceptual interface associated to the information repository can be readily exposed as a SOA service or distributed component. Distributed components and services implemented using the information pattern family, are treated as local components for all practical purposes. Complex artifacts such as stubs, IDLs, WSDLs or similar are not required.

The information pattern family provides the infrastructure required to ensure transparent and secure access to distributed components and services. Mobile applications can take advantage of distributed access to large repositories of information. Because of many considerations including resource constraints and data maintenance, it is not practical to store this type of information locally. Distributed access from mobile devices becomes a must-have requirement.

**Interoperability**: The information repository abstraction facilitates and promotes the integration of heterogeneous processes and technologies. The conceptual interface associated to the information repository abstraction can be readily incorporated as part of processes that use multiple technologies, languages, platforms, and data representation. By using a conceptual interface, the information repository can be transparently accessed via a web service, BPEL/BPM process and/or distributed interface.

The conceptual information stored as part of the information repository is independent of language, technology, protocol, and/or data representation. Information (I) can be mathematically expressed as group of concepts: $I = \{C1, C2, ,Cn\}$ that can be represented using arbitrary formats and technologies: XML, relational database, non-relational database, object database, flat file, binary representation, and so on. Conceptual information can also be transparently transferred between heterogeneous components and systems using any protocol or technology.

**UML/BPM/BPEL diagrams and applications**: The memory abstraction can be readily incorporated into UML/BPM/BPEL diagrams and production quality BPEL/BPM applications.

**Conceptual Framework**: The information repository concept, member of the information pattern family, should be implemented as part of a reusable conceptual framework able to provide the infrastructure required for dealing with complex real-world challenges. Such reusable implementation of the information pattern family is not only possible but also recommended because of its impact on reusability, cost, project timelines, quality, and so on. Software implementation is able to focus on the specific business and technical requirements to be met by the application. Most of the information requirements are provided by the conceptual framework and can be readily reused. A conceptual framework is very similar to all other communication frameworks employed by human beings (phone, email, instant messaging, Cable, etc) which provide the reusable infrastructure required for the interchange, storage and management of information.

**Conceptual Paradigm**: A conceptual paradigm helps understand the abstractions (i.e. concepts) found in nature. Entities like Gravity and Force should be studied from the standpoint of Concepts. The same principle applies to the natural concept of memory. It is challenging to find drawbacks, trade-offs and limitations for these natural abstractions, which is difficult to explain within the context of design pattern methodologies.

A conceptual paradigm, on the other hand, offers an explanation for the apparent inconsistencies. Since concepts are extracted from natural reality, and nature sets the ultimate standard, finding drawbacks and

130

trade-offs is not really feasible or necessary within a conceptual paradigm. For instance, consider the concepts of Gravity, Energy and Force. Trying to find drawbacks and limitations associated to these concepts is probably a futile undertaking. Mathematical perfection with no inconsistencies defines their natural existence. Also, the aforementioned concepts are unique and there are no similar natural concepts that can be used for comparison purposes. The same principle can be generalized to many other natural concepts and laws including the concept of memory.

The Mathematical Universe Theory should also be mentioned [31]. If such theory is true, *everything* in the Universe is governed by mathematical laws, including the mind and its memory mechanisms. Nature and all its processes seem to behave like a clock, with mathematical precision and perfection.

**Overhead:** Transferring messages between components introduces a small overhead when compared with traditional method/procedure invocation. As computers become faster and faster this becomes a non-issue. Also, the benefits of messaging outweigh the small performance cost.

## 11.8  Implementation

The memory abstraction is based on a straightforward conceptual interface that mirrors its natural contra part. It consists of a set of four messages:

Create (manufacture) conceptual information
Read (retrieve) conceptual information
Update conceptual information
Delete (discard) conceptual information

Since the memory abstraction is usually implemented as an internal component, the set of software requirements and messages is straightforward. In general, there is no need to be concerned about consideration such as concurrency, security, authentication, authorization, permissions, and so forth.

Consider for instance a mobile application running locally and intended for a single user without distributed data access. The aforementioned considerations usually do not apply.

Information repositories, on the other hand, usually need to handle other aspects which are specific to information storage technologies such as transactions, locking, security, connection pools, authentication, authorization, access control, permissions, and so forth. Many of these aspects are handled by the information pattern family, as part of a conceptual framework, which provide secure/remote access to distributed components and/or services. Some of the other aforementioned requirements can be readily handled by adding the relevant pieces of information (i.e. associations) to the messages. A few new messages may also be defined to implement locking, transactions, data security, access control, permissions and so forth.

Notice that conceptual interfaces are flexible and versatile enough to readily accommodate new messages and/or versions of existing messages. Because of decoupling such changes have no impact whatsoever on the messaging mechanism/interface. As opposed to method parameters, the amount of information passed in the form of associations is optimal: no more and no less than what is strictly required for efficient communication. A disciplined approach is able to ensure backward compatibility in terms of the messages being exchanged. Since a conceptual interface based on the information primitive is Turing complete, arbitrary technical and business requirements can be met.

An advanced conceptual interface is able to handle messages of arbitrary complexity. Consider the following message targeted to an automated reservation system: "Retrieve information about all the flights bound for Hawaii departing next week". Such interface need to handle concepts in several domains including: place (Hawaii, Denver, Orlando, etc.) and time (next week, next Tuesday, the 22dn, afternoon, etc.).

The Information Repository component relies on other components (Adapters) to deal with aspects such as technology, API, and representation. Messages received by the Information Repository component are forwarded to the appropriate adapter. From the standpoint of software, the storage technology, API, and representation can be independently altered without having any impact on functionality.

132

## 11.9    Known Uses

**Design patterns Implementation.** The information pattern family and the memory abstraction have been employed for the reusable implementation of well-known design patterns dealing with information persistency. In particular, Data Access Objects (DAO) and Animated or Live Entities. On the other hand, information persistency can be implemented via the memory abstraction without the need for traditional objects and configuration files. Consider that a large database usually requires a large number of DAO objects and descriptors to represent the stored data. Animated or Live entities usually require the implementation of memory capabilities in order to 'remember' and process persistent information: context information, dialog information, messaging and so on.

**Component and Conceptual Frameworks**: The information pattern family and the information repository abstraction are well suited for the implementation of complete object oriented frameworks able to handle, in very natural fashion, complex information challenges like persistency, transactions, locking, connection pools, caching, security, permissions, distributed data access, concurrency, and so on.

Frameworks implemented based on the information patterns are also able to operate at a higher level of abstraction: conceptual level. In order to accurately mirror the thinking patterns of the mind, a conceptual framework is required. The data persistency complexities are managed and hidden by the information repository abstraction. Software components and applications do not need to know how conceptual information is internally managed in order to successfully retrieve it and use it for processing purposes. Aspects such as technology, computer language, and data representation can be altered independently without having an impact on the information content itself (i.e. semantics) and the processing mechanism.

**Distributed Component and Service Model [4].** The information repository abstraction has been readily reused for the implementation of heterogeneous processes and technologies (BPEL/BPM). Distributed access to information repositories is fully supported via the information patterns which hide the complexities associated with distributed data persistency and component/service access. Concepts can be freely retrieved and shared among applications/services based on the proposed abstractions. Sharing and reuse of conceptual data among multiple organizations, departments, technologies and applications is facilitated by the proposed abstractions.

## 11.10   Related Patterns

Information repository or memory is related to the Data Access Object (DAO) pattern. The use of concepts and the associated conceptual interface is the main difference between both abstractions. Concepts provide an absolute separation (decoupling) between information and the entity or component processing it. DAOs are based on traditional O-O APIs. A conceptual approach eliminates the need for DAO descriptors and 'artificial' objects which ties the solution to a computer language, technology, data representation and/or DAO implementation.

Consider that a large database may contain a considerable amount of entities and relationships which need to be 'artificially' represented as objects and included as part of DAO descriptors and/or configuration files. Every entity is represented using the object abstraction, although not all of them are associated to physical objects. Most of the 'objects' only require getters and setters necessary to manipulate the information attributes and could be easily and realistically represented as concepts without information processing capabilities. Consider that every single one of these entities is represented and stored by the human memory as a concept.

## 12. DIALOG

### 12.1　Intent

The concept of Dialog represents the interchange of information between two or more entities. Such information exchange is accomplished via messaging between the parties involved. The abstraction improves decoupling, encapsulation, reusability and scalability by separating message, messaging mechanism, and component functionality. Components, messages and messaging mechanism are decoupled entities, fully independent and encapsulated. Information is usually exchanged in the form of concepts via a conceptual interface like the ones provided by natural languages.

### 12.2　Applicability

The interchange of information, in the form of dialog, happens all around us between individuals, communities, computer systems, components, and so forth. The dialog abstraction can be utilized in a variety of scenarios. In general, concepts are highly reusable entities. They can be applied to multiple problems and situations. As a concept, the dialog abstraction is not an exception. It can be applied to multiple scenarios including groups of local/distributed components and systems working cooperatively and engaged in exchanging information.

Consider the communication between human beings. Sophisticated mechanisms of communication (i.e. languages) have evolved over the ages to transfer information in the form of concepts. Advanced computer frameworks and telecommunication capabilities have been developed and refined to allow the dialog between individuals and organizations. A dialog is a highly evolved and efficient mechanism of exchanging conceptual information. It is able to naturally handle complex challenges such as redundancy, fault tolerance, security, distributed/asynchronous messaging, etc. For instance, during the course of a conversation, additional information can be requested: why do you mean by that? A sentence (message) may be asked to be repeated: can you repeat what you just said?

As stated earlier, the dialog concept can be applied in a variety of contexts and scenarios. In particular, the concept of dialog applies to the communication between heterogeneous components, systems and applications. Most of what can be learned about the concept of dialog, in the context of human communication, can be mirrored and applied to solve communication challenges in the context of concurrent/distributed computer applications and components. Both scenarios share the same exact concept. It can be said that both scenarios are conceptually equivalent; therefore they share a common approach, implementation and overall solution.

## 12.3    Motivation

The implementation of information exchange (i.e. dialog) based on traditional O-O APIs  present a variety of challenges including coupling, reusability, versioning, interoperability, lack of encapsulation, scalability, and so on.    Consider for example, the design and implementation of a typical mobile application using traditional O-O APIs.  The proposed application needs to provide capabilities for accessing, displaying, and updating arbitrary information stored locally on a database and remotely via web services. Like for most mobile applications, concurrent processing of information is also a requirement.

The conventional O-O APIs will present a variety of challenges and limitations including:

a) Strong coupling which ties the solution to a specific platform, technology, data format, multithreading mechanism, and/or computer language. Information and processing mechanism are also tightly coupled.

b) Lack of encapsulation usually associated with not using messaging as the communication abstraction and mechanism. A web of tightly coupled component interdependencies gets created. Versioning of applications and APIs introduce unnecessary complexity.  The threading mechanism is usually 'artificially' implemented as a separate object. A single thread may also be artificially associated with multiple components.

c) Lack of reusability which usually results from strong coupling, lack of encapsulation and the lack of reusable concepts such as the ones provided by the information pattern family.

d) Complexity dealing with asynchronous communication, concurrency, thread management, synchronization, race conditions, deadlocks, and so on.

e) Complexities dealing with distributed/SOA technologies which require the manipulation of distributed artifacts such as stubs, IDLs, WSDLs, RPCs, or similar.

f) Quality and testing issues. Testing of traditional multithreaded APIs and applications is a complex, risky and challenging activity. It is fairly easy to introduce bugs. On the other hand, it can be fairly difficult and time consuming to avoid, reproduce, catch, and fix bugs within the context of traditional multithreaded APIs. Bugs may appear sporadically under very specific multithreading conditions that are hard to avoid and reproduce. Large multithreaded applications and/or large teams, complicate the problem further. Such quality issues have a negative impact on overall software risk, especially in the context of mission critical applications where software failure may result in loss of life or injury: control systems for health care, automotive, aviation, and so on.

g) Scalability and interoperability limitations brought about by strong coupling, lack of encapsulation and the use of distributed artifacts.

## 12.4   Participants

In reality, and as part of a realistic information model, participant components can be divided into two categories: a) entities that can process information (Components) and b) Entities that cannot (Concepts). Relatively speaking, very few entities in reality are able to independently process information. All the others can be represented as concepts.

a) Components. Collection of independent entities that interchange information as part of the *dialog*. Such entities can be systems, applications or *Live* or *Animated entities*. They are able to behave and process information (messaging) independently from the rest of the system, which usually means that the component uses its own independent processing mechanism or thread of execution.

b) Messaging concept. The interchange of information between participants is achieved via the messaging abstraction as specified by the concept of Messaging: sender, receiver, message and messaging mechanism are decoupled, encapsulated and fully independent. In the context of a realistic model, messages can take many forms all of which can be modeled using computer software: a number, a text/email message, a document, a spoken sentence, a letter, energy (light, sound, electric impulse, analog signal, etc.), biochemical message, and so on. All forms of messaging are modeled: synchronous, asynchronous, streaming, distributed messaging, two-way messaging, secure messaging, and combinations of these forms.

c) Optional memory subcomponent. Each participant component usually consists of a memory subcomponent responsible for persistent information storage and management. A lot of the information is stored in the form of concepts (conceptual information). A separate chapter covers the memory abstraction in more detail.

d) Dialog related concepts. As part of the dialog implementation, several additional concepts may need to be stored and manipulated. Such information includes the following concepts: contextual information, dialog topic, conversation state, and so forth.

## 12.5  Diagram

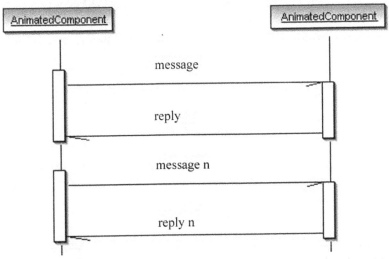

**Fig. 1 Asynchronous Dialog between two Animated/Live Entities.**


## 12.6  Collaboration

The dialog abstraction and its implementation are based on other abstractions that seek to accurately mirror reality:

a) Concept of Messaging.  Sender, receiver, message, and messaging mechanism are decoupled entities, encapsulated and fully independent.

b) Live or Animated entities that interact with each other and interchange information (i.e. *messaging*) within the context of a dialog. Live/Animated components rely on Messaging as the mechanism of communication to establish a dialog with other components and applications (Fig. 1).

Animated or Live components are able to engage in elaborated patterns of collaboration and dialog in order to exchange information as part of complex and realistic processes.

c) Live or Animated entities usually include a memory subcomponent that provides persistent storage capabilities for conceptual information. All the information (I) stored in memory can be expressed as a group of concepts and information associations: $I = \{C1, C2, , Cn\}$ where $Ci = \{a1, a2, , an\}$. The memory subcomponent provides a conceptual interface (CI) to maintain and update such persistent information.

The proposed dialog abstraction is capable of modeling all forms of messaging: synchronous, asynchronous, streaming, distributed messaging, secure messaging, and combinations of these forms. In reality, information itself, encapsulated as a message, can assume many forms as well. Information is exchanged in the form of concepts via a conceptual interface. In other words, the messaging abstraction carries messages which represent concepts.

In the case of asynchronous communication, a Live or Animated component processes incoming messages, on at a time, via its independent processing mechanism or thread of execution (Fig. 2-4). It relies on the information primitive to process incoming messages. In other words, the Animated component is constantly processing incoming information via its independent thread of execution, which mainly waits for incoming messages and processes them by invoking the information primitive: *processInformation (message)*.

Animated or Live components are able to engage in elaborated patterns of collaboration and dialog with other animated components, in order to exchange information as part of complex processes. The dialog abstraction can be readily incorporated into heterogeneous distributed BPM/BPEL processes and applications.

## 12.7 Consequences

**Decoupling:** The dialog abstraction helps maximize decoupling. Participant components, messaging mechanism and conceptual information (concepts) are completely independent (decoupled) within

140

the context of the dialog pattern. Messaging is the only channel of communication between components which accurately mirrors reality.

**Encapsulation:** This pattern helps maximize encapsulation. Dialog participants and concepts are totally encapsulated. Again, messaging is the only channel of communication between components.

**Reusability:** This pattern helps improve reusability. The dialog abstraction is fully implementable. Most of the functionality required to implement the dialog abstraction can be reused. A generic implementation can be achieved based on the information pattern family. The information pattern family, including the dialog abstraction, also improves and encourages reuse because components can be integrated from multiple platforms, languages, communication protocols and technologies. In other words, technologies, languages, protocols can be freely mixed and matched within the context of the dialog pattern.

The proposed dialog abstraction can also be leveraged to provide reusable implementations of related design patterns[2]. For instance, a reusable MVC implementation is feasible based on information pattern family, including dialog. A generic implementation of MVC can be achieved. The same principle applies to the implementation of other design patterns where the dialog concept is relevant.

**Distributed Component/Service Model (SOA):** The information patterns, including the dialog abstraction, can be employed for the specification and implementation of a complete distributed component/service model (Turing Complete). The dialog pattern provides transparent access to distributed applications, components and services. The proposed abstraction hides and/or minimizes the complexities associated with concurrency and distributed component access. Stubs, IDLs, WSDLs or similar artifacts add complexity and are not required.

**Multithreaded artifacts**: Traditional multithreading has been replaced by realistic abstractions. In reality, component functionality and threading/processing mechanism are inherently linked and part of a single encapsulated unit. They should not be artificially modeled and implemented as separate entities. Animated components minimize the

141

complexity and issues associated with traditional multithreaded APIs. Race conditions and deadlocks are reduced. Keep in mind that the messaging abstraction and its asynchronous queuing mechanism ensure that messages are placed in the queue and processed sequentially by the Animated/Live component. The messaging abstraction, usually implemented by a conceptual framework, ensures that access to the shared resource (message queue) is properly controlled.

**Interoperability**: As part of a dialog, components and applications that use multiple technologies, languages, platforms, and protocols can be incorporated. All these aspects can be altered independently. The information abstractions involved are independent from a specific language, technology and/or protocol. Platforms, languages, technologies and protocols can be transparently mixed and matched within the context of a dialog. For instance, the information can be interchanged regardless of what communication technology or protocol is being employed: sockets, .Net, HTTP, RMI, REST, SSL, EJBs, etc. All these technologies and protocols can be transparently incorporated as part of a dialog.

**Scalability:** Traditional O-O APIs present scalability limitations [2, 14]. Because of tight coupling, client and server software need to be upgraded at the same time which is usually not feasible for large installations and/or operations running 24/7. Under the proposed dialog abstraction, client, server and messaging mechanism are fully decoupled. The versatility and flexibility of human communication is mirrored. Changes made to the messages have no impact on the messaging mechanism and infrastructure. They both are separate and decoupled concerns that can be changed independently. Client and server software can be upgraded independently.

Dialogs based on the proposed approach are able to transparently scale and handle arbitrary large infrastructures running 24/7. Gradual upgrade of servers and clients is feasible without disrupting the rest of the infrastructure. Once all the servers have been gradually upgraded, client nodes can be upgraded to take advantage of the new software functionality. It is assumed that the new software version is backward compatible in terms of messaging which is similar to human languages.

**BPM/BPEL processes and applications**: The abstractions that are part of the dialog pattern can be readily incorporated into production quality BPEL/BPM processes and applications.

**Conceptual Framework**: Although not a requirement, it is recommended that the dialog abstraction be implemented via a conceptual framework as a best practice. The information infrastructure (plumbing) is provided by the framework and its information patterns. Component implementation is able to focus on the business logic. In general, under traditional APIs, users need to re-implement the distributed and asynchronous communication mechanism for each component which is the source of implementation complexity, shortcomings, costs, quality issues, and so on. The natural and realistic concepts, part of the information pattern family, are usually overlooked.

**Natural Language Dialogs (IVR):** As part of the natural evolution of computers and computer systems, it should be expected that the man-machine interfaces/dialogs will be based on natural languages. Such transition is already happening for many applications. IVR applications are becoming ubiquitous. The dialog abstraction and the conceptual interfaces are well suited for a smooth transition from conventional applications to applications able to support emerging IVR capabilities.

Processing conceptual information coming from another component or application becomes equivalent to processing the same information coming from a human being. Because a conceptual interface is being used, the same concepts apply to both scenarios. Messaging is also the communication abstraction for both. No major changes to the conceptual interface are required to handle messages communicated using a natural language. The main challenge becomes transforming sentences to software messages which is a very manageable problem.

Notice that concepts, including messaging, are a key aspect for having a smooth application transition to meet emerging requirements. Natural languages are not only more efficient and effective for communication; they can also positively impact cost and reach. A lot of information can be transferred with a single or very few sentences, making the interface more efficient. People are able interface with the application using their native language. Automatic mechanisms of translation are feasible which improves overall software cost, timeframe, quality, and reach.

## 12.8   Implementation

The dialog abstraction can be implemented using arbitrary computer languages and technologies. On the other hand, it is recommended that the dialog implementation be based on a conceptual framework consisting of the information pattern family able to readily deal with the associated complexities: asynchronous messaging, distributed component/services access, concurrency, security, fault tolerance and so forth. The conceptual framework implements the information infrastructure required to satisfy complex production requirements. Reusing such type of framework positively impacts cost, quality, timelines, overall complexity, and so forth.

The dialog abstraction represents a conceptual interface. Imaging yourself having a dialog with another individual or group of individuals. Conceptually the dialog between computers, application and components is equivalent to the coordinated dialog between human beings. Obviously the same concept (dialog) applies to both scenarios. As a consequence, common considerations and implementation follow. As part of the conversation, several pieces of information (i.e. concepts) need to be kept internally by all the individuals involved. Such information represents another concept: the context of the conversation (Ctx). It is kept in memory and can be expressed as a group of concepts:

$$Ctx = \{C1, C2, , Cn\}$$

This group of concepts includes:

**Subject:** topic or subject of the conversation
**State:** state of the conversation

As part of the dialog, synchronization is a fundamental aspect to consider. If during a conversation you ask a question, you need to wait for a reply. At this time, you need to keep in mind that you are waiting for a reply. Once a message comes, you need to verify that the message is indeed the reply that you were waiting for. The reply may never come or

144

an unrelated message may come instead. You may also need to resend the original question. By keeping the state of the conversation, the dialog can be synchronized and information can be successfully exchanged in a methodic (i.e. coordinated) fashion. Most of the process involved is performed without even thinking about it.

Similar considerations apply to a group of components engaged in a dialog. In terms of implementation, a serial or ID needs to be added to the message and the reply. In this way, the reply can be matched with its corresponding message. Depending on specific requirements, a timeout period may also be needed before resending the message or giving up based on a specified number of retries.

For instance, a GUI component may need to display the current GPS location. In order to do so, an asynchronous message is sent to controller component. In turn, the controller sents an asynchronous message to the GPS component. Once the GPS component gets a position fix, it sends an asynchronous reply message to the GUI component. Besides the subject of the dialog, the message and its reply include an ID or serial number which is matched by the GUI component before displaying the position information. This realistic dialog illustrates the typical conversation that takes place between the components of an asynchronous MVC implementation as part of a mobile application. Notice that the GUI component may receive and process many other unrelated messages and/or events before receiving the expected location reply. The controller and GPS component may also receive and process many other unrelated messages. Obtaining a GPS fix may take several minutes.

A dialog that relies on the phone system, or similar communication framework, introduces additional challenges. The phone conversation may get disconnected. A poor connection may occur. The connection may need to be restarted. The same sort of challenges applies to a group of components and/or heterogeneous applications cooperating as part of distributed dialogs.

All types of intricate patterns of fault-tolerant dialogs can be implemented using the proposed information pattern family and its dialog abstraction which provide a realistic (robust) communication infrastructure required. There are several aspects to consider including synchronization, fault tolerance, distributed messaging, asynchronous messaging, redundancy, and so forth.

## 12.9　Known Uses

**Design patterns.** The dialog abstraction has been used for the implementation (i.e. reusable implementation) of well-known design patterns like Gang of Four design patterns (GoF), MVC (Model View Controller), Master-Worker, etc [2]. Exchange of information (i.e. dialog) between participants is a ubiquitous concept applicable to multiple scenarios. It should not come as a surprise that several pattern implementations can reuse the concept and its implementation. As a consequence, the dialog abstraction can be employed to provide and/or facilitate a reusable implementation of related design patterns.

Notice that the dialog abstraction, and the other members of the information pattern family, provide the information infrastructure able to deal with concurrency, asynchronous messaging, distributed service/component access and so forth.

For instance, MVC can be implemented using multiple Animated/Live components exchanging information as part of a dialog. Each component participant (Model View Controller) is implemented as an Animated/Live component which provides transparently handling of concurrency and asynchronous messaging. The proposed of implementation is not only natural and realistic but also required at times because of the concurrency requirements, such as the ones imposed by some mobile architectures. A distributed implementation of MVC, where dialog participants run on heterogeneous systems, is also readily accommodated.

**Distributed Component and Service Model.** As mentioned earlier, the information pattern family, including the dialog abstraction, are well suited for the implementation of a complete distributed component/service model (Turing complete) able to handle complex real-world considerations such as security, redundancy, interoperability, fault tolerance, concurrency, asynchronous messaging, scalability, and so on.

The information pattern family which includes the dialog abstraction is able to provide transparent access to distributed components/services

146

regardless of technology, platform, language, data format, communication protocol, and so on. They also help deal with a complex set of problems related to remote access and multithreading artifacts within the context of distributed applications engaged in information exchange (i.e. dialog).

**BPM/BPEL frameworks and technologies.** The dialog abstraction has been used to model and implement arbitrary business processes in a realistic and accurate fashion. In particular the abstraction can be used for the comprehensive implementation of business process technologies (BPEL/BPM), frameworks, and applications.

Consider that the concept of dialog between independent participants is prevalent as part of real business processes. The dialog abstraction can be reused to implement the required functionality in very natural ways while at the same time improving overall complexity and reusability.

## 12.10 Related Patterns

The dialog pattern is related to Model View Controller (MVC) in terms of functionality. In fact the pattern can be reused for a realistic implementation of MVC where the components are implemented using the Animated/Live component abstraction and interchange information using the dialog pattern. On the other hand, the dialog abstraction is not limited to GUI related patterns dealing with a View component. It can be applied to any type of dialog between components, applications and systems (local and distributed); including dialogs where communication is achieved using computer synthesized speech and/or voice recognition (IVR).

The dialog abstraction usually involves only two Animated/Live components engaged in a two-way communication. However, multiple Animated/Live entities may participate as part of the dialog. Obviously, the proposed pattern relies heavily on the messaging abstraction to implement most of the required communication functionality: messaging infrastructure including distributed messaging, security and access control.

# 13.   INFORMATION PATTERN FAMILY

Every aspect of reality can be represented as a concept (C). The concepts that belong to the information pattern family can be classified based on the fundamental information aspect as follows:

a) **Animated or Live Entities (A)**. Components or entities able to process information via the information primitive: *processInformation (message)*. They can also interact with other entities (animated/unanimated) as part of real-world processes. Animated or Live entities often utilize an independent processing mechanism or thread of execution. They implement, through software, the Information Machine abstraction which makes them Turing complete. A memory subcomponent often provides information persistency capabilities.

b) **Messaging (M)**. Concept that represents the interchange of information between Animated or Live entities. All modalities of messaging are modeled including synchronous, asynchronous and streaming. Messaging can be classified into two major categories depending on the type of information being exchanged: conceptual and non-conceptual.

c) **Information Association (a)**. Basic building block of information. A concept consists of a group of information associations: C = {a1, a2, , an}

d) **Unanimated Objects (O)** . Physical objects unable to process information. All of them can be represented as concepts (C). Object attributes are expressed as information associations.

e) **Dialog.** Interchange of messaging between two or more Animated/Live entities. Usually, the interchange is accomplished in the form of concepts: conceptual interface. A conceptual interface represents a higher level of abstraction in terms of the messaging being exchanged. Human languages represent examples of conceptual interfaces. Advantages of conceptual communication, that can be mirrored, include efficiency, completeness, conciseness, expressiveness, and true realistic correspondence [30].

149

f) **Process.** Animated and unanimated entities interact and/or interchange information (i.e. messaging) in the real world, as part of natural or man-made processes. Such processes are modeled and simulated using the information process abstraction. In some instances, physical laws or concepts like gravity and force need to be modeled as part of these processes.

g) **Group (G).** Abstraction that represents a collection of concepts: $G = \{C1, C2, , Cn\}$ Concepts can be grouped or organized into more complex information structures: *groups*.

The information pattern family represents a Turing-complete group. Arbitrary computer technologies can be implemented using this family of concepts which includes SOA, ESB, BPEL/BPM and so forth. They also provide a complete information infrastructure required to build reusable components, applications and frameworks able to deal with arbitrary real-world problems. Keep in mind that information is a concept, a highly reusable one. It applies to every aspect of reality. It should not come as a surprise that the information pattern family is applicable to every technology dealing with information. Consider also that the logical mind, part of a living being, can process conceptual information using a single all-encompassing abstraction: Concept (C).

As shown, reality consists of many other entities in addition to traditional objects. In particular, abstractions like messaging, concepts, and Live or Animated Entities, are usually overlooked by traditional APIs. Notice that artificial abstractions and their inherent limitations/shortcomings, such as traditional distributed artifacts and multithreading, are not part of a realistic information model. When it comes to software, the old cliché still applies: Keep it real.

The information pattern family can also be classified into two major groups:

a) **Animated or Live Entities (components).** Physical entities able to process information via the information primitive. In relative terms, there are very few entities able to process information in the real world: living beings, computers, automated systems, machines, and so forth. One out of seven categories when considering the classification above. The ratio becomes even smaller if we take into account all the entities in the universe as a whole. Notice that the messaging concept represents the one and only *real* mechanism of communication.

b) **Concepts**. Entities unable to process information: C = {a1, a2, , an}.

As mentioned earlier, the distinction must be made between the conceptual representation and the entity itself which are two separate and independent aspects. Concepts are mental representations based on information and separate from the physical entities or objects being represented. Animated or Live Entities also represent an abstraction, a concept. As such, they cannot process information. On the other hand, the physical entities classified as 'Animated or Live Entities' can process information.

There are several other classifications applicable to the information pattern family. In terms of functionality, there are three main areas: Storage, Transference and Processing.

a) **Information Container (Storage)**. Patterns that store or consist of information as their main purpose: Unanimated Objects, Information Associations, Concepts (unable to transfer and process information), Groups, Information Repository (Memory). These patterns are related to how information is structured.

b) **Information Transference (Messaging)**. Patterns associated with the communication and transference of information: Messaging and Dialog.

c) **Information Processing**. Patterns associated with the processing of information: Animated/Live Entities and Process.

There may be other classifications applicable to the information pattern family. In terms of the information structures there are three levels of ascending complexity (or dimensions) in which the information is grouped:

a) **Information Association (a).** Basic building block of information.

b) **Concept (C).** Group of information associations. $C = \{a1, a2, ,an\}$

c) **Group (G).** Collection of concepts some of which may be groups themselves. $G = \{C1, C2, ,Cn\}$.

Notice that groups can be organized into more complex groups. On the other hand, such structures are still represented using the group abstraction regardless of the level of complexity. Arbitrary data structures can be implemented using the three concepts above. For instance, a tree structure, which can be represented as a group, may consist of several concepts and subgroups. Structures of any level of complexity can be represented. Consider all the conceptual information (I) stored in the mind: concepts and associations forming a complex web (graph) of interrelated entities. It can be precisely represented with mathematical simplicity and completeness as a group of concepts:

$I = \{C1, C2, , Cn\}$

# 14.    CONCEPTUAL FRAMEWORK

A Conceptual Framework is designed for the rapid implementation of Object Oriented applications including Java and Android applications. The framework addresses the following goals:

A) The framework architecture is based on the information pattern family, including the concept of Messaging: framework components are able to interchange information and perform computations by sending, receiving and processing messages. A single messaging (information) primitive provides simplicity, strong encapsulation, loose coupling and scalability; framework components can be interchangeably plugged into complex framework applications using a conceptual architecture based on messaging. All modalities of messaging are accommodated: synchronous, asynchronous, streaming, distributed messaging, two-way messaging, secure messaging, and combinations of these forms. The framework takes full advantage of the power and simplicity of the information primitive which is Turing complete.

B) The proposed framework relies on a conceptual paradigm and interfaces (CI) which provides a higher level of abstraction. The conceptual framework uses messaging to implement and/or facilitate the reusable implementation of well-known design patterns like Gang of Four design patterns (GoF), MVC, DAO, Master-Worker, and J2EE Design patterns. The framework itself is conceived and implemented, from the ground up, based on Concepts and design patterns. The framework also facilitates and accelerates the implementation of applications based on the aforementioned design patterns.

C) The framework conceptual architecture, based on the information pattern family, implements a complete distributed component/service model which is able to provide transparent, secure and fault-tolerant access to distributed components and SOA services: distributed framework components are treated as local ones. Patterns implemented by the framework (messaging, animated/live components, adapters, remote proxies and facades) make this possible by hiding the complexities associated with remote APIs and artifacts. Built-in components for message encryption, authentication and logging are provided.

153

D) The framework and the information pattern family are reused to implement SOA, BPM/BPEL and ESB technologies. Consider that the concept of information is highly reusable. These technologies deal with information requirements and infrastructure which the conceptual framework already implements. The framework also provides transparent integration with other technologies via reusable adapters, proxies and the implementation of related design patterns. These technologies include Model View Controller (MVC) implementations, DAO implementations, EJBs, JSP, AJAX, JMS, XML, and so on.

E) The information pattern family and the framework itself offer high reusability and low overhead (small size footprint). As a consequence, the framework is very lightweight and able to readily run on smartphones under Android. It uses pure Java, therefore other mobile platforms based on Java are also viable. Because of resource limitations, not many other Java frameworks are able to run efficiently on mobile devices.

F) The framework conceptual architecture improves and simplifies design/development efforts. There is a tight correspondence between UML design diagrams and the framework messaging-based applications and components needed for the implementation. The framework provides wizards and automated capabilities for generating framework applications. Framework components can be readily added to BPM/BPEL diagrams and processes. In future versions of the framework, it should be possible for repetitive application modules to be generated directly from the UML design diagrams.

G) The framework messaging architecture facilitates testing and debugging efforts. Live/Animated components are fully decoupled and encapsulated. They can be tested as independent units by sending messages to the independent component and verifying the expected reply messages via a testing harness. Messages exchanged between components can be automatically logged by the framework which facilitates the debugging process.

154

## 14.1    Framework Core Components

The framework design is based on a conceptual paradigm: components able to process information and concepts need to be specified. Based on the information pattern family, a conceptual framework implements a straightforward and compact group of core components able to provide support for a comprehensive information infrastructure:

**Factory:** implements the factory method pattern. It is responsible for manufacturing and updating framework components and Concepts (C) – including messages. It may also be assigned responsibility for providing reusable Singleton and Prototype functionality: conceptually, a factory should be able to manufacture 'one of a kind' and make copies (i.e. clones) of specific components. The implementation of the factory abstraction should already have all the information (blueprints) required to do so. Such functionality can be reused across the board for all the framework components and concepts.

**Messenger:** component responsible for transferring messages from the sender to the recipient (receiver). All modalities of messaging are supported including asynchronous and secure messaging. It delegates responsibility to other framework components for the implementation of security, encryption, authentication, and authorization of the messaging being exchanged.

**Logger:** component that provides built-in logging capabilities. It handles the information logged by the framework. The framework can be configured or directed to log all the messages interchanged between components which facilitates debugging, testing and implementation efforts. It can also automatically log all framework operations. Problems can be quickly identified and resolved by checking the messaging being automatically logged.

**Registry:** component responsible for maintaining the framework registry. It allows framework components to locate other components. This component also implements a naming mechanism to uniquely identify each component being added to the registry.

Live/Animated components are fully encapsulated and decoupled entities whose only realistic mechanism of communication is via inter-component messaging. The registry functionality supports mechanisms for framework components to find and cooperate with each other.

**Resource Manager**: component responsible for handling the information stored in the properties resource file (or data source) which is used to initialize/configure components and concepts when they are first created.

**Exception Handler**: Components can forward detected exceptions to this component for handling. Custom exception handlers are supported and can be incorporated.

**Printer:** Component responsible for printing capabilities. It is able to print detailed information about a concept (C) or component regardless of complexity. The XML format is usually employed since the entity being printed may represent a complex hierarchy of concepts and/or objects. A printer component provides additional convenience while building, testing and debugging applications.

In terms of the framework concepts involved, a complete framework and its core components are able to handle arbitrary concepts extracted from reality. There are several special classes of concepts that need to be managed: Messages, Groups, Events, Information Associations, Exceptions, Errors, and Warnings. Notice that these entities do not require information processing capabilities and are accurately represented as concepts which can be readily shared across local and remote components, processes and applications. Similar to all the other Live/Animated components, the framework core components can be incorporated as part of BPEL/BPM processes and tools. Distributed access to these local core components may be allowed if necessary.

Think about the significant simplification and reduction in the number of core components (objects) required to provide a comprehensive framework implementation as a direct result of using a conceptual paradigm and interfaces. Each core component also implements a straightforward conceptual interface which runs seamlessly from mobile devices all the way up to enterprise servers.

## 14.2    Conceptual Framework for Android

The Android Architecture, like every other computer technology, is about information. The proposed pattern family, part of a conceptual framework implementation, has been reused to provide comprehensive information infrastructure capabilities for Android. Most of the functionality implemented by the framework runs under the Android platform without any software modifications. The following design principles apply to the Android implementation of the framework:

a) The framework itself is designed and implemented based on a conceptual paradigm. Every framework pattern and core component implements a conceptual interface based on single information primitive and a compact set of messages.

b) The philosophy behind Java is straightforward: "write once, run everywhere". Obviously, such idea has many benefits in terms of software portability, costs, time frames, quality, and so on. A conceptual framework is consistent with the Java philosophy.

As mentioned earlier, most of the framework components and patterns have been reused to run under the Android platform without any variation.  In general, the framework implementation avoids, as much as possible, nonstandard Android APIs and configuration files because of incompatibility and portability limitations. They are also the potential source for additional complexities, cost, timeframe delays, quality defects and so forth.

c) The conceptual framework based on the information pattern family offers a high level of reusability. It can be employed to implement arbitrary information technologies and related components. A compact set of framework core components results in a lightweight implementation (small size footprint) able to accommodate the resource constraints imposed by mobile platforms.

Because of resource limitations, not many other Java frameworks are able to run efficiently and seamlessly on mobile platforms.

d) The framework offers a complete set of components based on pure Java and able run across all Java platforms, including mobile devices: Logger, Registry, Factory, Messenger, Resource Manager, Printer, and Exception Handler.

h) A limited number of framework components need to be specific to the Android platform since their functionality is not provided by the standard Java SDK. The list includes GPS, voice recognition, voice synthesis, device configuration and GUI components. To provide Android specific functionality, the conceptual framework relies on independent Live/Animated components to encapsulate the Android specific functionality. For instance, there is a framework component that implements a conceptual interface and communicates with the Android GPS API. This reusable component can be employed for the application requirements related to GPS functionality.

If the framework application needs to run on a different platform, Android specific components can be easily replaced. Since a conceptual interface and framework are being used, it is just a matter of substituting the framework component with another component built to support the new platform. No additional software changes are required since both components implement the same conceptual interface.

It is just like taking a part (component) from your car and replacing it with one from a different manufacture, designed based on the same specification (conceptual interface). A part built based a newer and improved design should also seamlessly work since conceptual interfaces are designed to be backward compatible. Traditional APIs not based on messaging and concepts do not provide this level of versatility, versioning flexibility and interoperability. Bear in mind that conceptual interfaces are straightforward relying on a single primitive and a small set of predefined message types.

i) The utilization of a conceptual framework has practical consequences in terms of Android development, design, debugging and testing. Most of the component development is independent of the platform and can be performed using high-end computers and development environments. This characteristic is a direct result of relying on pure Java and avoiding Android specific APIs and configuration files as much as possible.

158

Building, debugging and testing applications on the device itself or via the Android emulator can be time consuming and hindered by performance limitations. A limited number of Android specific components need to be developed/tested as separate units avoiding the use of the device and/or Android emulator as much as possible during the development and testing phases.

Android is not based on the standard Java SDK. There are several differences to consider:

a) Java Database Connectivity (JDBC) is not supported. However, the Memory or Information Repository abstraction is implemented via an Android Adapter. From the standpoint of the application, nothing changes. The same conceptual interface required to access persistent information still applies.

b) Java GUI APIs are not supported. The conceptual framework provides reusable components based on the Android GUI APIs. These components implement and/or facilitate the implementation of several framework abstractions: messaging and dialog. These abstractions allow the interchange of messaging between GUI components and other parts of the system.

c) The J2EE Design patterns implemented by the framework are not supported because Android does not implement the corresponding J2EE APIs.

# 15.    DESIGN PATTERN IMPLEMENTATION (GoF)

The information pattern family has been utilized as the basis for the reusable implementation of well-known design patterns like Gang of Four design patterns (GoF), DAO, MVC, J2EE Design patterns, Master-Worker, and so forth [2]. Pattern implementation deals with information interchange, storage, and processing. Consider that the information pattern family constitutes a Turing-complete group able to provide the infrastructure necessary for the implementation of arbitrary technologies. Pattern implementations can use the ubiquitous information abstractions to achieve a realistic solution, while at the same time improving overall complexity, reusability, encapsulation, cost, timelines, and so on.

Several design patterns will be used to illustrate how this is accomplished. The same concepts apply to the implementation of many others. Concepts also provide a more accurate and straightforward implementation. Although synchronous messaging is shown, all forms of messaging are supported.

Design patterns implemented using Concepts, can be reused as building blocks. A generic pattern implementation becomes possible. Complex frameworks and applications can be built based on these building blocks which share a simple way of interconnecting them (i.e. common messaging interface).

## 15.1    Proxy

Concepts facilitate the reusable implementation of Proxy. Under the conceptual paradigm, Proxy is mainly responsible for forwarding information (input message) to the real subject. Notice that all the participants are completely independent (minimum coupling). Encapsulation is maximized. Messaging is the only mechanism of communication between participants.

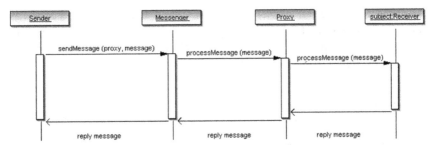

**Figure 1. Implementation of a reusable Proxy based on Concepts.**

## 15.2    Adapter

Under messaging and the conceptual model, the main purpose of Adapter becomes the transformation of information (messages) between message sender and receiver so that these components can be interconnected. For instance, you may need to implement a HTTP Adapter so that your local component can communicate with a remote component via the HTTP protocol. The same principle applies to arbitrary communication technologies and protocols (sockets, web services, REST, RMI, .Net, EJB, etc.)

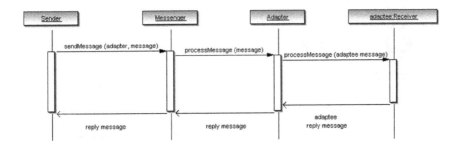

**Figure 2. Implementation of Adapter based on Concepts.**

161

## 15.3    Façade

Concepts facilitate the implementation of the Façade pattern. Façade is mainly responsible for forwarding the message to the appropriate subsystem. In our particular scenario, Façade needs to forward the message to the appropriate remote component.

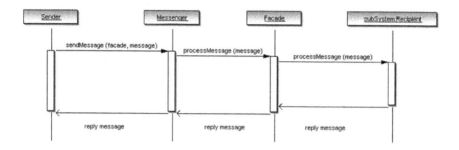

**Figure 3. Implementation of Façade based on Concepts.**

## 15.4    Strategy

Under a conceptual paradigm, Strategy is mainly responsible for forwarding the message to the component that implements the concrete strategy.

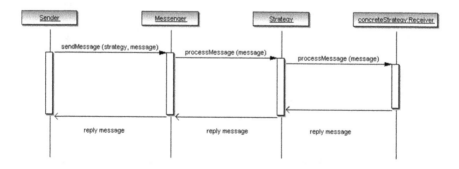

**Figure 4. Strategy implementation based on Concepts.**

## 15.5 Bridge

When a conceptual approach is used, Bridge is mainly responsible for forwarding the message to the concrete implementer.

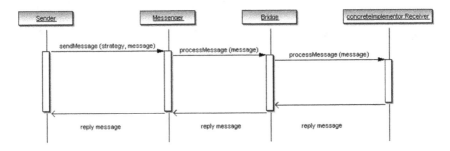

**Figure 5. Implementation of Bridge based on Concepts**

## 15.6 Command

Concepts facilitate the implementation of Command (Figure 6). Under the conceptual paradigm, Command is responsible for processing the request/message. It may also queue or log requests (RequestLogger).

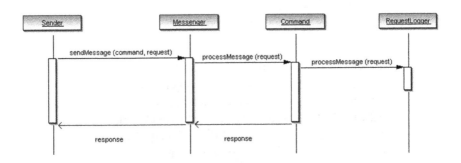

**Figure 6. Implementation of Command based on Concepts**

## 15.7    Decorator

When Concepts are used, Decorator is responsible for implementing new functionality. Decorator is also responsible for forwarding messages (related to the existing functionality) to the decorated component.

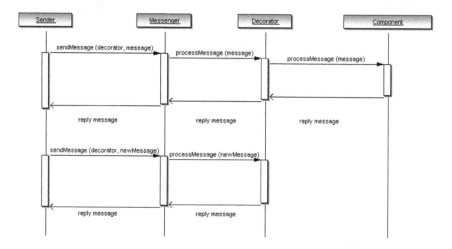

**Figure 7. Implementation of Decorator based on Concepts**

## 15.8    Factory

Based on a conceptual approach, a realistic implementation of the Factory pattern serves four main functions:

a)  Creation and manipulation of other components and Concepts (C), which includes the handling of internal attributes. Optionally, a name (component Id) may be assigned during creation which is used for registration via the framework Registry. Registration allows fully independent/decoupled components to find each other in the context of distributed and local processes.

b)  Initialization and/or configuration of components when they are first created based on the information stored in the properties resource file (or data source). The Factory implementation relies on the Resource Manager to provide the needed functionality.

164

c) Singleton Pattern. A realistic implementation of the Factory pattern may also provide Singleton functionality by creating a one-of-a-king component.

d) Prototype Pattern. The Factory implementation may also be responsible for creating copies of a specific component or Concept (clone). It makes sense for the Factory implementation to be able to 'manufacture' clones of a specific component.

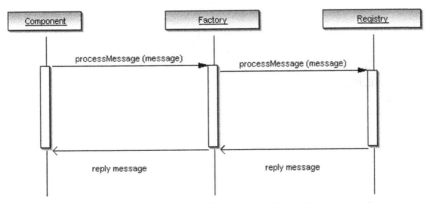

**Figure 8. Implementation of the Factory pattern based on Concepts**

The following straightforward messages should be part of a conceptual interface for the Factory pattern implementation:

a) **CREATE:** create an instance of the component of the specified class. A name (component Id) may be assigned to the component during creation. The component may also be registered with the framework via the Registry component. The component is initialized via the Resource Manager using the properties resource file or data source.

a.1) **CREATE (SINGLETON):** create a singleton instance of a class. The functionality is implemented via the Registry component which keeps track of Singleton classes. Subsequent attempts to create an instance of the same class will result in the Singleton being returned: no additional instances will be created. Concurrent access to the Registry information is properly controlled by the Registry component.

b) **READ (ATTRIBUTES):** Retrieve the group of attributes and attribute values part of the object. This functionality is mainly required by internal framework components and specialized applications.

c) **REMOVE**: Remove a component from the framework registry.

c.1) **REMOVE (SINGLETON)**: Remove a Singleton instance from the framework registry.

d) **CLONE**: Create a copy of a specific component or concept. Every application component can be cloned by reusing the functionality provided by the Conceptual framework. The user does not need to re-implement it for each class. The clone functionality can be implemented by using a version of the CREATE message: CREATE (CLONE).

## 15.9   Prototype

A realistic implementation of the Prototype pattern can be provided by the Factory pattern. Factory should be able to 'manufacture' copies of arbitrary application components and Concepts by processing the CLONE message (See Factory):  Prototype returns a copy of the object or concept when the CLONE message is received.

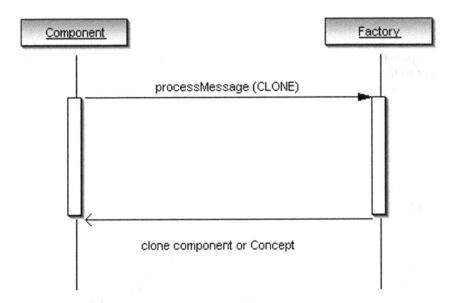

**Figure 9. Implementation of prototype functionality via the Factory pattern**

## 15.10 Model View Controller (MVC)

The information pattern family can be leveraged to implement the Model-View-Controller (MVC) pattern. Its members provide concurrency and messaging capabilities. In particular Messaging, Animated/Live components, and the Dialog pattern support most of the required capabilities. Under a conceptual model, MVC components are completely encapsulated and decoupled entities. They can be implemented as independent Animated/Live components. All forms of messaging are supported including asynchronous and distributed messaging. MVC components can also run as distributed components on separate computers. This may become useful for specialized distributed applications.

Support for concurrency and asynchronous messaging are particularly useful on Mobile devices where multiple components are usually running concurrently and resource constraints need to be taken into account. The information pattern family supports a concurrent and distributed implementation of MVC.

167

Messaging is the only mechanism of communication among MVC components. GUI events are encapsulated as framework messages and sent to the controller for processing. The controller may then interchange messaging with components part of the model. For instance, once a button is pressed a corresponding event (message) is sent to the controller. The same mechanism applies to any other event generated by the GUI. Updates to the graphical user interface are performed via messages sent to the GUI by the other components. Conceptual interfaces that rely on a compact set of messages can be employed for the communication between MVC components. In particular, between the graphical user interface (View) and the other MVC components.

Functionality that is not pure Java (platform specific) can be encapsulated as a Live/Animated component or group of Live/Animated components. Later on, the component(s) can be readily replaced by a component based on pure java or another platform-specific component without having any major impact on the rest of the system. The use of messaging, Dialog pattern, and Live/Animated components allows such level of interoperability, encapsulation and decoupling as part of a MVC implementation.

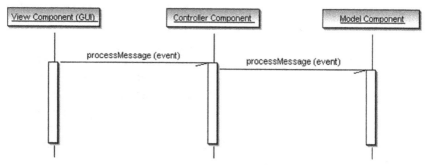

**Figure 10. Implementation of MVC based on Concepts. Messages are sent from the GUI in the form of events.**

# 16.    J2EE DESIGN PATTERN IMPLEMENTATION

Enterprise Java Beans (EJBs) is one of the technologies that can be used to access remote components. The next section will illustrate how Concepts and several other J2EE design patterns can be combined to implement transparent access to distributed EJB components. The same principles apply to other communication technologies and protocols.

## 16.1    J2EE Business Delegate

When Concepts are used, Business Delegate is mainly responsible for forwarding the message to the remote component via EJBAdapter and J2EESessionFacade. The behavior is very similar to Proxy.

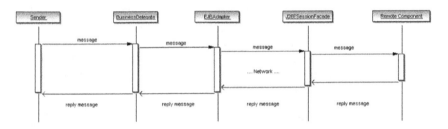

**Figure 1. Implementation of J2EE Business Delegate based on Concepts**

## 16.2    J2EE Session Façade

When Concepts are used, Session Façade is mainly responsible for forwarding the message to the appropriate remote component.

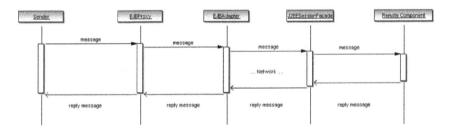

**Figure 2. Implementation of J2EE Session Façade based on Concepts**

169

The following are the design patterns involved. For clarity sake the messenger component and the intrinsic *processMessage()* method have been removed from the UML diagram.

1) Business Delegate: the message is sent to the remote component via the business delegate.
2) EJBAdapter : adapter responsible for interfacing with the EJB API. It transfers the message to J2EESessionFacade.
3) J2EESessionFacade: forward the message to the appropriate remote component.

The J2EE session façade is usually responsible for security as well (messaging authorization and authentication). Notice that under a messaging paradigm, this can be made transparent to message sender and receiver. In other words, sender and receiver do not need to be too concerned as to whether or not secure messaging is being used and how it is being implemented. The conceptual framework should provide the required security mechanisms ("plumbing"). Using a real world analogy, in general you and your friend should not be concerned if the service provider is encrypting your phone conversation because of privacy and security considerations.

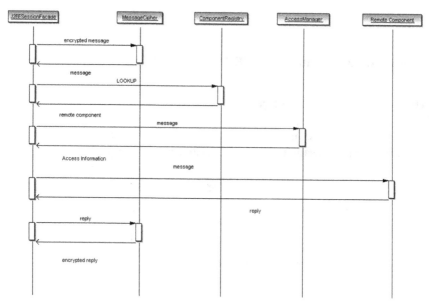

**Figure 3. Implementation of J2EE session façade based on Concepts**

170

Before the message is forwarded to the Receiver, J2EESessionFacade performs decryption, authorization and authentication on it. The following are the components involved:

MessageCipher: component responsible for decrypting the input message and encrypting the reply message.
Component Registry: allows the system to register and look up components by name.
AccessManager: responsible for granting/denying access to remote components. It authorizes and authenticates each message received.

## 16.3   J2EE Service Locator

When messaging is used, Service Locator is mainly responsible for locating the service (home interface) by interfacing with the JNDI Adapter. JNDIAdapter is a messaging adapter that interfaces with the JNDI API.

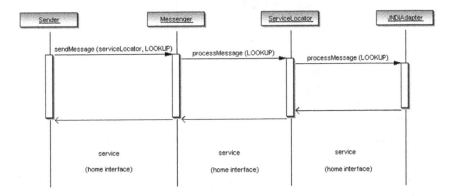

**Figure 4. J2EE Service Locator**

# 17.   Distributed Component and Service Model

The information patterns are well suited for the implementation of a complete distributed component and service model (Turing complete) able to handle complex real-world considerations such as security, redundancy, fault tolerance, multithreading, scalability, and so on. Conceptually, communicating with a distributed component is not that different from communicating with a local one since the same Messaging concept [2] is being used. The proposed information abstractions provide transparent access to distributed components regardless of the technology, platform, computer language, data representation and protocol being used. They also help deal with a complex set of problems associated with remote access and traditional multithreading in the context of distributed applications.

Let us use a real-world analogy to illustrate the problem and its solution. Consider your phone system, postal service, or email/chat system. You are able to communicate with a friend by simply sending a message to the intended recipient. In the case of the phone system, you are able to communicate with your friend regardless of the technology being used. For instance, you may be using a land line while your friend is using wireless, internet or satellite technology. All these technologies are able to interoperate in a seamless fashion. You can communicate with a friend across the room or thousands of miles away. You and your friend do not need to be concerned as to how your conversation is transmitted (technologies, communication protocols, security mechanisms, etc).

The service provider is responsible for putting together the infrastructure or *framework* to make it possible. Such framework consists of interconnected *components* to transmit voice, video and/or text to the receiver. For instance, the framework will probably include bridges and *adapters* to transport information and transform it into the appropriate signal or message format. A similar principle applies to the postal service and the internet service. You are able to send a message or letter regardless of the technology used to transport the message. Your letter may be carried via air, ground or ship. A similar principle applies to your internet service.

The communication between distributed components and services should be accomplished in a similar fashion. All these systems share the same concepts, and messaging in particular. There is no *real* reason for the complexities and shortcomings mentioned above; other than the lack of fundamental concepts as part of traditional models and technologies. Therefore, the information pattern family provides the proposed distributed model with the building blocks (realistic concepts) required to overcome the problems and shortcomings. Obviously, if true correspondence [30] is to be achieved, *all* the relevant concepts must be mirrored as part of a comprehensive solution: model design and implementation.

The limitations and drawbacks associated with traditional distributed and SOA technologies have been studied and documented in the technical literature. In particular, several references deal with complexity [13, 14, 15, 20], interoperability [13, 14, 15, 20], coupling [20] and proprietary limitations [13,14]. These limitations have a negative impact on software schedules and cost [20, 13].

Messaging is about transferring or exchanging information. As a concept, messaging is simple, effective, efficient, versatile, robust, scalable, interoperable, etc. Messaging can also be made reliable, secure (authenticated and/or encrypted), redundant and fault-tolerant. Just consider the amount of vital information exchanged every single moment. All these qualities become part of a robust distributed component/service model and implementation once the messaging concept is fully grasped and mirrored. The software model and its implementation "absorb" these inherent messaging qualities. The proposed distributed model can be utilized, as part of a conceptual framework, to implement arbitrary production-quality applications and technologies including SOA, REST, ESB, Master-Worker, and BPEL [10]. It demonstrates the feasibility, completeness, and advantages of the proposed model.

The information pattern family and other patterns can be combined to implement access to remote components and services. They are able to provide transparent and secure access to remote components/services regardless of the protocol and communication technology being used: remote components are treated as local components.

173

Messages can be transferred via web services, EJBs, RMI, HTTP, REST, Sockets, SSL or any other comparable communication interface. Concepts and patterns (Messaging, Animated/Live component, Adapters, Proxies and Facades) make this possible by hiding the complexities associated with remote APIs.

The following UML diagram illustrates how this is accomplished. In the real world, you can communicate with a friend across the room or thousands of miles away via a phone conversation. You and your friend do not need to be concerned as to how the telephone conversation is transmitted. It is transparent to you. The phone company provides the messaging framework to make it possible. By mimicking this behavior, the information pattern family is able to provide transparent communication between local and remote components/services.

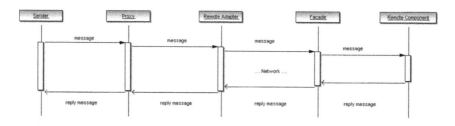

**Figure 1. Access to distributed components and services based on Concepts**

The following are the Concepts and design patterns involved. For clarity sake the messenger component and the intrinsic information primitive (processMessage(Message)) have been removed from the UML diagram.

1) Proxy: the message is sent to the remote component via a reusable proxy applicable to arbitrary remote components.
2) Remote Adapter: adapter responsible for interfacing with the remote API.
3) Façade: forward the message to the appropriate remote component. It usually provides security capabilities as well.
4) Information patterns: the information pattern family provides realistic abstractions for transferring and processing of information.

174

## 17.1 Security, Naming and Access Control

The proposed distributed component/service model can deal with security challenges in a straightforward manner. It provides end-to-end security, non-repudiation and message-level security (as opposed to transport level security). It can also be used for selective encryption so that only sensitive portions of the message are encrypted. Well-known security mechanisms fit well with the proposed model. On the other hand, Messaging is not limited to a specific message format (XML, SOAP, binary, etc.). Any message format and Restful service can be accommodated which includes proprietary and custom message formats. Bear in mind that the information machine is Turing complete. Therefore, any arbitrary distributed computing model or technology can be implemented based on the information abstractions and single primitive.

Most of the security aspects can be made transparent to message sender and receiver (figure 9 and 10). For instance, sender and receiver do not need to be overly concerned as to whether or not security is being used and how it is being implemented. The conceptual framework provides the required security components and mechanisms ("plumbing"). Using our real-world analogy, in general you and your friend do not need to be concerned if the service provider is encrypting your conversation because of privacy and/or security considerations. The framework can also rely on declarative security which avoids the need for error-prone security coding. Finally, custom security mechanisms can be readily accommodated based on specific requirements. For instance, the sender may decide to use a mutually agreed security mechanism (encryption and/or authentication) without relying on the security facilities implemented by the framework.

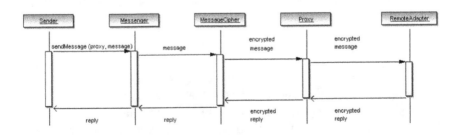

**Figure 2. Secure messaging (client side)**

175

Going back to the proposed analogy, the communication framework maintained by the service provider will require some sort of *registry* (phone book) so that participants can locate each other. Each entity will have associated a phone number or *ID*. A straightforward naming mechanism is all that is required. In some cases we may need to provide a city code and/or country code. The postal service, your internet service provider and Messaging also use straightforward naming schemes. In the case of distributed Live/Animated components, they can be readily located based on component name, class, and URL.

Other service providers take advantage of the framework and use custom *authentication/authorization* mechanisms. Your banking institution, for instance, makes use of the phone system and has *Access Control* mechanisms for authorization and authentication purposes. We are required to provide some piece(s) of information to authenticate our identity before being granted access to an account. Using another analogy, you will not be able to gain phone access to a government official to discuss classified matters. Access will not be allowed, unless of course, you have been granted the right privileges. In that case, you will be able to discuss only matters for which you have been granted access. The communication will probably take place over secure channels.

Similar mechanisms can be readily mirrored by the proposed model. Actually, the proposed distributed model, based on the Turing-complete information primitive, is able to implement arbitrary security schemes. For example, access to remote components can be granted depending on several factors: a) role of the sender a) type of access granted to the sender based on its role b) type of message being exchanged c) name or class of the receiver. Security is usually implemented within the context of a conceptual framework.

The additional components required for the implementation of the proposed model and associated communication framework mimic the functionality outlined above. The façade component is usually responsible for security (messaging authorization and authentication). Before the message is forwarded to the receiver, Facade performs decryption, authorization and authentication on it.

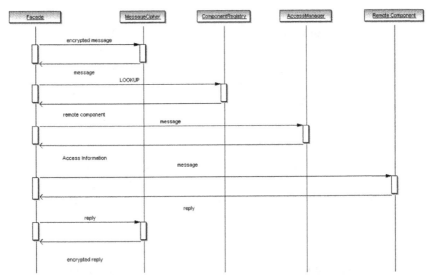

**Figure 3.** Secure access to remote components and services based on Concepts (server side)

The following are the components involved:

**MessageCipher**: component responsible for decrypting the input message and encrypting the reply message. This component can be configured to use a specific encryption scheme.

**Component Registry**: allows the system to register and look up components by ID.

**AccessManager**: responsible for granting/denying access to remote components. It authorizes and authenticates each message received. If the access manager is unable to authenticate the message, it never reaches the receiver.

Animated/Live entities, messaging, dialogs, and messages are key players in daily life. Business applications are just another example. Information is constantly exchanged between participant entities as part of predefined processes.

177

For instance, you can send a check to a company to pay a bill. The company initiates an electronic transaction to deduct the money from the bank account. The bank processes the transaction and transfers the money. A monthly statement, including all the transactions, is mailed at a later time. Checks, transactions, electronic funds, and statements represent just a few examples of the countless messages being exchanged between system components as part of daily business transactions. It should become obvious the ubiquity of the proposed concepts as part of distributed processes and the faithful correspondence [30] between the proposed model and reality. Also, notice the accurate correspondence between the model and proven/robust communication frameworks that make modern life possible for wide audiences at a massive scale.

## 17.2    Performance, Scalability, and other considerations

The proposed distributed component/service model is simple yet versatile and robust. It is able to handle complex issues associated with distributed applications. The model is fully compatible with common scalability and availability mechanisms (clustering, load balancing, failover, caching, etc). A conceptual framework and infrastructure based on the information pattern family play an important role in supporting these mechanisms. For instance, distributed applications/components based on the proposed model can readily run on a cluster of computers to improve performance, reliability, and availability.

The proposed approach helps improve interoperability. It provides the flexibility of transparently combining heterogeneous platforms, protocols, languages, and technologies. Information patterns separate the critical information aspect from how such information is stored, represented, transferred, and processed. All these aspects can be altered independently without impacting the actual information. Information primitive and patterns are technology agnostic: computer language, platform, protocol, data format and so on. Concepts of the form $C = \{(x1, y1), , (xn, yn)\}$ can be freely interchanged between systems and components. Arbitrary technologies, implemented based on the proposed model, can be readily incorporated as part of an integrated information process: sockets, .Net, HTTP, RMI, REST, SSL, EJBs, and so forth. They can be mixed and matched depending on the specific architecture requirements.

178

During the peer review process, it was proposed that Messaging could be applied to improve scalability [2]. Because of tight coupling between client and server, conventional distributed/service technologies based on distributed artifacts require that client and server application be upgraded at the same time. This is usually not feasible and presents significant scalability limitations for infrastructures running 24/7 and/or expecting to accommodate a large number of computer nodes.

On the other hand, Messaging does not present such limitation because client, server and communication mechanism are fully decoupled. Servers can be upgraded one by one without an impact on the client application and the rest of the infrastructure. Once all the servers have been gradually upgraded, clients can be upgraded to take advantage of the new software functionality. As a consequence, an infrastructure based on Messaging can scale well and handle an arbitrary number of servers and clients 24/7. It is assumed that the new software version is backward compatible in terms of the messaging being exchanged.

In terms of garbage collection, a straightforward garbage collection mechanism can be employed to support the implementation of a distributed computing model based on the information patterns. A leasing approach, for instance. Keep in mind that few extra overhead components need to be maintained when using Messaging and the proposed model. The mechanism implemented can also take advantage of the garbage collection mechanism provided by the computer language at hand.

## 17.3    Fault-tolerant capabilities

The abstractions part of the information pattern family can be readily replicated to provide a fault-tolerant information infrastructure. Animated/Live components behave like state machines. Therefore they can be extended to provide fault-tolerant capabilities in a very natural fashion by replicating components and coordinating their interaction via consensus algorithms [6, 16].

Consider that nature is very keen in addressing fault-tolerant challenges in terms of message, individual, and process redundancy. The survival of species depends on having robust fault-tolerant mechanisms in place. The information pattern family is able to mirror these mechanisms.

Using a real-world analogy, consider the scenario where a critical task is given to a group of team members by the team leader. Redundancy is provided so fault tolerance can be achieved: the critical task can get completed even if some of team members fail to complete their share. The leader will interchange messages with the members via phone, internet, face-to-face conversations to assess progress and deal with failures. Once the task is completed by a quorum of team members, the leader will be able to compare the preliminary results and arrive to final results based on consensus.

The information patterns can be utilized to implement fault-tolerant capabilities. The replicated *state machine approach* is a general method for implementing fault-tolerant systems by replicating components and coordinating their interaction via consensus algorithms. Live/Animated components (i.e. information machine) happen to behave like a state machine: *input* message, *output* message and component *state* are part of the model. An information machine can emulate any arbitrary state machine. Consider that the information primitive is Turing-complete and can be used to implement arbitrary models including state machines. The following fault-tolerant aspects apply within the context of Concepts:

*Redundancy*: It is possible to use several replicas of the component (information machine) to achieve fault tolerance. Input messages are sent to all the component replicas (Animated/Live components). Each component replica is running on a separate host. Instead of replicating a monolithic system, Live/Animated components are replicated. In other words, fault tolerance can be modeled and implemented at the component level in a straightforward fashion. Message redundancy and process redundancy are also possible. Actually, as a consequence of the proposed model, redundancy can be realistically provided for each member of the information pattern family.

*Consensus*: The output coming from a *quorum* of Live/Animated replicas can be compared to detect failures or achieve consensus. The leader component (part of the client application) is responsible for checking progress on a regular basis and gathering/comparing the outputs.

*Auditing and failure detection*: Non-faulty component replicas will always have the same component state and produce the same outputs.

*Replica-group reconfiguration*: This is done in case of a new replica component being added to the group or in case of a component malfunction. In the latter scenario, the faulty component needs to be removed from the replica group.

*Component State Transfer*: Before a new component replica is added to the group, the component state must be the same. The component state must be copied from a non-faulty component replica.

*Checkpoints*: A duplicate component state is saved so that the inputs processed up to a point can be discarded.

The proposed distributed model takes a holistic and realistic approach based on information and the Turing-complete primitive. All other relevant concepts are part of the model. It views fault tolerance from the information perspective. As part of the proposed model, there are several entities that can be replicated. Actually, all the members of the information pattern family can be replicated to achieve fault tolerance: components, messaging, dialog, association, information process, information repository, and group.

Think about an organization or group of individuals working cooperatively. In order for the group to accomplish its goals, redundant processes are put in place to monitor vital areas. The group also relies on multiple individuals to accomplish key processes - redundancy at the individual level. As part of such processes, individuals are constantly engaged in multiple dialogs, possibly redundant, where vital information is exchanged via messaging. Furthermore, sentences and information associations can be made redundant. Individuals also rely on redundant information repositories and experts to find information and accomplish their common goals.

The proposed distributed/service model can mirror all these scenarios as related to arbitrary processes. As mentioned earlier, it is also geared towards the implementation of fault tolerance at the component level (Live/Animated component) as opposed to the system level. Actually, Live/Animated components are by nature ready to be replicated as part of fault-tolerant systems without any required changes to the component itself.

Redundancy of information happens at all levels: from the information association and message, all the way to the information process. For instance, when a person says: Are you sure, without a doubt, that it is safe to cross the street? - Positive? Or perhaps something in a different context: Are you absolutely sure that the reactor is cooling down? No doubt about it? Notice the information redundancy, at the association level, as part of the first sentence.

Consider the true correspondence between the proposed distributed model and the reality it seeks to represent, specifically when it comes to mirroring fault tolerance aspects. Every aspect, including fault tolerance, should be viewed from the information perspective – the fundamental concept. The proposed distributed model can be leveraged to provide complete fault tolerance capabilities, in a very realistic fashion, by replicating one or usually several members of the information pattern family. Reference four [4] demonstrates a reusable implementation of the Master-Worker pattern which features BPEL and fault-tolerant characteristics.

In summary, the proposed distributed component/service model is able to *naturally* manage complex real-world challenges and requirements: security, interoperability, fault tolerance, parallelism, concurrency, scalability, reliability, and so on. All relevant concepts are mirrored by the realistic Turing-complete approach and information primitive. As a consequence, distributed/concurrent processes and applications gain substantial improvements in several areas including reusability, quality, cost, timeframe, and maintainability.

182

# 18. INFORMATION MACHINE AND TURING COMPLETENESS

This section discusses the proposed mathematical model and demonstrates its Turing-completeness. The mathematical model consists of three (3) main concepts.

- a) **Information Machine (A):** an automatic machine able to perform computations via the information primitive which defines the machine's single function (or purpose). The machine A is defined by a two-tuple A= (*processInformation(message)*, I). A is Turing complete.

- b) **Information (I, M):** processed in the forms of messages (M), also called information packets or chunks (IC). A message (M) is expressed by a n-tuple M= (b1, , bn) where b1, , bn are symbols in a finite alphabet ($\sum$). Information machines include a memory subcomponent able to store and retrieve information. The information stored (i.e. known) by the machine is represented by I = (IC1, ,ICn), where IC1, ,ICn are information chunks (or packets) . ICi = (b_{i1}, , b_{in}); b_{i1}, , b_{in} $\in \sum$; i = [1.. n].

- c) **Information primitive:** *processInformation (message)* represents a function $f: \sum* \to \sum*$

A Turing machine is specified as a 7-tuple M= (Q,$\Gamma$,b,$\Sigma$ ,$\delta$,q$_0$, F). Given an arbitrary Turing machine, let us demonstrate that an equivalent information A-machine can be built based on the information primitive $f$:

```
// Pseudocode implementation based
// on the information primitive (f).
// The message consists of a single symbol.

void processInformation (symbol) {
    Transition transition;   // Consists of next state, operation/symbol to be written,
                             // and tape movement ('L' or 'R')

    // Transition table being replicated.
    transition = transitionTable[currentState, symbol];
```

```
if (transition.operation != 'N')
    updateTape(transition);            // Update the machine tape

if (transition.movement == 'L' || transition.movement == 'R')
    moveHead (transition.movement); // Move the head

currentState = transition.nextState ; // Part of the information stored in the
                                      // machine's memory
    return;
}
```

The machine tape can be implemented as an array, vector, or any other comparable data structure. It is part of the information (I) stored in the machine's memory subcomponent. The machine's transition table, current state, initial state, and set of final states are also part of (I). For any arbitrary Turing machine, an equivalent information machine (A) can be built, which demonstrates that (A) is Turing complete. As a consequence, and based on the Church-Turing thesis, any computable function or algorithm can be computed by using the information machine (A). $f\colon \sum^* \to \sum^*$ is a generalization of *processInformation(symbol)* applicable to messages (information chunks) of finite length $(\sum^*)$. Animated/Live components represent a software implementation of Turing-complete A-machines. In other words, Animated/Live components based on the information primitive can be used to implement any computer technology, protocol, language and/or framework including secure, distributed, and fault-tolerant technologies. Consider that there is a fundamental aspect, expressed by the primitive *f*, and associated with every computer technology: *information*. A Conceptual framework, based on the information abstractions, has been utilized to implement a complete set of technologies including distributed components, SOA, REST, ESB, BPEL, and so forth [4, 10].

There is a second approach that can be employed to demonstrate Turing completeness. Let us demonstrate that the information primitive *f* can be utilized to implement the same functionality implemented by a Turing complete language or process technology.

184

Let us consider an arbitrary process, function, or procedure (*p*) written in an arbitrary Turing complete language (or process technology like BPEL): *output = p (x1,x2,... ,xk);*

*x1, x2, ... ,xk* are the parameters processed by the function, procedure or process. *Output* is optional since procedures do not return a value.

An Animated/Live component can be implemented to provide equivalent functionality regardless of the complexity associated to the procedure, function, or process. Notice that *f* is a generalization of any arbitrary function or procedure (*p*). Within the context of a realistic model, instead of using parameters (*x1, x2, .... ,xk*), the information is passed to *f* as a fully decoupled *message* with attributes *x1,x2,...., xk*. In other words, the realistic information primitive expressed by *f*, can be utilized to implement any arbitrary functionality (or algorithm) provided by a Turing-complete language or process technology.

Based on the earlier discussion, it should also be fairly obvious that the information primitive and Animated/Live components can be used to compute any arbitrary mathematical function expressed as *(y1, y2, .......,yn) = f (x1, x2, ............,xm)*. An Animated/Live component is equivalent to a Turing machine (or computer) in terms of processing power. On the other hand, it is necessary to emphasize the fundamental and ubiquitous aspect: *information.* There are multiple reasons for such assertion, including practical, implementation, and pedagogical aspects. In terms of practical considerations, software processes based on the information primitive, are improved in terms of simplicity, encapsulation, reusability, coupling, scalability, quality, cost, and so on. Not to mention the fact that the proposed model seeks to mirror reality as an overriding design principle, and therefore it aims to be in perfect harmony with reality. From the pedagogical standpoint, it should be fairly obvious how to communicate that Animated/Live components, information processes, computers, and computer technologies in general, have a single purpose: *processing of information.* All these entities, extracted from reality, are responsible for a *single* function (literally):

*processInformation (message);*

Conceptually, these entities are *implementable information machines (or computers)*. As described above, the proposed information machine is able to compute any arbitrary mathematical function $f$. Therefore, information machines are also 'mathematical' machines. Notice the strong interrelationship between the physical world (reality), information, Mathematics, and Computer Science. Reality and our physical world happen to be completely mathematical should we ask? Animated/Live components, information processes, computers, and computer technologies, regardless of complexity, can be expressed in complete, simple and precise mathematical terms as demonstrated by the proposed Turing-complete realistic model and its associated information primitive $f$.

In regards to the proposed question, George Boole's remarkable realization gives us invaluable insight into the matter[1, 22]:

"The truth that the ultimate laws of thought are mathematical in their form, viewed in connexion with the fact of the possibility of error, establishes a ground for some remarkable conclusions. If we directed our attention to the scientific truth alone, we might be led to infer an almost exact parallelism between the intellectual operations and the movements of external nature. Suppose any one conversant with physical science, but unaccustomed to reflect upon the nature of his own faculties, to have been informed, that it had been proved, that the laws of those faculties were mathematical; it is probable that after the first feelings of incredulity had subsided, the impression would arise, that the order of thought must, therefore, be as necessary as that of the material universe. We know that in the realm of natural science, the absolute connexion between the initial and final elements of a problem, exhibited in the mathematical form, fitly symbolizes that physical necessity which binds together effect and cause."

It can be demonstrated that Boole's Conceptual Machine $(A = (\beta(m), I))$ is Turing Complete. The A-machine relies on its memory subcomponent for storage and retrieval of conceptual information (I). The scope of the information primitive $\beta(m)$ has been substantially simplified (i.e. narrowed) to the implementation of logical processing as specified by Boole's Algebra of Logic: logical operations (AND, OR, NOT, Boolean equality, and so forth) applied to information represented using the concept construct (C). Basic flow of control is also required to execute procedures (P). Set theory and operations represent a Boolean algebra.

186

The machine is able to understand/produce sentences (S) and execute procedures (P) in the natural language (L). Implementing Boole's machine is straightforward (mirrors mathematical formulation). For convenience and versatility sake, the machine can also execute procedures (P) that use a syntax similar to the one employed by traditional computer languages. Also for convenience, advanced flow of control is recommended (while, for, and so forth). For any arbitrary Turing machine (M= $(Q,\Gamma,b,\Sigma,\delta,q_0, F)$), a procedure (P) can be built to simulate it which proves Turing Completeness.

```
// Procedure (P) that implements a Turing Machine.
// It is written using a conceptual language targeted to be
// run by a Boole's machine.


Procedure simulateTuringMachine {


Concept TM;              // Turing Machine
Concept Transition;      // Consists of next state, operation/symbol to be written,
                         // and tape movement ('L' or 'R')
Concept stateTransitions; // Transitions associated to a specific state


// This specific procedure implements logical negation (bitwise)
// A procedure (P) can be written, for the conceptual machine, to
// emulate any arbitrary Turing machine – simply by changing
// the TM initialization section to match M= (Q,Γ,b,Σ ,δ,q0, F)


// Initialize Turing Machine (TM)


TM->initialState = TM->currentState = "q0";
TM->finalStates = {"q1"};




// Initialize Transition Table


// State q0 (transitions)
Transition->operation = "W"; Transition->newSymbol = '1';Transition->movement = 'R'; Transition->newState = "q1";
TM->transitionTable->q0->0 = Transition;
```

```
Transition->operation = "W";Transition->newSymbol = '0';Transition->movement =
'R'; Transition->newState = "q1";
TM->transitionTable->q0->1 = Transition

...


while (!(TM->currentState ∈ TM->finalStates)) {

  TM->symbol = readTape ( );

  // Retrieve transitions associated to the current state

  stateTransitions = TM->transitionTable[TM->currentState];
  Transition = stateTransition [TM->symbol];        // Retrieve transition for symbol

  if (Transition->operation != 'N')
    updateTape(transition);                          // Update the machine tape


  if (Transition->movement == 'L' || Transition->movement == 'R')
    moveHead (Transition->movement);        // Move the head

  TM->currentState = Transition->nextState ;
  }


}
```

A variable or index (I) can be utilized to access Concept associations. If the value of I is $x_i$ ($i = [1 .. n]$), C[I] retrieves the value of C->$x_i$. Boole's Conceptual Machine mimics the mind and features cognitive abilities including learning and logical reasoning.

"The idea of a learning machine may appear paradoxical to some readers. How can the rules of operation of the machine change? They should describe completely how the machine will react whatever its history might be, whatever changes it might undergo. The rules are thus quite time-invariant. This is quite true. The explanation of the paradox is that the rules which get changed in the learning process are of a rather less pretentious kind, claiming only an ephemeral validity. The reader may draw a parallel with the Constitution of the United States." Alan Turing [3].

188

Boole's Algebra of Logic ($\beta$-function) represents the Constitution that provides the machine with abilities of logical reasoning: The Laws of Thought, which are time-invariant. On the other hand, the information ($I$) learned in the form of concepts (C), is ephemeral – including learned procedures (P) to solve problems or perform tasks. The mathematical formulation clearly shows it: $A = (\beta(m),\ I.)$

"Computability logic believes that logic is meant to be the most basic, general-purpose formal tool potentially usable by intelligent agents in successfully navigating real life. And it is semantics that establishes that ultimate real-life meaning of logic." Giorgi Japaridze

# 19.   BPM/BPEL TECHNOLOGIES

The information pattern family and conceptual framework can be used to model arbitrary business processes in a realistic and accurate fashion. They can be reused for the comprehensive implementation of business process technologies (BPEL/BPM), frameworks, and applications. The information process abstractions can also be readily incorporated into UML/BPM/BPEL diagrams in order to design and implement applications with comparable functionality to traditional business process applications. There is a direct correspondence between the proposed abstractions and specific modeling diagrams and tools.

Because of the simplicity of the proposed model, a simple information primitive needs to be implemented: (*processMessage (message)*). Any BPEL/BPM technology can be utilized and/or extended to implement the information primitive required. For convenience, the examples that follow use the BPEL implementation provided by the Jt conceptual framework [10]. The BPEL diagrams have been produced using the Eclipse BPEL designer. By using these tools and frameworks, complete production quality applications can be generated with comparable capabilities to the ones provided by traditional distributed and process technologies.

The following simple process (HelloWorld) sends a message ("hi") to a local component. Notice the compact syntax. *processMessage()* is not included but assumed implicitly:

*reply = component(message);*

This is equivalent to *reply= component.processMessage (message);*

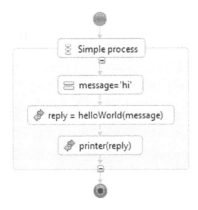

**Fig 1. Simple example of the information process (synchronous messaging)**

The following BPEL syntax represents the component invocation (using the Jt BPEL extensions):

```
<bpel:invoke   component="helloWorld"
   inputVariable="message"
   outputVariable="reply">
</bpel:invoke>
```

The component helloWorld has been defined as a class instance:

```
<bpel:variable
   name="helloWorld"
   type="java:Jt.examples.HelloWorld">
</bpel:variable>
```

As part of a process, all forms of messaging are supported: synchronous, asynchronous, streaming, distributed messaging, two-way messaging, authenticated, encrypted, and combinations of these forms. For instance, asynchronous messaging requires the attribute *synchronous="false"* as part of the component invocation.

191

The following process invokes a web service. A synchronous message is sent to a remote component/service via its local MDP proxy. The reply message is printed. The same can be accomplished by using the *messenger* abstraction instead of a proxy (not demonstrated here). If an exception is detected during the service invocation, the process prints it. Conceptually, the remote service/component invocation looks like:

*proxy.processMessage (message);*

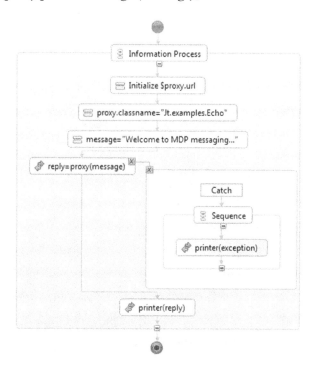

**Fig 2. Remote component/service invocation using the process design pattern**

The following BPEL code represents the remote service/component invocation. The proxy needs to be initialized beforehand with the name and address associated to the remote component/service. Exception handling is also demonstrated:

```
<bpel:invoke component="proxy" inputVariable="message"
    outputVariable="reply" exception="exception">
  <bpel:catch faultMessageType="java:java.lang.Exception">
    <bpel:sequence>
      <bpel:invoke component="printer"
                   inputVariable="exception">
      </bpel:invoke>
    </bpel:sequence>
  </bpel:catch>
</bpel:invoke>
```

## 19.1   Master-Worker Pattern

The following example provides a reusable BPEL implementation of the well-known Master-Worker design pattern, based on the process abstractions (also known as divide-and-conquer). Using the proposed realistic paradigm, the process can be conceptualized as the process associated with a *team* of animated components. Tasks are assigned to a team of members to complete. Team members can be local or remote components/services. All forms of messaging are supported: asynchronous, synchronous, distributed, two-way, secure, etc. The user of this pattern, only needs to provide the logic associated with the member (task itself). Most of the complexities associated with the development of distributed processes are handled by using the proposed approach and abstractions: distributed communication, security, multithreading challenges, etc.

The following section of the process (Leader) assigns tasks to the team members by sending an asynchronous message (task) to the member. A task table (taskTable) is maintained to keep track of the task assignments and the corresponding team member assigned to each particular task.

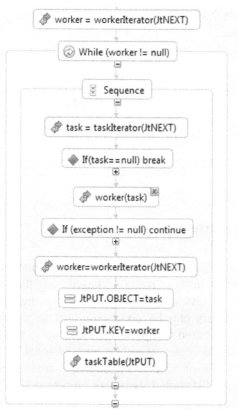

**Fig 3. Task assignments within the process (via asynchronous messaging).**

The following section of the process (*Leader*) checks on progress, on a regular basis via synchronous messaging. Notice that progress notifications sent to the *team leader* via asynchronous messaging is also feasible. Once the task is completed, the task results are retrieved; the member is removed from the work-in-progress list (worker) and added to the list of available members. In case a member is unable to complete a specific task, the task is reassigned to another available member. This simple example can be modified to provide sophisticated redundancy, fault-tolerant and decision-making capabilities, like the ones required by any modern organization or corporation.

Keep in mind that the proposed model contains the complete set of abstractions (Turing complete as demonstrated) required to model arbitrarily complex organizations and information processes. For

194

instance, a hierarchy consisting of layers the supervision can be added, in order to monitor and supervise the work. Each layer consists of *Live/Animated* components acting as *team leaders*, *supervisors* or *managers* and interchanging information (via messaging) with other participants in order to make process decisions. Additional redundancy and fault tolerance characteristics can be achieved by assigning the same task to a *team* of members instead of individuals. Once the task is completed by a quorum of team members, the *team leader* will be able to compare the preliminary results and arrive to final results based on consensus.

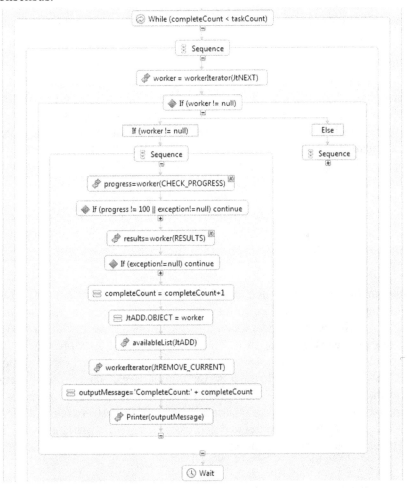

**Fig. 4 Task progress and results tracking via synchronous messaging.**

## 20.  COMPARISON WITH RELATED SOFTWARE MODELS

The proposed model can be compared with several other related approaches. Krueger introduces the following taxonomy of different approaches of software reuse based on the central role played by abstractions [44]: High-Level Languages, Software Components (including OO) ,Software Schemas, Application Generators, Transformational Systems and Software Architectures. The proposed approach is related to software components and software architectures. Design patterns also represent a related approach to software reuse [11].

The real world consists of other entities besides objects/components and design patterns. Concepts can be used to represent every single aspect of our reality. They are not limited to the representation of physical objects/components. Not every concept is a design pattern either. Information is a concept, a very broad one, applicable to every problem and situation. It is not an object or a design pattern. The same principle applies to many other concepts: Energy, Gravity, Force, Time, Sentence, Reservation, natural laws and so on. These entities are concepts, not objects or design patterns. On the other hand, every abstraction including design patterns and objects/components can be represented as a concept. Think that all these abstractions were first created and manipulated by the conceptual mind in the form of concepts.

As mentioned earlier, the terms object and component are used interchangeably. From an information perspective, the fundamental aspect is whether the object or component is able to process information in the real world. If so, the object or component is represented and implemented using an Animated/Live component. In reality, most entities are unanimated objects or components, unable to process information. The term should not be confused with how it is used (precise semantics) in the context of component-based software engineering (CBSE) and related technologies. A comparison with the CBSE approach can be found later in the section.

Other examples of concepts are part of the information pattern family: Messaging and Information Process. These ubiquitous concepts have been studied and formalized from the standpoint of design patterns [2,4].

196

However, as concepts, they are different from objects and design patterns for several reasons, among them:

- Nature and its processes already exhibit an inherent design and a set of associated natural concepts. A similar principle applies to man-made processes and entities.

- Concepts represent information but have no information processing capabilities. While mimicking reality, the proposed model recognizes that there are two classes of entities (participants) based on the fundamental information aspect: a) Entities that can process information (Animated/Live components) b) Entities that cannot (Concepts). Furthermore, most entities in the world around us should be represented as concepts because they are unable to process information. Adding information processing capabilities to these entities is artificial, unrealistic, and not really beneficial.

- It is challenging to find drawbacks and trade-offs for the concepts extracted from nature, which is difficult to explain within the context of design pattern methodologies.

For comparison purposes the following quote should also be carefully considered: "We can note in passing that one of the biggest problems in the development of object-oriented SW architectures, particularly in the last 25 years, has been an enormous over-focus on objects and an under-focus on **messaging** (most so-called object-oriented languages don't *really* use the looser coupling of messaging, but instead use the much tighter gear meshing of procedure calls – this hurts scalability and interoperability)." Alan Kay et al. Tighter gear meshing of procedure calls has also been characterized as "The complex machinery of procedure declarations" while discussing problems associated with traditional APIs [26].

Since information is the foundation of our perceived reality, the presented model proposes that computer systems, like our minds, should tackle arbitrary problems from the standpoint of information. Such approach has interesting and perhaps unexpected consequences. There are clear differences between the conceptual approach and related abstractions (objects and design patterns) in regards to how participant entities are modeled.

Based on the proposed model, entities in reality can be classified into two groups based on the fundamental information aspect: a) Entities that can process information (Animated/Live components) b) Entities that cannot (Concept). Furthermore, traditional OO APIs usually rely on tighter gear meshing of procedure calls which is the source of a variety of issues including the ones mentioned above: complexity, coupling, interoperability limitations, and scalability limitations. This applies to implementations based on objects and design patterns. In contrast, the proposed approach relies on natural abstractions: Animated/Live components and Messaging.

Let us carefully observe reality and conclude that most entities are unable to process information (unanimated objects). Actually, speaking in relative terms, very few entities are able to process information: living beings, computer systems, automated systems, machines, and so on. All these entities can be modeled using the Animated/Live component abstraction. A large majority of the entities in the physical world are unanimated. Such entities are unable to process information and therefore can be represented as concepts (C) with no information processing capabilities. This represents a main difference between the proposed model and related abstractions (Objects and Design Patterns).

Consider a bank application dealing with accounts, bank statements, transactions, and so on. All of these entities can be represented as concepts (C) because they are only able of conveying information. The banking system via an Animated/Live component, like a teller component, is the only entity that needs to process information in the form of the aforementioned concepts. All the other entities can be represented using concepts. As a consequence of the proposed model, a complex system can be specified, in a highly realistic fashion, using very few components with information processing capabilities. Obviously, the proposed model provides realism and simplicity among other advantages. The described behavior attempts to mirror the one exposed by the mind, which provides the processing mechanism able to manage a large variety of concepts. Concepts are also mental representations based on information associations, which mimics our thinking patterns.

Now consider all the entities contained in an arbitrary database. They only contain information without processing capability whatsoever. All the entities inside a database can be represented using a single

198

abstraction (concept) for processing purposes. Such conceptual representation also results in the significant reduction of the number of *real* components required for system implementation. In the scenario of the banking example discussed above, all the required entities (accounts, transactions, statements, etc) can potentially be stored and manipulated using a single abstraction: concept (C).

Since concepts represent pure information – independent of computer language, technology, platform, and protocol – they can be freely interchanged between heterogeneous systems, applications systems, and components. In contrasts, traditional objects that *artificially* couple information and processing mechanism, as a single entity, are unable to provide this degree of interoperability.

By classifying entities into two groups, the number of components necessary for implementation is significantly reduced: A few encapsulated Animated/Live components, able to process information, dealing with all the other entities represented as concepts (C).

The conceptual approach also eliminates unrealistic abstractions, artifacts, and primitives which are ultimately redundant. In other words, only realistic concepts and information primitive are part of the model. Overall system simplification is achieved. As an additional consequence, the complex web of tightly coupled and unrealistic component interdependencies is also eliminated. You may want to spend a minute or two wrapping your mind around this concept, a direct result of the realistic model. It should also illustrate the key differences between Concepts and the two related abstractions: Objects and Design Patterns.

As discussed earlier, traditional objects consist of a fixed number of attributes. On the other hand, concepts are dynamic entities which do not have a fixed number of associations. Instead, associations can be created dynamically. A sentence, for instance, can have a variety of structures (and associations). In this sense, objects are more concrete than concepts. In turn, every physical object can be represented as a concept (C).

Carefully consider that nature and natural processes already have an inherent design to them. In order to achieve true correspondence and realism [30], we must mirror it as part of the software design. Obviously, there is no point in 'reinventing' a design that already exists as part of natural creation. This realization will result in additional key differences between the proposed model and the related abstractions in terms of design approach, identification of trade-offs/drawbacks, context, and so forth.

Design patterns tend to focus on finding trade-offs and drawbacks associated with their utilization in a particular context. On the other hand, Concepts are extracted from reality in the form in which they exist. For instance, consider the concepts of Gravity, Energy and Force. Trying to find trade-offs and drawbacks associated to these concepts is probably a futile undertaking. Improving upon nature just seems unrealistic. The Designer of nature obviously seems to have a true knack for perfection. Also, the aforementioned concepts are unique and there are no similar natural concepts that can be used for comparison purposes. The same principle can be generalized to many other concepts and natural laws extracted from reality: reflection, refraction, messaging, message, light, and so forth. On the other hand, trade-offs are applicable when dealing with man-made designs, products and processes.

Aristotle defined the idea of perfection based on three associated concepts: as that which is complete, that which is so good that nothing could be better (unequaled), and that which has attained its purpose (effective). Arguably, idealized natural concepts meet the criteria and are therefore flawless. The proposed model helps understand why trade-offs and drawbacks are not found. Since concepts are extracted from natural reality, and nature sets the ultimate standard (golden standard), finding tradeoffs or drawbacks is not really feasible or necessary. Our best effort is limited to studying and mimicking such concepts in order to achieve a realistic representation and the associated software improvements. The idealized concept of messaging (transference of information) meets the above criteria. Less than perfect messaging can be encountered in real life. However, it represents a different concept: imperfect or faulty messaging.

In the case of man-made concepts like reservation and account, these entities only consists of factual and accurate information (truth) about specific aspects of reality. In a sense, they also represent idealized entities. Additionally, man-made processes and entities rely on natural ones. The same set of natural entities and concepts apply, including nature's laws. For instance, in order to convey messages, as part of human communication (man-made language), we need to rely on the natural concept of messaging.

It is best to view and study the information pattern family, and similar abstractions, from the standpoint of concepts. The same principle should apply to many other concepts found in the real world. By doing so, the perceived inconsistencies disappear. In general, while studying concepts, it is not necessary to specify or look for trade-offs/drawbacks. Concepts should be modeled, mirrored, and implemented as they exist in the real world (verbatim).

Design patterns are typically applicable to a specific context. On the other hand, concepts are applicable to a variety of contexts (highly reusable entities). For instance, the concept of information is very broad, applicable to arbitrary contexts. Every single aspect can be represented as information, expressed using the concept construct (C). Messaging and message also represent concepts applicable to a wide variety of contexts. However, Concepts can be leveraged for the reusable implementation of design patterns [4,5,2], usually as part of a framework.

In general terms, the main goal of a comprehensive conceptual design, becomes identifying and mirroring the complete set of concepts found in reality relevant to the problem or application. For example, if you are designing an application to provide communication between distributed applications, computers, and/or components, all the main relevant concepts must be included. Obviously, messaging is one of them since we are thinking about communication or exchange of information. Consider how the mind communicates with other components of the body, how the neurons in the brain communicate with each other, or how living beings – members of a group – interchange information to cooperate in accomplishing common goals. Messaging is a ubiquitous concept.

Failing to recognize one or more of the fundamental concepts will probably produce an incomplete design and solution: key concepts will be missing, limitations and shortcomings will follow. Within the context of a conceptual design, the responsibility of a designer is similar to the work of a realistic painter, writer, or sculptor: identifying the main concepts relevant to the reality being depicted in order to provide an accurate and realistic representation. The design choices are also limited within the context of a realistic design effort. The described difference is probably associated with the fact that the software design is based on something that already exists – natural or man-made entity/process – as opposed to designing a building, piece of furniture, or machine part which are entities that did not originally exist. We are not referring to machine parts where a natural model is available, like a robotic arm. On the other hand, it helps illustrate the difference since the process of designing a robotic arm also differs from the design of a building or piece of furniture, in terms of the preexistence of a model with an inherent design.

Improving on nature's design, arguably perfect, is probably unrealistic. On the other hand, imitation of the natural design via conceptualization is an attainable goal, consistent with Biomimetics, which produces substantial benefits in terms of software engineering processes and methodologies (see Model Evaluation and Metrics). A similar principle applies to man-made processes which already have and inherent design and may need to be automated as part of computer systems. Conceptualization entails the extraction of realistic concepts, relevant to the application, from natural and man-made reality. As you will find, such process will produce a streamlined set of implementable concepts, part of the information pattern family, which can be readily extracted and reused from a conceptual framework already implemented.

Going back to the taxonomy proposed by Krueger, software architectures represent reusable software frameworks and subsystems that capture the overall software design. There are key distinctions between these and the proposed approach. Software frameworks/subsystems tend not to focus on implementation/model realism based on natural concepts, or mathematical foundations. On the other hand, the proposed Turing-complete model recognizes that natural processes already have an inherent architecture and design based on a realistic set of concepts that need to be extracted, through conceptualization, as part of the software effort. The universe of abstractions (i.e. entities) is realistically and

202

unequivocally divided into two main categories depending on the ability to process information: Animated/Live entity (A-machine) or concept (C).

Architectural frameworks and abstractions tend to focus on *specific* application domains. In contrast, the proposed approach mimics the mind's conceptual framework which is based on the broad concept of information. The approach also relies on other natural concepts like Animated/Live entity, and messaging. In consequence, the conceptual model can be leveraged to implement *arbitrary* information technologies. In particular, concepts have been leveraged to implement a complete conceptual framework, reusable in *arbitrary* application and technologies.

Software architectures and abstractions that focus on specific application domains are typically more concrete than concepts. For example, consider a framework for the domain of banking applications similar to the one discussed earlier. It would consist of specific domain abstractions such as Account, Transaction, Statement, and so forth. Like every other abstraction found in reality, these also represent information (Concepts). In other words, they are more concrete entities part of the broader concept of information. By recognizing this, a *single* reusable software component, part of a conceptual framework, may encapsulate the functionality required to store and retrieve arbitrary pieces of information (Concepts). Such component would mimic the human memory which is able to store and retrieve arbitrary concepts (C). Therefore, high levels of reusability are accomplished by relying on the concept instead of the more concrete entity. In other words, the general solution applicable to the concept is also reusable and applicable to the concrete entity (special case).

The Turing-complete mathematical model represents a key difference between the conceptual approach and related software architectures/abstractions. The straightforward mathematical foundation, based on only three (3) natural concepts, present several qualities including simplicity, efficiency, completeness, and reusability. As a consequence, a Conceptual framework can be implemented with only two fundamental classes: Animated/Live component and Concept (C).

A total of 12 key classes (NKC = 12) are required to implement such framework, reusable in arbitrary application domains, and able to naturally handle complex real-world challenges such as distributed component/service access, security, redundancy, interoperability, fault tolerance, concurrency, scalability, and so on [2,4,5,10] (see Model Evaluation and Metrics).

Traditional software architectures/frameworks are implemented using a computer language [11].Framework implementation usually relies on traditional APIs, gear meshing of procedure calls, multithreading, and distributed artifacts. It is a common practice to represent every entity using the object abstraction, with associated information processing capabilities. On the other hand, concepts are language/platform agnostic. No artificial 'components', primitives, or abstractions are added to a realistic implementation based on natural concepts.

Multiple technologies and implementations fall under the umbrella of component-based software engineering (CBSE), including EJB, CORBA, and COM+. CBSE technologies do not focus on providing a unified mathematical foundation or integrated model based on natural concepts. Like the proposed conceptual model, component communication is accomplished through well-defined interfaces. Typical CBSE technologies rely on distributed artifacts, multithreading and traditional APIs based on gear meshing of procedure calls. Therefore, they inherit limitations and drawbacks that have been studied and documented in the technical literature [13, 14, 15, 20]: complexity, interoperability, coupling, versioning, and proprietary limitations.

Alan Kay's comments in terms of coupling, interoperability, and scalability also apply to typical CBSE technologies and components. In contrast, there is a single conceptual model based on a realistic approach mirrored from the mind and precise mathematical foundation: single information machine abstraction (Animated/Live entity), information primitive, and single concept construct (C). Founded on natural concepts and realism, messaging is the *single communication interface* between Animated/Live components.

The concept of messaging must never be mischaracterized or confused with gear meshing of procedure calls. Solutions based on the proposed approach can readily interoperate regardless of technology, platform,

204

protocol, and/or computer language (including CBSE technologies). The approach inspired by nature, also contributes to the resolution of the aforementioned software engineering challenges in straightforward and natural ways (see appendix on Traditional APIs).

In summary, the proposed approach is clearly different from related software models and reusability approaches in terms of mathematical model, Turing-complete information machine, single information primitive, single concept construct (C), overall realistic approach based on natural concepts, conceptual framework mimicked from the mind, and realistic implementation/correspondence.

# 21.    STATE OF THE ART (PROBLEM DOMAINS)

The conceptual paradigm has a transformative impact by advancing the state of the art as related to a variety of computing and *information* technology domains. Several complex problems are addressed.

**Distributed/Fault Tolerant Computing Technologies including SOA**: the conceptual paradigm can be leveraged for the implementation of a *complete distributed component/service model* able to handle arbitrarily complex real-world problems including scalability, security, reliability, interoperability, redundancy, and fault tolerance. Artificial abstractions, based on "gear meshing of procedure calls", are replaced by a streamlined set of realistic concepts (information pattern family). The implementation of traditional distributed applications/services is a complex endeavor, costly, and time consuming [13,14,15,20,4,5]: a) Complexity and rigidity. b) Lack of decoupling, encapsulation and reusability. c) Scalability limitations. d) Lack of interoperability. e) Technology, language, platform, protocol, and data format dependencies. The new approach addresses these problems.

**Concurrency and Parallelism related technologies**: the conceptual approach solves, in a very natural fashion, complex problems associated with parallelism and artificial abstractions like multithreading. The implementation of traditional multithreaded/parallel applications is a complex undertaking, costly, prone to error, and hampered by risks/issues [4,5]: a) Complexity. b) Strong coupling. c) Lack of encapsulation and reusability. d) Scalability and interoperability limitations. e) Complex quality issues that include race conditions, deadlocks, thread management defects, and so on. f) Risks associated with the previous challenges. All modalities of messaging, including asynchronous messaging, are accommodated by the proposed approach in a very natural, realistic, and straightforward fashion.

**Object-oriented technologies and component frameworks**: complex problems associated with OO technologies are resolved by leveraging the conceptual paradigm. "Gear meshing of procedure calls" is replaced by the natural concept of messaging. The list of problems addressed by the paradigm includes complexity, coupling, encapsulation, reusability, versioning, interoperability, scalability, and so on. The proposed approach can be employed to build a reusable conceptual framework, which has a positive impact on overall complexity, cost, timeframes, and quality.

**Design Patterns:** The conceptual paradigm has an impact on design pattern methodologies in terms of modeling and implementation. In particular, as related to pattern participants. In reality, entities can be classified into two main categories: a) entities that can process information (Live or Animated Entity) , b) passive entities that cannot (Concept). There are several key differences between design patterns and concepts. Not every concept represents a design pattern or an object. The conceptual approach can be leveraged for the reusable and realistic implementation of design patterns. After all, their implementation has to deal in one way or another with the omnipresent concepts of information and information exchange. Messaging is a ubiquitous concept that should never be overlooked in favor of artificial "gear meshing of procedure calls".

**Business Process Technologies (BPEL/BPM) and Enterprise Service Bus (ESB):** Since these *information* technologies are based on the previous technologies, the conceptual paradigm has an impact on their design and implementation. Redundant/artificial abstractions and primitives are replaced by natural concepts and single information primitive part of the conceptual approach (information pattern family). Such artifacts only add *unnecessary complexities*. A distributed component/service model implemented using the proposed approach already includes all the technology pieces/concepts required for the complete implementation. They can be readily reused without incurring any additional time and/or costs.

**Computer Languages and AI/Cognitive Architectures:** The conceptual paradigm is a perfect fit for the comprehensive implementation of a computer language NATURAL) able to mirror the natural language. Due to the proposed approach, such language is not only feasible but highly beneficial. Based on Biomimetics principles, the communication between man and machine should happen at the conceptual level ('optimal' level).

The way we instruct computers and robotic systems to perform tasks do not need to be different from how intelligent beings are instructed. The same concepts apply to both scenarios: information, messaging, conversation subject, context, message, procedure, task, and the other concepts found in reality. Obviously, both situations are conceptually equivalent or isomorphic.

Consider that procedures and concepts represent pure information and therefore they represent something that you *learn*. In other words, conceptual knowledge (information) is acquired by *learning* new concepts and procedures based on associations with concepts already mastered. By using the proposed language, the computer can be taught arbitrary concepts and procedures in the same way human beings learn. This is a direct consequence of the proposed paradigm which directs us to think from the standpoint of information, in conceptual terms. The concepts of *information, procedure,* and *learning* work together – they are in correspondence, harmony, and unity with reality.

Consider the broad impact and wide range of applications for the proposed language: health care systems, IVR systems, AI/robotic architectures, mobile, appliance interfaces, information retrieval systems based on web technologies, database interfaces, safer driving, systems to assist people physically impaired/sick/aging, and so on. Machine learning based on concepts should also be included. All these areas of application help improve society and quality of life. In general, a natural computer language can be applied to a large variety of automated devices and computer systems. It addresses the wide gap between human communication and man-machine communication by incorporating concepts and a conceptual approach – key ingredients for realistic communication.

**Software Engineering Technologies:** It should become obvious that a wide variety of software engineering technologies and design methodologies are affected by the conceptual paradigm as described above. Keep in mind that the conceptual paradigm based on the fundamental information concept, affects arbitrary *information* technologies. By having a transformative impact on these ubiquitous technologies, the conceptual paradigm has the potential for substantially impacting the overall quality of our lives and society as a whole.

Probably, it should be expected based on Biomimetics principles as related to the human mind.

The list above is not comprehensive by any means. In general, it should become clear that the conceptual paradigm has a broad impact on diverse *information* technologies. For instance, the following question should be asked: if the mind is able to process conceptual information using a single language construct (Concept), why do we need to have redundant/artificial abstractions and data structures as part of information technologies? Consider that in order to process information the logical mind does not need to know the internal representation/format of a concept – only its meaning as defined by associations with related concepts.

Also, consider that information and water are, in a sense, related concepts: information should *flow* like water among technologies and systems. Think about the substantial amounts of conceptual information that effortlessly flows between human beings which would be cumbersome if so many artificial/redundant abstractions became entangled in the process. Again, nature is leading the way. Questions like the previous one – direct consequence of the proposed model – are yet to be explored in more depth.

# 22.    MODEL EVALUATION AND METRICS

The proposed approach can be evaluated and compared with other approaches based on the following aspects which are a direct result of its mathematical model:

a) **Information machine (A):**  An automatic machine able to perform computations via the information primitive which defines the machine's single function (or purpose). The machine A= (*processInformation(message)*) is Turing complete.

d) **Information primitive**: Single function *processInformation (message)* where the message represents conceptual information (C).

e) **Concept (C)**: pure information expressed by a single language Construct, C = {a1,a2, ,an} where a1,a2, ,an are information associations.

**Simplicity.** This aspect can be measured using the number of primitives and abstractions required by the mathematical model. The proposed approach requires a single Turing-complete information primitive and one language construct (Concept). The complexity metric measured by Weighted Methods Per Class (WMC) is minimized [37],[38]: WMC = 1, for *every* single component class. The method level complexity [40] can be measured as well: one input parameter (message).

Now consider the simplification in terms of the measurable number of classes (NC) required for implementation: in reality most entities can be represented as pure information (Concept), unable to process information. NC represents a system level measurement of complexity [40]. It is related to the number of key classes (NKC) [41].

As indicated earlier, complexity can be measured by calculating the number of abstractions required for implementation (NC/NKC). All redundant abstractions and primitives add complexities (WMC & NC) and are ultimately unnecessary.   The information pattern family constitutes a small, but complete, set of realistic abstractions able to implement arbitrary technologies and applications – in particular, a complete distributed/component service model. Picture the application represented as a graph G = (V, E) where V represents the component classes and E represents the inter-dependencies between such classes.

Under the proposed approach, the order of the graph (cardinality (V) = NC) is minimized by mirroring the reality being represented.

The number of key classes required for the reference implementation of a conceptual framework can be quantified:

a)   Main framework classes (2): Animated/Live Component, and Concept.

b) Additional core classes (5): Factory, Messenger, Component Registry, Memory, and Exception Handler.   Support classes include a Resource Manager, an XML Adapter and a Logger.

c) Distributed Infrastructure classes (5): Façade, Message Cipher, Access Manager, Proxy, and Adapter (see UML diagrams).

A total of 12 key classes (NKC = 12) are required to implement the Conceptual framework and the proposed distributed component/service model. A proxy and an adapter (NKC+=2) need to be implemented in order to plug a new technology into the distributed information infrastructure provided by the conceptual framework. Adapters and Proxies for widely used technologies are already provided.

The concept of inheritance is not part of the mathematical model which is conceived from the information standpoint. Consider the *real* meaning of the concept within nature. As a consequence, the Depth of the Inheritance Tree metric is zero (DIT=0). The Number of Children is also zero (NOC=0). On the other hand, class inheritance is readily accommodated in the few cases when it becomes beneficial for implementation. In such cases, inheritance is kept to a minimum (shallow): DIT<=3 and NOC<=3.  The top class of the hierarchy is not taken into account because all components are required to inherit from it.

**Completeness.** Turing-completeness has been demonstrated via formal proof (see Information/Conceptual Machines and Turing Completeness). The proposed approach is able to accommodate all the concepts found in reality. Again, the information pattern family constitutes a compact, but complete, set of abstractions able to implement arbitrary technologies and applications. In particular, they can be leveraged for the implementation of a complete distributed component/service model.

**Efficiency.** This aspect can be quantified by determining the number of abstractions and primitives that are part of the model and the associated implementation. The proposed model leaves no room for unnecessary redundancy and inefficiencies: one Turing-complete primitive and one language construct (Concept). The model also relies on a streamlined set of information patterns, perhaps optimal. As discussed earlier, the number of class components (NC) is minimized since most entities represent Concepts unable to process information. Efficiency can also be measured based on application footprint (see size and application footprint).

As discussed earlier, efficient message-level security can be transparently built in as part of the distributed model and framework – in lieu of transport level security, which is computationally more expensive.

In general, keep in mind that nature and natural processes are highly efficient. They have evolved and improved for ages. By mirroring natural concepts, the proposed model and its implementation 'absorb' nature's qualities including efficiency. Obviously, this is consistent with the motivations behind Biomimetics principles.

**Effectivety.** It can be evaluated based on the number of real-world problems solved by the proposed model. Also, consider Turing-completeness which allows for the implementation of arbitrary information technologies. Again, nature is very effective in solving information related challenges – a quality that is readily absorbed by the distributed model. Alan Kay's comments should be carefully considered during the evaluation.

The proposed model has produced tangible and measurable results: several production quality applications and a reference implementation of the conceptual framework have been built based on the approach which demonstrates its viability and applicability [10],[2],[4],[5]. Several technologies have been designed and implemented by levering the proposed model, including SOA, REST, ESB, Master-Worker, and BPEL. The conceptual framework represents proof of concept(s) and reference implementation.

212

**Size and application footprint.** A compact set of concepts and single information primitive results in a streamlined implementation. The size of the conceptual framework can be accurately measured in terms of key classes (NKC=12) and file size. The current reference implementation of the framework takes about 512K which is very small (lightweight) when compared against traditional frameworks with similar functionally. The framework provides a complete information infrastructure [2],[4],[5]. In the realm of technology, smaller is often better and more efficient.

The conceptual framework is able to comfortably run on mobile devices where resource constraints are prevalent and need to be taken into careful consideration. Small application footprint are a direct consequence of other aspects including simplicity, straightforward mathematical model, reusability, and the compact/complete set of concepts part of the information pattern family. Requiring a streamlined set of components, as part of the design/implementation, is also a contributor because most entities are realistically represented as concepts (pure information). Like the mind, the application is able to do more with less – so to speak – by relying on a conceptual approach. This aspect is also related to the aspect of efficiency discussed earlier and can be evaluated quantitatively: 512K lightweight footprint.

**Coupling and Encapsulation**. By relying on messaging, encapsulation is maximized and coupling is minimized: the only realistic mechanism of communication between fully encapsulated components is via messaging. The number of interdependencies between components can be measured by counting the number of procedure calls required between components. The conceptual model does not present the web of coupled interdependencies required by traditional technologies/APIs based on "gear meshing of procedure calls". Again, picture the application represented as a graph $G = (V,E)$ where V represents the components and E represents the interdependencies between such components. Under the proposed approach, the size of the graph (cardinality (E)) is minimized.

Coupling between object classes (CBO) is a related complexity metric [37]. An ideal Animated/Live component is fully encapsulated and decoupled (CBO = 0): messaging is the only realistic mechanism of communication between components. A messenger subcomponent is responsible for providing the messaging functionality, when necessary.

213

Coupling between Animated/Live component and messenger is not taken into account because it is a subcomponent. In reality, Animated/Live component and its Messenger subcomponent are part of the same entity (i.e. unit). Calls to built-in classes provided by the computer language are not taken into account either since they should remain the same regardless of the approach being employed to implement the component. They can also be refactored to leverage messaging and mimic the real world (CBO = 0).

Due to complete component encapsulation, some Animated/Live components, depending on the complexity of their responsibilities, may grow to be large in terms of methods and lines of code. Such scenario can be mitigated by splitting the code and creating support subcomponents. Access to the support subcomponents is limited to the main (i.e. key) component of this hierarchy. From the system perspective, and for all practical purposes, the main component and its supporting components are viewed as a unit – single component.

**Reusability.** Based on empirical studies, it is widely accepted that encapsulation and decoupling (CBO) improve reusability [37], [39]. Therefore, by improving CBO metrics, the proposed model is bound to enhance reusability. The measured CBO value is below the recommended limit (CBO <= 5) [39].

The concepts part of the information pattern family need to be implemented once. Usually they are implemented as part of a Conceptual framework. After the initial implementation, the framework can be reused over and over again for the implementation of arbitrary technologies and applications. The same cannot be said about models and technologies based on artificial abstractions like distributed artifacts and multithreading which hinder reusability in multiple ways [2],[4],[5].

Animated/Live components that rely on the information primitive and messaging can be readily reused regardless of technology, computer language, platform, protocol and so on. Because of their encapsulation and decoupling properties, they can be reused at the component level: a single Animated/Live component can be extracted from another library/application and reused. The web of dependencies produced by gear meshing of procedure calls is effectively eliminated. Animated/Live

214

components can also be readily exposed as SOA services or distributed components.

**Scalability and Interoperability.** As documented in detail and expressed by Alan Kay, the lack of messaging imposes scalability and interoperability limitations [2],[4],[5]. Most technologies based on distributed artifacts present such limitations. They have a tangible and negative impact on the overall quality.

Scalability is usually measured in terms of the number of computer nodes that can be accommodated. An infrastructure based on the proposed distributed model can scale well and handle an arbitrary number of computers (servers and clients) 24/7 – without imposing limitations [2].

As discussed in detail, the conceptual approach based on the information pattern family is platform, technology, language, and protocol agnostic. Also, it does not present proprietary limitations. Consider a distributed application implemented based on a specific technology. Interoperability can be measured based on the number of technologies that can interoperate with the given technology (INTEROP).

For instance, a technology based on distributed artifacts like Java RMI can only interface with a client implemented using Java RMI: limited interoperability (INTEROP = 1). A similar situation applies to .NET and EJB. On the other hand, an Animated/Live component can interoperate with an application/component implemented using any arbitrary language and communication technology/protocol:

Interop = Cardinalty (computer languages) *
    Cardinality (communication technologies).

The Interop metric is much higher, without limitation. Especially, if the totality of computer languages and communication technologies is considered. Future technologies and protocols can be readily accommodated as well – through the use of suitable adapters.

For example, let us say that the distributed application needs to support Java, Android, C#, C++, and C. HTTP, Sockets, SOAP, and SSL are the communication technologies/protocols to be implemented:

Interop = 5 * 4 = 20   (based on the example)

An adapter is required for each technology to be supported. Think about the adapters that allow you to transparently connect your computer to the internet infrastructure regardless of the technology/protocol being used: Wireless, TCP/IP, modem adapter, cable adapter, and so forth.

**Correspondence (Realism).** Although perhaps more subjective, this aspect is worth mentioning. Careful attention should be paid to whether or not the real entity is able to process information. As emphasized before, concepts are passive entities unable to process information. To attain true correspondence there must be one-to-one correspondence between the implemented abstractions and the concepts extracted from conceptualization. In other words, the list of abstractions should perfectly match the extracted concepts in terms of quantity and individual names (semantics).

For instance, if the ubiquitous concept of messaging is missing from the design and/or implementation – replaced by gear meshing of procedure calls – there is lack of realistic correspondence. Also, the presence of artifacts, like distributed/SOA artifacts, indicates the lack of correspondence. The same can be said about redundant abstractions and primitives that do not match the behavior exhibited by real-world entities from the information standpoint (Concept versus Component). The information pattern family can be employed as a useful checklist and classification tool during conceptualization: concepts can be extracted and classified according to the checklist. The realistic correspondence between abstractions and their implementation can also be evaluated.

In summary, a complete model should include all the relevant concepts extracted from reality, and only those concepts without unnecessary redundancy. In the ideal scenario, model, design, and implementation should be in perfect correspondence with each other. In particular, when viewed and evaluated from the information standpoint. Such accurate correspondence is based on solid philosophical and scientific grounds as expressed by Scientific Realism and the associated Correspondence Theory of Truth[30]: the truth of a representation is determined by how it corresponds to reality. Consider that as consequence of correspondence with natural reality, the model absorbs nature's qualities which can be evaluated and often measured in quantitative terms. Also, outperforming nature is probably unrealistic as this evaluation and Biomimetics principles illustrate.

It can be argued that the combined set of metrics discussed also measures correspondence in regards to specific aspects. In reality, Animated/Live entities are fully decoupled (CBO=0) and can rely on a single function to process incoming information received via messaging (WMC=1). Entities do not override the functionality inherited from their parents (DIT=0 and NOC=0). Realistically, most entities do not have parents to inherit from. Scalability limitations are 'artificially' created. Therefore, the proposed model corresponds to reality in regards to these five measured aspects. On the other hand, traditional components based on gear meshing of procedure calls, lack correspondence in terms of CBO, WMC, DIT, NOC, and scalability.

**UML modeling**: there are 'artificial' gaps or inconsistencies between UML modeling tools and the subsequent component implementation. In particular, in terms of sequence and communication diagrams. This aspect should be evaluated. UML diagrams call for the messaging concept to be employed – either synchronous or asynchronous. On the other hand, the implementation usually relies on gear meshing of procedure calls which turn out to be the weak area once again since there is no solid justification for such discrepancy.

By relying on the proposed approach, based on realistic messaging, the gap and inconsistencies are eliminated. Also, to achieve realism and correspondence, every component part of the UML diagram, must share the same messaging interface and information primitive acting on a single message. Messaging represents a single concept that must have a realistic and uniform implementation across the board. Unanimated objects need to be modeled as concepts (C), without artificial processing capabilities. In summary, model, UML diagrams, implementation, *and reality* must match (true correspondence).

217

**Quality.** There are several metrics that can be applied to measure quality, including the number and severity of the software defects detected. Providing and analyzing detailed empirical data is outside the scope of the current effort. On the other hand, and based on empirical studies, there are well-known interdependencies between quality and the complexity metrics presented above: WMC, CBO, DIT, and NOC [37], [38]. They are below the recommended limits [39][41]: WMC <= 25, CBO <= 5, DIT<=5, and NOC<=5. As a consequence, quality is improved by leveraging the proposed model. It is also well-known that improvements in reusability result in better quality measurements.

Another area would be the elimination of multithreading artifacts which results in better quality by overcoming the complex problems presented earlier [2],[4],[5]. Lack of scalability and interoperability should arguably be viewed as measurable quality issues (defects) that are overcome by leveraging the proposed model. In any case, they represent limitations to be overcome – part of a complete model evaluation.

**Maintainability.** Based on an empirical study, maintainability is improved by enhancing complexity metrics [42], [37]: WMC, CBO, DIT and NOC. This aspect is related to software quality, risk, and overall timeframe/cost.

**Cost and Timeframe.** All the aspects described above have an impact on cost and timeframes which can be accurately measured during project implementation. Given a system consisting of n classes (NC), cost, and time can be calculated:

Total Cost = $\sum$ Cost(component$_i$); i <= NC

Total Time = $\sum$ Time(component$_i$); i <= NC

The function Cost() measures the design, implementation, testing, debugging, and maintenance costs associated to a specific component. Time() measures the amount of time required.

The interdependency between reusability and cost/timeframe is direct and well known. For instance, by reusing a conceptual framework there

218

is a significant improvement in terms of cost and timeframes because it needs to be implemented once – if it is not already available. The cost/timeframe of such implementation is also minimized due to the streamlined amount of realistic concepts to be implemented (information pattern family). Quality (software defects) also has a direct and measurable impact on cost/timeframe.

Consider the many classes, redundant primitives/APIs, and descriptors that *will not* need to be implemented thereby improving overall complexity, NC, total cost, and timeframe (NKC = 12):

a) Artifacts such as stubs, IDLs, WSDL descriptors, and similar required by traditional distributed components/services.

b) Classes and primitives associated to unrealistic abstractions. For instance, a single class (C) is required to interchange conceptual information between heterogeneous systems.

c) "The complex machinery of procedure declarations" associated with traditional APIs and parameter passing [26]. Another characterization for the gear meshing of procedure calls whose artificiality, complexity, and limitations get exacerbated in the context of heterogeneous multithreaded and distributed/SOA technologies.

d) Classes responsible for supporting information infrastructure capabilities: messaging (all forms), Animated/Live components (concurrency/parallelism), message-level security (authentication/encryption), component registry, access control, façade, technology adapters, distributed proxies, and so on. These capabilities are provided by the reusable conceptual framework. On the other hand, several of them cannot be readily reused and usually need to be reimplemented under traditional technologies. For instance, high-risk security functionality and distributed proxies usually cannot be reused.

Backus provided the following criteria for classifying models of computing [26]. Such classification is a useful tool that can also be applied to evaluate the proposed model.

**Mathematical Foundations:** "Is there an elegant and concise mathematical description of the model? Is it useful in proving helpful facts about the behavior of the model? Or is the model so complex that its description is bulky and of little mathematical use?"

Absolutely. A very concise and straightforward mathematical model that clearly expresses all the concepts associated with the model and their interrelationships.

**History sensitivity.** "Does the model include a notion of storage, so that one program can save information that can affect the behavior of a later program? That is, is the model history sensitive?"

Yes, it is history sensitive. Information is the model's fundamental concept. All relevant information operations are part of the model including store, retrieve, update, and delete. System behavior is impacted by conceptual information already known.

**Clarity and conceptual usefulness of programs.** "Are programs of the model clear expressions of a process or computation? Do they embody concepts that help us to formulate and reason about processes?"

Absolutely. Actually, the conceptual approach is based on foundation of realistic concepts extracted and mirrored from reality. In other words, the conceptual approach incorporates exactly the same concepts found in real-world processes. In particular, consider the concepts part of the information pattern family. There is a one-to-one correspondence between reality and the concepts employed. As a consequence, the implementation is clear and conceptually useful. This aspect is related to the level of abstraction.

**Type of semantics.** "Does a program successively transform states (which are not programs) until a terminal state is reached (state-transition semantics)? Are states simple or complex? Or can a "program" be successively reduced to simpler "programs" to yield a final "normal form program," which is the result (reduction semantics)?"

The proposed approach is based on the semantics of concepts as expressed by their definitions – associations with other concepts.

Based on his criteria, Backus characterizes three classes of models for computing. He underscores that the classification is "crude and debatable": The conceptual approach can also be categorized and evaluated using his criteria.

> **"Simple operational models.** Examples: Turing machines, various automata. Foundations: concise and useful. History sensitivity: have storage, are history sensitive. Semantics: state transition with very simple states. Program clarity: programs unclear and conceptually not helpful."

> **"Applicative models**. Examples: Church's lambda calculus, Curry's system of combinators, pure Lisp, functional programming. Foundations: concise and useful. History sensitivity: no storage, not history sensitive. Semantics: reduction semantics, no states. Program clarity: programs can be clear and conceptually useful."

> **Conventional programming languages.** "Foundations: complex, bulky, not useful. History sensitivity: have storage, are history sensitive. Semantics: state transition with complex states. Program clarity: programs can be moderately clear, *are not very useful conceptually.* "

**Conceptual model.** Based on Biomimetics principles and the conceptual framework utilized by the mind. Foundations: very concise and useful. It is able to accommodate all concepts that are part of reality. History sensitive: history sensitive, concepts can be stored. Semantics: no states, natural semantics of concepts as expressed by their definitions – associations with other concepts. Program clarity: programs can be very clear based on realistic concepts, are useful conceptually. The model operates at a higher level of abstraction (Conceptual).

By mirroring human languages, a computer language can be proposed to process procedures written using the natural language. Information and concepts can be *learned* based on concepts already mastered. A procedure is a concept (information) that can be learned. It is expressed as a sequence of steps. Each step is expressed using the natural language based on concepts already known. From a conceptual perspective, it cannot get clearer than this.

As expected, nature's approach excels in all the areas proposed by Backus – naturally. In particular, in the areas of conceptual usefulness and mathematical foundations. All the metrics presented can be applied to the implementation of a distributed component/service model *and* the heterogeneous technologies/applications that leverage it. They demonstrate in quantitative terms the qualities 'absorbed' by an approach that attempts to mirror nature's information model and concepts; which is consistent with Biomimetics principles.

# 23.   A NATURAL LANGUAGE OF CONCEPTS

The conceptual paradigm can be extended to propose a hypothetical Conceptual Language (NATURAL) able to mirror capabilities from the natural language to provide communication between man and machine. The principles involved are not only applicable to the communication between components, applications, and systems. Let us think about such a language using a conceptual design methodology (CD), which calls for the specification of concepts and components required for the solution.

In terms of components, a single main Animated/Live component $A = (\beta(m), I)$ should be required to understand and process messages (C) in the proposed conceptual language, via the information primitive. This mimics the mind's behavior while processing verbal communication. The message represents a sentence in the natural language. In order to identify the relevant concepts associated to the problem, consider the usual analogy in which you talk to a friend to accomplish a specific task or procedure. The first concept that comes to mind is the concept of procedure. A procedure (P) is defined as the sequence of steps (S1, S2, ,Sn) required to accomplish a specific task. It can be expressed using the conceptual notation:

$P = \{S1, S2, , Sn\}$ where S1,S2, ,Sn represent the steps to be executed.

Each step (S) is also a concept. It comes in the form of sentences in the natural language and can be represented using the conceptual form:

$Si = \{a1, a2, , an\}$

For example, the following straightforward procedure can be expressed using the conceptual form described above:

if today is my wife's birthday, please notify me

or

Please notify me on my wife's birthday

In order to perform the task, your friend will need to know the meaning of the following concepts and associations: Today, wife, wife's birthday, notify, me. Let us safely assume that your friend knows all or most of them. Any piece of information that is not known can be requested as part of a dialog. For instance: When is your wife's birthday?

The process just described can be generalized to handle any arbitrary procedure. The procedure is executed sequentially, one step at a time as described above. As usual, bear in mind that concepts are highly reusable entities and can be applied to diverse scenarios. The concept of procedure is not an exception. In summary, the definition of the proposed language consists of the following main concepts:

a) Procedure: $P = \{S1, S2, , Sn\}$
b) Step: $S = \{a1, a2, , an\}$ where a1,a2, are information associations that reference other concepts part of the hypothetical language.

Since the steps are expressed using the natural language, there will be many other concepts to consider, taken from reality. The context of the conversation is one important concept to take into consideration. Words like 'this' and 'it' will have specific meaning depending on the context. The example above will require concepts like today, wife and birthday. New concepts can be incrementally added to the language based on their information domains and the intended application. The conceptual deductive approach presented a methodology to classify information (I) into information domains of limited scope using a divide-and-conquer strategy.

For instance, a restricted information domain can deal with time related concepts (*when*): 'next Tuesday', 'tomorrow', 'today', and so forth. Another information domain can deal with location related concepts (*where*): 'Hawaii', 'Orlando', 'Seattle', 'home' and so forth. Yet another information domain may deal with concepts related to people (*who*): 'friends', 'family', 'wife', 'daughter', 'son', 'me' and so on.

As demonstrated, a conceptual approach can be utilized to ask an intelligent person to perform a specific task or procedure. Based on the concepts of realism and Biomimetics, there is no real reason why the natural language cannot be mirrored using the proposed approach. Nature is yet again ahead. Let us catch up. *Conceptually*, there is no difference between human and man-machine communication. The same concepts and principles apply to both scenarios including information (I), messaging, dialog, information associations, and the other concepts found in reality. Both situations are conceptually equivalent or isomorphic.

Actually, we must say that computer systems *need* to bridge the 'communication gap' and be improved by mimicking human languages. Such technology will have an impact on many other technologies including man-machine interfaces, IVR systems, robotics, information retrieval systems based on web technologies, database interfaces, and so on. Machine learning based on concepts should also be included.

At this point, you may be wondering about how the computer is supposed to execute the given procedure. In reality, it should mimic your friend's thinking patterns in regards to how the conceptual information is processed. Based on the proposed approach, Information (I) can be represented as a group of concepts: $I = \{C1, C2, ,Cn\}$. Suppose that the given procedure should be executed on your mobile phone.

At some point in time, before running the procedure, you need to communicate the following pieces of information (associations):

My name is George Boole.
My wife is Mrs. Mary Boole.
Her birthday is on July 11.

Using the conceptual notation (C):

$C1 = \{(\text{name, George Boole}), (\text{wife}, C2)\}$
$C2 = \{(\text{name, Mary Boole}), (\text{birthday, July 11})\}$

All the representations are semantically equivalent. On the other hand, the concepts and information associations may be easier to visualize using the syntax employed by the proposed conceptual language:

C1-> name = George Boole

C1->wife = C2

C2->name = Mary Boole

C2->birthday = July 11

if (today == C2->birthday) then notify C1;   //if today is my wife's birthday please notify me)

Again, the mobile device may not have enough information and request additional items: George, what is Mrs. Boole's birthday? Based on the concepts and information associations above, the mobile device will be able to execute the procedure, one step at a time.  The example should also illustrate the algebraic and logic properties of the process which I like to visualize as the Algebra of Concepts (or meaning): concepts are substituted by semantically equivalent concepts (same meaning). Obviously, it should remind us of Mathematics and Algebra:

$X = 1$

$Y = X$

Therefore, $Y = 1$

It is the same mathematical principle. Concepts and information associations are manipulated instead of numbers and letters. In the end, all of them are symbols. Is logical thinking a *mathematical process*? A matter of mathematical, logical and symbolic manipulation, inside the mind? These two are related to the question: Can machines think?

George Boole gives us insight into these questions based on his remarkable conclusions [1,22]:

"The truth that the ultimate laws of thought are mathematical in their form, viewed in connexion with the fact of the possibility of error, establishes a ground for some remarkable conclusions. If we directed our attention to the scientific truth alone, we might be led to infer an almost exact parallelism between the intellectual operations and the movements of external nature. Suppose any one conversant with physical science, but unaccustomed to reflect upon the nature of his own faculties, to have been informed, that it had been proved, that the laws of those faculties were mathematical; it is probable that after the first feelings of incredulity had subsided, the impression would arise, that the order of thought must, therefore, be as necessary as that of the material universe. We know that in the realm of natural science, the absolute connexion between the initial and final elements of a problem, exhibited in the mathematical form, fitly symbolizes that physical necessity which binds together effect and cause."

The distinction should be made between thinking and the other functions performed by the mind. Boole is specifically referring to logical thinking, mathematically modeled by what is known today as Boolean Algebraic Logic or Boolean Logic. Obviously the mind is constantly processing information (messages) coming from other components of the body in order to perform critical functions: vision, walking, breathing, and so on. However, none of these functions involve logical thinking. The mind is able to process two main categories of information: conceptual and non-conceptual [30]. Logical thinking strictly refers to conceptual information.

You might want to ask: where did the local procedure variables go? I am not sure just yet. On the other hand, who needs them? Or, hypothetically they might go extinct to put it in Darwinian terms. Consider that human beings do not seem to require variables while thinking, which should call our attention based on the concepts of realism and Biomimetics. Also, natural languages are dynamic and versatile entities changing constantly by adding new words and concepts (symbols). They do not consist of a fixed number of constructs which should also call our attention.

A procedure is a concept, pure information; A fact that has some interesting consequences. There is a tendency to think of a program in terms of an active party performing operations on information (data).

Strictly speaking, it is incorrect to say that a procedure or program is executing. In reality, programs or procedures do not execute (or run). As concepts, they are passive entities (pure information). Therefore they can only be executed by the host computer. A *program* is *information*. No wonder perhaps, since information is the fundamental aspect.

The human mind learns procedures to perform new tasks based on concepts already mastered. A procedure can be learned by means of written or verbal communication. The proposed language mirrors and shares the same abilities. Information (data) becomes the 'program' so to speak. Take for example a cooking recipe which is a concept (data). On the other hand, it also represents a procedure (program) that defines a written sequence of steps to be followed *by* the mind.

Obviously, natural languages have many advantages. Consider the concepts of expressiveness, conciseness, richness, efficiency, 'simplicity', realism, teaching tool for the mind's learning abilities, higher level of abstraction and so forth. In the abstract, obviously the proposed language mirrors and absorbs these *natural* qualities. It is really tough to compete with natural languages when it comes to information exchange and processing. Many of the listed qualities are closely related to the fact that natural languages operate at a higher level of abstraction: the *conceptual* level. It can take just a few concepts to communicate elaborate ideas. A significant amount of information can be communicated with one concise message:

Please make reservations to Hawaii for the whole family departing next Thursday on Pacific airlines. Don't forget to make arrangements for Copernicus (family pet).

Concepts and information associations make it possible. Messaging should not be overlooked either. Try to emulate the exchange using other forms of communication or interface and the difference should become evident. No wonder, given the fact that human communication has evolved and improved through the ages becoming the ultimate mechanism of interchanging conceptual information. It has a significant head start in an evolutionary sense.

Notice that the proposed design has been completely done at the conceptual (abstract) level, within the mind only. It was also possible to use other concepts to assess, in the abstract, the capabilities of the proposed language. A conceptual computer language is beneficial and recommended based on the qualities of the natural language which will be absorbed by a realistic implementation.

As a general rule of thumb and part of a conceptual design, when facing a design task the main concepts involved with the problem need to be methodologically identified and extracted from natural reality. Failing to do so, leads to an incomplete design/solution with unrealistic and/or unnatural characteristics that will eventually face the selection forces of Darwinian evolution in the realm of technology. The concept of messaging is probably a good example: overlooking it becomes a costly hindrance in many respects.

The implementation of the proposed language is a separate matter that should be forthcoming. However, the abstract nature of the design and the assessment do not diminish their usefulness. A good conceptual design should bring forth a comparable implementation. In particular, when the 'same' solution has already been devised and proven in the natural world in the form of conceptual human languages: natural languages. Although no small task, the main implementation challenges become the faithful imitation of nature's existing communication model based on concepts. A divide-and-conquer engineering approach ensures steady improvements over time.

Since a new computing model and language are being discussed, it probably makes sense for a new computer to host it: Heuristic, Algebraic, and Logical Computer or Holistic, Algebraic, and Logical Computer. Information expressed as a group of concepts ($I$={C1,C2, , Cn} ) }; n measures the number of known concepts (n = cardinality (K)).

An early version of the implemented system should be able to handle 100 concepts or so, in several domains: Time (when), Location (where), national airlines, job titles. Such a system should be able to answer relatively simple but useful (common) queries in the natural language:

Can you please find all the Pacific flights for Hawaii that depart next week?

Retrieve all the papers that have been published in the last ten years on Artificial Intelligent.

Please find all the teaching positions that opened this week in Florida.

A relatively small number of information domains and concepts are involved. It is assumed that the system also has access to databases or web interfaces hosting the requested information. Once an information domain is implemented, it can be reused for arbitrary applications based on the proposed language. The mind is able to reuse the same concepts across daily activities. As shown above, the straightforward domains of time and location can be applied to diverse applications: Mobile reservation, Information Retrieval, and other applications dealing with these information domains.

The proposed system should be useful in the realms of search engines, man-machine interfaces and business processes technologies (BPM/BPEL), based on its natural expressive qualities, proposed 'learning' abilities, and so on. Additionally, it should be helpful in aiding people that are unable to read due to physical challenge, sickness or other reason. For instance, it should be useful if you find yourself at the airport and you do not speak the language. A multilingual system would be able to assist you using your native language, even perhaps via automated translation which should impact cost, implementation timeframe, and application reach.

An initial version of the language targeted to mobile devices (100) should provide enough capabilities to control most of the phone functionality: weather, news, calls, calendar, trivia, electronic reader (eReader), SMS messaging, GPS, directions, CallerID, voice activated (IVR) features, speech synthesis, safe driving, and so on. All personal information can be safely stored by the device: family members, address, preferences, payment information, passwords, health information, primary physician, and so forth.

As an example of a custom application, a healthcare professional would be able to instruct a device or smartphone using the proposed language and appropriate information domains (who, where, when, etc.):

- Please remind Mr. Smith to take his medicine every four hours. Make an appointment for him to see the doctor on the 22nd and remind him.

- In case of an emergency call his family, his doctor, and paramedics. If requested, give his location and health history to the paramedics.

- Several preexisting procedures would be required: remind, call, make an appointment, etc.

The proposed system can describe in detail, using the natural language, a specific procedure and/or the logical deduction based on the known conceptual information. The proposed system can 'learn' new concepts based on the definition of the ones already mastered, much the same as your friend is able to learn new information and make new associations. For instance, it can learn the meaning of Tomorrow and Hawaii, by making new associations based on information already known:

Tomorrow is the day after today (Time domain)

Hawaii is an island in the United States (Location domain)

If the above is what the series 100 can do, we can only imagine what the series 10,000 will do, after its conceptual information bank has been increased couple of orders of magnitude. The proposed language can scale to accommodate multiple domains and a large bank of concepts.

The aspect of ambiguity becomes a bigger issue as the number of information domains and concepts increases. Hypothetically, the series 10,000 should be able to 'learn' autonomously by reading and associating new concepts to the large bank of known ones. Similar to what the minds does when learning a new word or idea based on its definition, which provides associations to known concepts.

For the engineering and practical perspectives, the challenges are somewhat similar to the computer graphics arena. The early systems were able to display a small amount of objects using a limited level of realism. After a few years of progress, the level of realism achieved is significant, based on additional processing power and improved realistic techniques. The analogy can be applied to the proposed language based on its conceptual capabilities and the incremental divide-and-conquer strategy discussed.

An increase in 'conceptual understanding' should result in a better and more realistic system over time. A system able to master a substantial amount of concepts associated to the reality surrounding the application domain, and able to follow learnt procedures using logical deductions based on acquired knowledge. The mind is able to handle a substantial amount of conceptual information as the basis of highly intelligent behavior. On the other hand, regardless of how far the language is able to evolve, it represents a substantial improvement when compared with other languages not based on a conceptual paradigm.

## 23.1   Boole's Logical Engine and Module for Information Inference, Navigation, and Decision-making

The proposed mathematical model will be leveraged to produce a realistic software design and implementation: Module for information inference, navigation, and decision-making. This single module is responsible for processing of conceptual and non-conceptual information based on the following functionality which mimics the mind's behavior. In order to design a complete solution, a conceptual design approach will be followed: all relevant realistic concepts need to be extracted and incorporated. When defining the *concept* of *processing information*, there are three (3) main associated concepts: storage, retrieval, and logical processing. These three concepts specify the ways in which information can be processed by the logical mind.

## 23.2   Participants

**Boole's Logical Engine (Boole's LE)**: module's single main component responsible for logical processing of information: implementation of the conceptual deductive approach founded on Boole's Algebra of Logic defined by the single $\beta$-function. It implements the conceptual component abstraction *(LE = ($\beta$(m), I))* and provides inference capabilities. The engine relies on the memory subcomponent for the storage and retrieval of conceptual information and knowledge (K).

The scope of the information primitive has been substantially simplified (i.e. narrowed) to the implementation of logical processing as specified by Boolean algebra: logical operations (AND, OR, NOT, Boolean equality, and so forth) applied to information represented using the concept construct (C). Basic flow of control is also required to execute procedures (P).

The Boole's LE is able to understand/produce sentences (S) and execute procedures (P) in the natural language (L). A conceptual machine that implements Boole's Algebra of Logic (Laws of Thought) via the described engine is called a Boole's conceptual machine. Such machine is Turing complete and as powerful as any universal computer (see demonstration of Turing-Completeness).

**Memory subcomponent**: The conceptual machine's memory subcomponent is responsible for storing and retrieving conceptual and non-conceptual information (I). Information is received and processed in the form of chunks of information (messages). Acquiring new knowledge or information (i.e. learning) is tightly intertwined with the concepts of storing and retrieving information via the memory subcomponent.

## 23.3   Collaboration

Notice that by relying on the conceptual design methodology, an otherwise 'complex' problem has been reduced (i.e. conceptualized) to a complete and streamlined set of concepts (including operations) which also happen to have a straightforward and reusable implementation from an engineering standpoint.   All other abstractions, primitives, and components add unnecessary complexities. Messaging is a ubiquitous natural concept, part of the model. The functionality described above provides the conceptual machine with its 'core' cognitive abilities:

233

**Memory**: the module is able to store and retrieve all forms of information (I): conceptual and non-conceptual.

**Logical Reasoning**: the Boole's LE provides the system with reasoning capabilities by implementing the conceptual deductive approach ($\beta$-function) which has been demonstrated via formal proof (see Conceptual Deductive approach). The approach is based on well-known backward chaining methods of reasoning, employed by AI systems and founded on Boole's Algebra of Logic [1, 22]. It basically consists of navigating the graph of knowledge (K) to retrieve information and/or make new inferences based on concepts/associations already learned.

**Learning**: the module is constantly interacting, and learning from the environment via messaging. The module can readily learn (or be taught) new concepts (C) and procedures (P), which are stored in memory, based on information associations with concepts already mastered. Learning literally means acquiring new information or knowledge. In the case of conceptual information, the 'web' of knowledge (K) is augmented by adding new information in the form of concepts and/or associations. Procedures (P) to performed tasks are concepts as well (i.e. information). The conceptual information known to system can be expressed as a group of concepts: $K = \{C1, C2, \ , Cn\}$; n measures the number of known concepts (n = cardinality (K)). Conceptual knowledge (K) is also a graph (or web) where nodes represent concepts and edges represent information associations: $K = \{V, E\}$. The size of the graph (Size (K) = cardinality (E)) gives us a measure of the amount of conceptual information known (learned) by the system.

Learning may also occur by levering the Boole's LE and inferring new facts or conclusions from the information already known. The graph (K) is navigated to retrieve known concepts, reason, and/or perform learned tasks – as demonstrated by the deductive approach. Obviously, memory and logical reasoning are crucial in supporting the module's learning abilities.

The aforementioned capabilities are categorized as 'core' because they provide the foundation for all other cognitive processes including natural language processing/production, decision making, and problem solving.

234

**Natural Language (L)**: Language is a concept (C) that consists of a set of symbols and their associated definitions: L = {((symbol1), Definition (symbol1)), , ((symboln), Definition (symboln))}. It also represents information that can be learned. By levering its learning and logical abilities, the module is able to master and communicate using one or multiple languages. Notice that the concept of language (L) represents pure information without information processing capabilities. Therefore, its implementation does not require any additional components. The language (L) is an integral part of the machine's conceptual knowledge (K). Symbols in the language (words) and their meaning (definitions) are learned.

Messages are communicated in the form of sentences (S) in the language (L). A procedure (P) is a concept (C) defined as a sequence of steps to be executed: P = {S1, , Sn} where each step (or statement) is expressed in the form of a sentence (S). The Boole's Logical Engine is the component responsible for providing language functionality by executing the learned procedures (P) required for language understanding and production.

In summary, the following main concepts have been extracted through conceptualization: a) Storing of information. b) Retrieving of information. c) Logical processing of information (i.e. reasoning). The core concepts provide the foundation for other cognitive processes including natural language (L) processing, decision making, and problem solving. These processes are performed based on logical processing (i.e. reasoning) and the knowledge (K) stored in memory. Also, procedures (P) are known or can be learned as a way of making decisions and solving specific problems. Consider that Boole's conceptual machines (A = ($\beta$(m), I)) are Turing complete. Ponder that decision making and problem solving are obviously tightly intertwined with logical thinking (i.e. reasoning).

All of the aforementioned concepts cooperate in unity and harmony according to the principles of conceptual design (CD). They can also be expressed in precise mathematical terms and implemented using a straightforward and realistic approach. Logical processing of information, the fundamental concept implemented by the machine, has been mathematically formalized using Boole's algebra of logic (Laws of Thought).

Acquiring new knowledge or information (i.e. learning) can be mathematically modeled using set theory, a Boolean algebra. Information (I), Conceptual Knowledge (K), Language (L), Procedure (P), Sentence (S), Message (M), can be expressed mathematically using the concept construct (C).

Like the human mind, the innate potential of Boole's conceptual machine is virtually unlimited in terms of how much the machine is able to learn and the problems it can tackle. The innate abilities of communication with its environment, learning, and reasoning provide the machine with such potential. On the other hand, there is another side to this coin, as clearly expressed by the two-tuple formulation $(A = (\beta(m), I))$:the machine's effective computing power (i.e. reasoning power) is also determined by how much knowledge is mastered by it (I/K).

Like the mind, without enough knowledge (I/K), the virtually unlimited potential of the conceptual machine goes unrealized (underutilized). Conceptually, the human mind is an entity of beautiful simplicity – naturally. A Mathematical entity acting under the Boole's "Laws of Thought", equivalent to Turing's analogy about the time-invariant U.S. Constitution [3].

It should also be clear that information machines, like the mind, act like sponges, constantly soaking information and learning from the environment through messaging (message form). Based on the model's formulation, its motto seems to be 'know thy environment' which is arguably a perfect match for adaptation purposes. Obviously, accurate knowledge of the environment is paramount to the survival and advancement of species.   Additional sections will describe the above topics and participants in more detail.

## 23.4   Consequences

The consequences and qualities associated to the paradigm are derived from its mathematical model:

a) **Information primitive**: Single function *processInformation (message)* where the message represents conceptual (C) or non-conceptual information.

b) **Concept (C)**: pure information expressed by a single language Construct, C = {a1,a2, ,an} where a1,a2, an, are information associations.

An Information/Mathematical machine (A) is a Turing-Complete automatic machine able to perform computations via the information primitive which defines the machine's single function or purpose. A can also be expressed as $A = (f(m), I)$, where $f$ represents any computable function. A Boole's Conceptual machine can be expressed by $A=(\beta(m), I.)$, where the function $\beta(m)$ represents logical processing of information as defined by Boole's Algebra of Logic. It should be obvious why information is the model's fundamental concept. Every aspect should be viewed from the standpoint of information.

The mind, and related information concepts, work as a holistic entity (i.e. unit) part of the order of nature – in agreement with Occam's razor in terms simplicity, efficiency (economy) and conciseness (elegance): "Nature does not multiply [Concepts] unnecessarily ...".

**Machine Learning:** *information is learned.* Concepts, including procedures to perform tasks, are *learned*. By leveraging the conceptual approach, the proposed NATURAL language, will be able to provide cognitive/AI systems with learning abilities. The system can be readily taught new concepts and procedures based on information associations with concepts already mastered. Once concepts are 'learned', they can be applied in new contexts and problem domains. For instance, the concepts associated with Time (when), Location (where), and people (who) can be reused for multiple application/problem domains. Such is the broad nature of concepts.

There are no set limitations for the amount of information (knowledge) that the system can learn. Such learning capabilities are behind other aspects such as effectively, adaptability, and versatility. For instance, the system can readily adapt and cope with new environmental conditions based on the knowledge (K) being acquired. We can probably say that information/conceptual machines, based on an approach mirrored from the mind, are in fact learning machines. Well, it just seems natural.

**Logical Reasoning**: The conceptual model, which mimics the mind, will provide the system with reasoning capabilities based on the conceptual deductive approach which has been demonstrated via formal proof. As mentioned earlier, the approach is based on well-known backward chaining methods of reasoning, employed by AI systems and founded on Boole's Algebra of Logic [1, 22]. It basically consists of navigating the graph of knowledge (K) to retrieve information and/or make new inferences based on concepts/associations already learned. If you look at reasoning from a conceptual standpoint, it literally means "to form conclusions, judgments, or inferences from facts or premises".

In other words, logical processing of information. Facts and premises are part of the knowledge (K) already acquired, and expressed in the form of concepts (C). Language (L) is a subset of system Knowledge (K). In consequence, the conceptual paradigm in conjunction with a natural computer language should help close the cognitive gap between human and machine in terms of learning and logical processing abilities.

**Natural Conceptual Language:** As mentioned earlier, natural languages have many advantages: expressiveness, conciseness, richness, efficiency, 'simplicity', realism, conceptual usefulness, higher level of abstraction and so forth. The proposed computer language mirrors and absorbs the aforementioned qualities. Many of the observed qualities are closely related to the fact that natural languages operate at a higher level of abstraction: the *conceptual* level. In consequence, conceptual usefulness and expressiveness are effectively improved by writing programs in the natural language.

By improving interoperability [4,5] and relying on a natural computer language the issue of technology obsolescence is minimized or eliminated. Consider that natural languages are dynamic (i.e. organic) entities that evolve over time to meet changing information requirements, therefore avoiding obsolescence. Such adaptability and dynamism are bound to be absorbed (i.e. mirrored) by the proposed computer language. New symbols (i.e. words) can be readily added to (L) and defined based on other concepts already learned.

**Extensibility and Natural Language Processing (NLP):** Although the conceptual model and language do not tackle the general NLP problem, the proposed language can incrementally scale to address it by using a

238

divide-and-conquer methodology. Based on the model's solid mathematical/natural foundations, NATURAL10000, featuring 10000 concepts and therefore high cognitive/computing power, should be within human grasp – one information/concept domain at a time. Boole's Laws of Thought provides the mathematical foundations and corroboration for such belief [1,22]. The limited scope of a prototype language (NATURAL100) would not hinder its applicability to a variety of real-world areas/problems. We do not need to master all the words of a second language in order to have a meaningful/productive conversation or accomplish and task by executing a given procedure. It is always an incremental/continuous learning process.

**Realism and Correspondence**: By mirroring natural concepts, true realistic correspondence is achieved (Correspondence Theory of Truth[30]). In agreement with Biomimetics principles, Mother Nature knows best when it comes to information processing. Realistic imitation is the best approach for us, limited mortals, so to speak. By mimicking the conceptual mind, significant software improvements are realized, in several areas, including overall complexity, interoperability, communication gap between man-machine, machine learning, logical abilities, technology obsolescence, quality, cost, timeframes, and so forth. A separate chapter includes detailed model evaluation and metrics in support of many of the consequences above. Cognitive, learning, and logical abilities have been demonstrated via formal mathematical proofs.

## 23.5    Related Work

Several related computer languages/platforms have recognized the benefits and importance of programming in the natural language including Wolfram Alpha, and Inform 7. Authors have discussed their benefits and feasibility as well [45]:"We want to make computers easier to use and enable people who are not computer scientists to be able to teach new behavior to their computers". No widely used natural computer language exists yet. Several cognitive models have been proposed throughout the years including Unified Theories of Cognition, Society of Mind, and Neurocognitive Networks [22] (see Appendix on cognitive/AI models). However it should be stated that these related models do not focus on computer languages like NATURAL does.

## 24.    BACK TO THE FUTURE

In regards to the question "Can Machines Think?" It seems that George Boole helped answer it far ahead of his time. Over 150 years ago, to be more precise. Consider his conclusion:


A) "The laws of thought are mathematical".

In other words, thinking is a mathematical process. In particular, he was referring to *logical* thinking based on his mathematical proofs and findings: what is known today as Boolean Logic or Boolean Algebraic Logic.


B) On the other hand, computers are mathematical machines. Based on the Church-Turing thesis, any computable function or algorithm can be computed.

By combining the premises A and B, the following conclusion is deducted:


Computers can think logically.


As a consequence, and from pragmatic scientific and engineering perspectives, computers can realistically mirror the logical thinking (i.e. reasoning) mechanisms utilized by the mind to process information. Mathematical models based on Boolean algebra are able to accurately mimic logical thinking. Consider that the concept of "logical thinking" (reasoning), which is unambiguous, precisely describes what it is, and its logical nature. It would be contradictory otherwise. If you look at reasoning from a conceptual standpoint, it literally means "to form conclusions, judgments, or inferences from facts or premises". In other words, *logical* processing of information. Facts and premises are part of the knowledge already acquired, and expressed in the form of concepts (C).


Obviously, the conceptual deductive approach demonstrated is also based on Boole's algebraic logic. As discussed previously, it can scale to 'understand' reality and make decisions based on a large bank of

240

conceptual information via logical and algebraic manipulation. The title of Boole's seminal book (The Laws of Thought ...) and his conclusions are unequivocal. A number of other authors, in many fields, have put forth results and theories consistent or founded upon his work [23, 25, 28, 30, 31, 33]:seminal "ground for remarkable conclusions" that shed light on the inner secrets of the logical mind, the pinnacle in terms of information processing: $A = (\beta(x),\ I)$. As faith led him to believe, God's greatest creation!

# 25. CONCEPTUAL FRAMEWORK - CORE COMPONENTS

## 25.1 Reference Implementation (Requirements and Setup)

Jt is a reference implementation of the conceptual model. The software is included. It represents only one of the many potential implementations of the Concepts involved. The main framework functionality requires a single Jar (Jt.jar) with small memory signature of about 512K. To utilize the Jt framework, install the software according the packaged instructions.

Source code distribution and accompanying materials for this book can be downloaded from the following URL:

https://sites.google.com/site/conceptualparadigm/documents/Jt.zip?attredirects=0&d=1

It includes the latest version of the framework, examples, and working applications. The distribution has been archived using the .zip format. To extract the files, you will need a de-compression program such as WinZip. You will find a Readme file in addition to installation instructions. Feel free to employ your favorite IDE (Eclipse and Java 2 platform version 1.5 or better are recommended). A build.xml file for Ant is also included.

## 25.2 Messenger

The framework Messenger is responsible for transferring messages between Live/Animated components – from component sender to the receiver. All modalities of messaging are supported including synchronous, asynchronous, distributed, and secure messaging. The Messenger delegates responsibility to other framework components for the implementation of security, encryption, authentication, and authorization of the messaging being exchanged.

For convenience, a `sendMessage()` method is provided:

| Method | Description |
|---|---|
| `sendMessage(Object object, Object message)` | Send a message to the specified component. The `object` parameter can be a reference to the component or the component `id` specified during creation (see Factory). |

Also for convenience, the following attributes control the behavior of the Messenger:

| Attributes | Description |
|---|---|
| `synchronous (boolean)` | Specifies whether asynchronous or synchronous messaging should be employed. Synchronous messaging is the default. |
| `encrypted (boolean)` | Enables or disables encrypted messaging. By default, no encryption is performed. |

The methods above are provided mainly for readability and convenience. The same functionality can be accomplished via the information primitive. The Messenger in the following example sends messages to a component to retrieve weather information. Also, messages to a teller component are sent to retrieve account information. Other framework components are covered in later sections: Printer (`JtPrinter`), Factory (`JtFactory`), HTTP Proxy (`JtHttpProxy`), Concept (`JtConcept`) and so forth.

Messages can be or arbitrary types (Object). On the other hand, a separate class is often employed for representing messages. For convenience and readability reasons, the framework defines a class named `JtMessage,` which inherits from `JtConcept`.

243

Framework messages of the class `JtMessage` represent concepts (C). Also for convenience, a message ID can be readily specified during the creation of the message. For instance, the following statement creates a new message and specifies its message ID:

```
msg = new JtMessage (JtComponent.JtREAD);
```

The framework Messenger is also able to handle distributed messaging via framework Proxies. Such proxies need to specify a way of locating the distributed component; for instance, component URL, and class (or name) need to be provided to locate components via a HTTP Proxy.

## 25.2.1 Example

```
/**
 * Demonstrates the JtMessenger functionality
 */

public static void main(String[] args) {

    JtMessenger messenger = new JtMessenger ();
    WeatherService weather;
    JtPrinter printer = new JtPrinter ();

    JtConcept reply;
    JtHttpProxy proxy;
    JtFactory factory = new JtFactory ();
    String url =
        "http://localhost:8080/JtPortal/JtRestService";
    JtMessage msg;
    JtConcept ctx;

        weather = new WeatherService ();

        // Send a message via the framework messenger

        reply = (JtConcept) messenger.sendMessage(weather,
                            new JtMessage
                        (JtComponent.JtREAD));

    printer.processMessage(reply);

    // Asynchronous messaging is supported

    messenger.setSynchronous(false);

    messenger.sendMessage(weather,
        new JtMessage (JtComponent.JtREAD));
```

```
// Distributed messaging. Create
// an instance of the remote Proxy

messenger = new JtMessenger ();

proxy = (JtHttpProxy) factory.createObject
        (JtHttpProxy.JtCLASS_NAME);

// Specify URL and class name for the remote component

proxy.setUrl(url);
proxy.setClassname
            ("Jt.examples.WeatherService");


// Send the message (Read) to the distributed
// component that provides the Weather service.
// Weather information is retrieved.

reply = (JtConcept) messenger.sendMessage (proxy,
                            new JtMessage
                            (JtFactory.JtREAD));

    if (reply instanceof JtError) {
        System.out.println
            ("Exception detected:");
        printer.processMessage(reply);
    } else
        printer.processMessage (reply);


// Distributed messaging (encrypted and authenticated)

proxy = (JtHttpProxy) factory.createObject
        (JtHttpProxy.JtCLASS_NAME);

proxy.setUrl(url);
proxy.setClassname ("Jt.examples.service.BankTeller");

ctx = new JtConcept ();
factory.setValue(ctx, "username", "jt");
factory.setValue(ctx, "password", "messaging");


messenger = new JtMessenger ();
messenger.setContext(ctx);

// Specify that secure/encrypted messaging should be used.
// The Bank Teller component requires it.

messenger.setEncrypted(true);

// Send the message to the distribute bank teller component
// to retrieve account information. A concept (account)
// or an exception is returned.

msg = new JtMessage (JtComponent.JtREAD);
factory.setValue (msg, BankTeller.ACCOUNT, "12345678");
```

```java
    reply = (JtConcept) messenger.sendMessage (proxy, msg);



    if (reply instanceof JtError) {
      System.out.println ("Exception detected:");
      printer.processMessage(reply);
    } else
      printer.processMessage (reply);


    // Remove the proxy and all remote references.
    // The remote component should be ready to be garbage collected
    // after this operation.
    factory.removeObject(proxy);
}
```

## 25.3    Factory

The framework Factory (JtFactory) is responsible for manufacturing and updating framework components and Concepts (C) – including messages. It also provides reusable Singleton and Prototype functionality: the Factory is able to manufacture 'one of a kind' and make copies (i.e. clones) of arbitrary components.

The framework Factory interfaces with a Registry subcomponent (Singleton) to keep track of active system components. Components can be registered and located based on component ID. The Factory provides methods for the manipulation of the Concept construct (C) and its associations. During creation, components and concepts are configured by the Factory with the assistance of the Resource Manager (RM). The framework RM is responsible for managing resources found in the properties file or stream.

The framework Factory implements the following main messages as part of its conceptual interface (CI):

| Message ID | Description |
|---|---|
| JtCREATE | Create an instance of the specified class (CLASSNAME) and return it. If an id is provided (INSTANCE_ID), the new instance is added to the framework registry. Null is returned if the entry (INSTANCE_ID) already exists unless the message includes additional directives: If RETURN_IF_ALREADY_EXISTS is specified, the existing entry is returned. If REPLACE_IF_ALREADY_EXISTS is specified, the entry is overridden. Null is returned if the operation fails for any given reason. |
| JtREAD | Retrieve the specified instance (INSTANCE_ID) from the framework Registry. Null is returned if the instance (INSTANCE_ID) cannot be |

| | found. |
|---|---|
| JtGET_VALUE | Retrieve the value of an attribute or association. A reference to an Object is returned. |
| JtSET_VALUE | Set the value of the attribute or association. String values are automatically converted to the appropriate type by the framework. |
| JtDELETE | Delete the specified instance (INSTANCE_ID) from the framework Registry. |

The messages above have additional modalities. For instance, Singleton functionality is implemented via the SINGLETON directive (see Singleton handling in this section). For convenience, JtFactory supports the following methods which provide comparable functionality to the messaging interface just described:

| Method | Description |
|---|---|
| createObject (String classname) | Create a component of the specified class (classname) and return it. |
| createObject (String classname, Object id) | Create a component of the specified class and return it. Also, the component is added to the framework Registry using the id provided. It can be later retrieved from the framework Registry based on component id. |
| setValue (Object object, String attribute, Object value) | Set the value of the attribute or association specified by attribute. String values are automatically converted to the appropriate type by the |

| | framework. From String to integer, for instance. The `object` parameter can be either a reference to the component or the component `id` (See the `createObject()` method). |
|---|---|
| `getValue (Object object, String attribute)` | Retrieve the value of the attribute or association specified by `attribute`. A reference to an Object is returned. For instance, in Java/Android an int attribute will return an object of the class Integer. The `object` parameter can be either a reference to the component or the component `id` (See the `createObject()` method). |
| `lookupObject (String id)` | Retrieve a component from the framework Registry using its id and returns a reference to it. Null is returned if the component `id` is not found in the Registry. |
| `removeObject (String id)` | Remove the component specified by `id` from the framework Registry. Returns true if the component is removed; false otherwise. After removing the component from the registry, it becomes ready to be collected by the standard garbage collection mechanism. |

The methods above are provided mainly for readability and convenience. The same functionality can be accomplished via the information primitive. The framework Factory is responsible for providing Singleton functionality: class restricted to having a single instance. The following table of messages defines the conceptual interface (CI).

| Message ID | Description |
|---|---|
| JtCREATE (SINGLETON) | Create a Singleton of the specified class (CLASSNAME attribute) and return it. SINGLETON has to be included (WHAT attribute) as part of the message. The new component (Singleton) is added to the framework Registry. Null is returned if the Singleton cannot be created. Further attempts to create a component of the same class will result in the Singleton being returned. |
| JtREAD (SINGLETON) | Retrieve the Singleton of the specified class (CLASSNAME attribute). SINGLETON has to be used (WHAT attribute). Null is returned if a Singleton for the specified class is not found. |
| JtDELETE (SINGLETON) | Delete the Singleton associated to the specified class (CLASSNAME attribute). SINGLETON has to be used (WHAT attribute). |

The framework Factory is also responsible for proving Group (G) functionality. It relies on the `JtGroupFactory` support class for the implementation of such functionality (see Group Factory). A realistic implementation of the Prototype functionality is provided by the framework Factory. It 'manufactures' copies of arbitrary components and Concepts (C) by processing the CLONE message:

| JtCLONE | Build a clone of the specified component or Concept (INSTANCE attribute). |
|---|---|

The example below creates and manipulates several components and Concepts (C) via the framework Factory. The manipulation of Singletons is also demonstrated.

## 25.3.1  Example

```
/**
 * Framework component implementation of Factory Method.
 * It creates and manages framework.
 * The Concept construct is implemented via a factory
 * (Factory Method pattern). Concepts can also be
 * implemented using compiler capabilities
 * (Conceptual language) which is more concise
 * and clear. Such implementation would be similar
 * to the implementation of the object abstraction.
 */


public static void main(String[] args) {

        JtFactory factory = new JtFactory ();
        JtMessage msg;
        JtConcept Concept;
        JtPrinter printer = new JtPrinter ();
        Integer Int;
        String str;
        WeatherService weatherComponent;
        Object obj;



        // Use the factory to manipulate a
        // Concept (information associations)

        Concept = new JtConcept ();

        factory.setValue(Concept,
                WeatherService.summary, "Sunny");
        factory.setValue(Concept, WeatherService.maximum,
                new Integer (80));
        factory.setValue(Concept, WeatherService.minimum,
                new Integer (67));
        factory.setValue(Concept,
                WeatherService.precipitation,
                new Float (5.0));

        printer.processMessage(Concept);

        // Retrieve associations

        Int = (Integer) factory.getValue(Concept,
                WeatherService.maximum);

        System.out.println(WeatherService.maximum + ":" +
            Int);
```

```
Int = (Integer) factory.getValue(Concept,
    WeatherService.minimum);

System.out.println(WeatherService.minimum + ":" +
    Int);

str = (String) factory.getValue(Concept,
    WeatherService.summary);

System.out.println(WeatherService.summary + ":" +
    str);


// Create a framework component.
// Properties are loaded automatically
// from the properties file.

obj = factory.createObject
        (WeatherService.JtCLASS_NAME);

// A component can be added to the
// component registry during creation.
// A component ID (name) is assigned to it.
// The registry allows components to
// find each other using a component ID.

obj = factory.createObject
        (WeatherService.JtCLASS_NAME,
         "my component");

// Use the factory to retrieve the
// component from the registry.

obj = factory.lookupObject("my component");

// Remove component from the registry

factory.removeObject("my component");

// Demonstrate the handling of singletons (via
// JtFactory). It handles concurrency (
// Animated/Live components).

msg = new JtMessage (JtFactory.JtCREATE);
factory.setValue(msg, JtFactory.SINGLETON, new
    Boolean (true));

// Specify the classname as part of the message.
// Any arbitrary class may be specified.

factory.setValue(msg, JtFactory.CLASSNAME,
                WeatherService.JtCLASS_NAME);

// Create the singlenton.

weatherComponent = (WeatherService)
    factory.processMessage (msg);
```

```
// Retrieve the Singleton

msg = new JtMessage (JtFactory.JtREAD);
factory.setValue(msg, JtFactory.SINGLETON,
  new Boolean (true));
factory.setValue(msg, JtFactory.CLASSNAME,
  WeatherService.JtCLASS_NAME);

weatherComponent = (WeatherService)
  factory.processMessage (msg);


if (weatherComponent != null)
  System.out.println("Singleton (JtREAD): GO");
else
  System.out.println("Singleton (JtREAD): FAIL");

// Attempt to create another instance of
// the singleton class. The singleton
//instance is returned. No new instance is created

obj = factory.processMessage (msg);

if (weatherComponent == obj)
        System.out.println
          ("create singleton (JtCREATE): GO");
else
        System.out.println
          ("create singleton (JtCREATE): FAIL");

// Delete the Singleton

msg = new JtMessage (JtFactory.JtDELETE);
factory.setValue(msg, JtFactory.SINGLETON,
  new Boolean (true));
factory.setValue(msg, JtFactory.CLASSNAME,
  WeatherService.JtCLASS_NAME);

factory.processMessage (msg);

msg = new JtMessage (JtFactory.JtREAD);
factory.setValue(msg, JtFactory.SINGLETON,
  new Boolean (true));
factory.setValue(msg, JtFactory.CLASSNAME,
  WeatherService.JtCLASS_NAME);

weatherComponent = (WeatherService)
  factory.processMessage (msg);

if (weatherComponent == null)
        System.out.println
          ("Singleton (JtDELETE): GO");
else
        System.out.println
          ("Singleton (JtDELETE): FAIL");


}
```

## 25.4 Memory or Information Repository

The concept of Memory or Information repository represents the ability to store persistent information for later retrieval and use. Live or Animated entities *(A = (f(x), I))* usually rely on a memory component or subsystem to provide information (I) storage capabilities. The information contained in the memory is organized into concepts (I = {C1, , Cn}). By the same token, these concepts are classified into groups of related concepts: $G_i$ = {Ci1, Cij}. A single key association or attribute (ID) is required to identify a concept within a group.

For instance, conceptual information about a specific city can be stored in memory as part of the group (G) of cities. The city can be stored and retrieved from the group based on a key association (ID): city name.

In a sense, the main purpose of the Memory component is the implementation of its mathematical formulation: I = {G1, ,Gk}. Obviously, there are several possible implementations and internal representations. We should observe that information processing (i.e. computing) can be achieved without consideration of the specific storage mechanism and/or representation being employed (see specification of the Memory Concept). Consider the human memory, people are able to use the information stored in memory without knowing how the actual information is represented and stored. Computer software should mimic this characteristic in order to become more representation and technology agnostic.

The group of concepts (I = {G1, ,Gk}) can be expressed using arbitrary data representations and technologies including relational databases. Each group Gi can be represented as a database table. However, a traditional table, with a fixed number of columns, is not an ideal fit to represent dynamic entities such as Concepts (C) and Groups (G). The associations of a concept can grow dynamically. The group of concepts (I) is in fact a graph of information or network of concepts - similar in shape (isomorphic) to the neural network contained in the brain.

Based on Biomimetics, we can only *speculate* that the most robust "engineering" solution for storage and retrieval of conceptual information is hidden deep inside our brain and its neural network. In any case, the graph of information (I) can be implemented using relational database technology. Conceptually, the software engineer needs to think in terms of straightforward concepts and groups instead of database tables and their operations. For instance, instead of thinking in terms of joins between tables, the engineer thinks in terms of retrieving the concepts that belong to a given group: for example, retrieve all the players that belong to the specified team. The Memory concept, which operates at a higher level of abstraction, hides the implementation details and database operations that are required (joins and so forth) to retrieve the group information.

The framework Memory implements the following main messages as part of its conceptual interface (CI):

| Message ID | Description |
|------------|-------------|
| JtADD | Add a concept (CONCEPT) to the memory as part of a group (GROUP) of related concepts. The group (GROUP) specifies the name (ID) of the group and the attribute, part of the concept, to be used as the key (KEY_ATTRIBUTE). It applies to the other messages below. |
| JtREAD | Retrieve a concept (CONCEPT) part of a group (GROUP). CONCEPT contains the unique ID that identifies the entity within the group. |
| JtUPDATE | Update the concept (CONCEPT) part of a group (GROUP). The concept contains the new association values. |
| JtDELETE | Delete the concept |

| | (CONCEPT) part of a group (GROUP). CONCEPT contains the unique ID that identifies the entity within the group. |
|---|---|

A concept part of a group ($G_i$) may be associated with a concept part of a second group ($G_j$). For instance, you may have a group of players (P = {C1, , Cn}) and another group of teams (T = {c1, , $c_m$}). As part of the team concept ($C_i$), it is required to keep an association that represents the group of players part of the team.

A group of associations represents a special type of group (GA). As the name indicates, it contains associations between two arbitrary groups (P and T):

T = {C1, ,Cn}

P = {c1, , $c_m$}

GA = {$SG_1$, , $SG_n$} where $SG_i$ is a subgroup of GA and can be expressed as follows:

$SG_i$ = {$A_{i1}$, , $A_{ik}$} where $A_{ij}$ is concept as well (C = {a1, , an}). $A_{ij}$ references a concept in P. $SG_i$ represents the group of members of P associated with $C_i$.

Using the example provided, the subgroup $SG_i$ contains associations *(references)* to the players that belong to a specific team ($C_i$). In short, $SG_i$ represents the subgroup of players that belong to $C_i$. $A_{ij}$ may contain additional information about the association. For instance, it may contain the player position within the team.

The group GA contains all the associations between two arbitrary groups $G_i$ and $G_j$:

$GA = \{SG_1, , SG_n\}$ where $SG_i$ is a subgroup as specified above.

In other words, associations are organized into subgroups part of the group GA (special group of associations). Group of associations (GA) can be represented using a database table containing a reference to the subgroup and a reference to the concept: team reference $(C_i)$ and player reference $(c_i)$ based on the example provided. The following messages apply to groups of associations:

| Message ID | Description |
| --- | --- |
| JtADD | Add an association (ASSOCIATION) to the memory as part of a group (GROUP) which consists of three attributes: a) the subgroup (SUBGROUP). b) the attribute to be used as the key (KEY_ATTRIBUTE), c) the second group $(G_j)$ being referenced (MEMBER_GROUP). The same GROUP information applies to the other messages below. |
| JtREAD | Retrieve an association (ASSOCIATION) part of a group (GROUP). ASSOCIATION contains the unique ID that identifies the entity within the group/subgroup. |
| JtUPDATE | Update an association (ASSOCIATION) part of a group (GROUP). |
| JtDELETE | Delete an (ASSOCIATION) part of a |

| | group (GROUP). ASSOCIATION contains the unique ID that identifies the association within the group. |
| --- | --- |

The Memory implementation supports Transactions. Messages can be grouped together and processed as a unit within the scope of a transaction.

| Message ID | Description |
| --- | --- |
| JtBEGIN_TRANSACTION | Begin a transaction. This message must be sent to the Memory component before sending the group of messages part of the transaction. |
| JtCOMMIT | All changes to the Memory, produced by the group of messages, are committed as a unit. |
| JtROLLBACK | Terminate the transaction and return any Memory values that were modified to their previous values. In other words, the changes produced by the group of messages are undone. |

## 25.4.1 Example

```
/**
 * Demonstrates the Memory or Information Repository
 * abstraction and the conceptual interface used
 * for its implementation. This abstraction is responsible
 * for information (concept) persistency.
 */

public static void main(String[] args) {

        JtFactory factory = new JtFactory ();
        JtConcept player, team;
        JtMemory memory;
        JtPrinter printer = new JtPrinter ();
        JtMessage msg;
        Object reply;
        JtGroup players;
        JtGroup teams;
        JtGroup team_players;
        JtConcept Association;


        memory = new JtMemory ();


        // Define a concept (C)

        player = new JtConcept ();

        // Semantically equivalent to
        // player->email="Jen@test.com"
        factory.setValue(player, "email", "Jen@test.com");
        factory.setValue(player, "firstname", "Jen");
        factory.setValue(player, "lastname", null);
        factory.setValue(player, "status",
          new Integer(200));
        factory.setValue(player, "tstamp", new Date());
        factory.setValue(player, "mdate", new Date());

        // Add Concept to Memory. The concept needs to
        // be added to a group (class) of concepts.

        players = new JtGroup ("players");
        factory.setValue(players, JtMemory.KEY_ATTRIBUTE,
        "email"); // key Association


        msg = new JtMessage (JtMemory.JtADD);
        factory.setValue(msg, JtMemory.GROUP, players);
        factory.setValue(msg, JtMemory.CONCEPT, player);


        reply = memory.processMessage(msg);
```

```java
if (reply instanceof JtError)
        System.out.println("JtADD:FAIL");
else
        System.out.println("JtADD:PASS");



// Retrieve Concept from Memory. A group needs to
// be specified as well.

msg = new JtMessage (JtMemory.JtREAD);
// Key (concept ID)
factory.setValue(msg, JtMemory.CONCEPT,
  "Jen@test.com");
factory.setValue(msg, JtMemory.GROUP, players);


reply = memory.processMessage(msg);

if (reply instanceof JtError)
        System.out.println("JtREAD:FAIL");
else
        System.out.println("JtREAD:PASS");

printer.processMessage("Reply:\n");
printer.processMessage(reply);


// Update concept

msg = new JtMessage (JtMemory.JtUPDATE);
player = new JtConcept ();
factory.setValue(player, "email", "Jen@test.com");
factory.setValue(player, "firstname", "Jen'");
factory.setValue(player, "subject", null);
factory.setValue(player, "status",
  new Integer(300));
factory.setValue(player, "salary",
  new Double(1000.5));

//factory.setValue(player, "binaryValue", buffer);

factory.setValue(msg, JtMemory.GROUP, players);
factory.setValue(msg, JtMemory.CONCEPT, player);

reply = memory.processMessage(msg);

if (reply instanceof JtError)
        System.out.println("JtUPDATE:FAIL");
else
        System.out.println("JtUPDATE:PASS");


// Read information from Memory
// using a specific query. This message
// is only applicable when the data source
// is a relational database.

msg = new JtMessage (JtMemory.JtREAD);
```

```java
factory.setValue(msg, JtMemory.QUERY,
   "Select * from players");



if (reply instanceof JtException)
      System.out.println("JtREAD(QUERY):FAIL");

else
      System.out.println("JtREAD(QUERY):PASS");

reply = memory.processMessage(msg);

printer.processMessage("Reply:\n");
printer.processMessage(reply);

// Teams

teams = new JtGroup ("teams");
factory.setValue(teams, JtMemory.KEY_ATTRIBUTE,
   "id");

// Add a new team

team = new JtConcept ();

factory.setValue(team, "id", new Long(2));
factory.setValue(team, "name", "Team Red");


msg = new JtMessage (JtMemory.JtADD);
factory.setValue(msg, JtMemory.GROUP, teams);
factory.setValue(msg, JtMemory.CONCEPT, team);


reply = memory.processMessage(msg);

if (reply instanceof JtError)
      System.out.println("JtADD(team):FAIL");

else
      System.out.println("JtADD(team):PASS");

// Team players (associations between a team
// and its players). A subgroup needs to be
// specified.

team_players = new JtGroup ("team_players");
factory.setValue(team_players, JtMemory.SUBGROUP,
               new Long(2));


factory.setValue(team_players,
   JtMemory.KEY_ATTRIBUTE, "email");
factory.setValue(team_players,
   JtMemory.MEMBER_GROUP, "players");
```

261

```
// Associate a member with a team.  Each association
// references a member of the group of players

Association = new JtConcept ();

factory.setValue(Association, JtConcept.ID,
"Jen@test.com");
factory.setValue(Association, "position",
"Center");
factory.setValue(Association, "date",
            new Date ());

msg = new JtMessage (JtMemory.JtADD);
factory.setValue(msg, JtGroup.GROUP, team_players);

factory.setValue(msg, JtGroup.ASSOCIATION,
            Association); // Member ID


reply = memory.processMessage(msg);

if (reply instanceof JtException)
      System.out.println
        ("JtADD(team association):FAIL");
else
      System.out.println
        ("JtADD(team association):PASS");

// Update the group association using a
// new position and date

factory.setValue(Association, "position",
            null);
factory.setValue(Association, "date",
            new Date());

msg = new JtMessage (JtMemory.JtUPDATE);
factory.setValue(msg, JtGroup.GROUP, team_players);

factory.setValue(msg, JtGroup.ASSOCIATION,
            Association); // Member ID


reply = memory.processMessage(msg);

if (reply instanceof JtException)
      System.out.println
        ("JtUPDATE(team association):FAIL");
else
      System.out.println
        ("JtUPDATE(team association):PASS");

// Retrieve all members of a group

msg = new JtMessage (JtMemory.JtREAD);
factory.setValue(msg, JtGroup.GROUP, team_players);
factory.setValue(msg, JtMessage.WHAT,
  JtGroup.MEMBERS);
```

```java
reply = memory.processMessage(msg);

if (reply instanceof JtError)
        System.out.println
          ("JtREAD(all members):FAIL");
else
        System.out.println
          ("JtREAD(all members):PASS");

printer.processMessage(reply);


// Delete the association between a member
// and a team

msg = new JtMessage (JtMemory.JtDELETE);
factory.setValue(msg, JtMemory.GROUP, team_players);
factory.setValue(msg, JtMemory.ASSOCIATION,
"Jen@test.com"); // Member ID


reply = memory.processMessage(msg);

if (reply instanceof JtError)
        System.out.println
          ("JtDELETE(team association):FAIL");
else
        System.out.println
          ("JtDELETE(team association):PASS");


msg = new JtMessage (JtMemory.JtADD);
factory.setValue(msg, JtGroup.GROUP, team_players);

// The association only contains a
// reference to the Member.
// No additional information is included.

factory.setValue(msg, JtGroup.ASSOCIATION,
"Jen@test.com");


reply = memory.processMessage(msg);

if (reply instanceof JtException)
        System.out.println
          ("JtADD(team association):FAIL");
else
        System.out.println
          ("JtADD(team association):PASS");

// Delete the association between
// a member and a team

msg = new JtMessage (JtMemory.JtDELETE);
factory.setValue(msg, JtMemory.GROUP, team_players);
factory.setValue(msg, JtMemory.ASSOCIATION,
```

```java
    "Jen@test.com"); // Member ID


reply = memory.processMessage(msg);

if (reply instanceof JtError)
        System.out.println
        ("JtDELETE(team association):FAIL");
else
        System.out.println
        ("JtDELETE(team association):PASS");

// Delete Concept

msg = new JtMessage (JtMemory.JtDELETE);
factory.setValue(msg, JtMemory.CONCEPT,
  "Jen@test.com");
factory.setValue(msg, JtMemory.GROUP, players);

reply = memory.processMessage(msg);

if (reply instanceof JtException)
        System.out.println("JtDELETE(player):FAIL");

else
        System.out.println("JtDELETE(player):PASS");


msg = new JtMessage (JtMemory.JtDELETE);
factory.setValue(msg, JtMemory.GROUP, teams);
factory.setValue(msg, JtMemory.CONCEPT,
  new Long(2));


reply = memory.processMessage(msg);

if (reply instanceof JtError)
        System.out.println("JtDELETE(team):FAIL");

else
        System.out.println("JtDELETE(team):PASS");

// Remove Component

reply = memory.processMessage(
                new JtMessage (JtFactory.JtREMOVE));


}
```

## 25.5    Logger

The Framework Logger provides built-in logging capabilities. The framework can be configured or directed to log all the messages interchanged between components which facilitates debugging, testing, and implementation efforts. It can also automatically log all framework operations. Problems can be quickly identified and resolved by checking the messaging being automatically logged.

For convenience, the following attributes are provided by the framework Logger:

| Attributes | Description |
|---|---|
| logging (boolean) | Logging flag which specifies whether logging is enabled or not. As a result, the feature can be enabled and disabled at will. |
| logLevel (integer) | Log messages can be assigned a level and selectively logged. This attribute specifies the current log level: messages of level below the specified level are not logged. Valid values are between the constants `JtMIN_LOG_LEVEL` and `JtMAX_LOG_LEVEL`. The default value is `JtDEFAULT_LOG_LEVEL`. If the current log level is equal to `JtMIN_LOG_LEVEL`, all messages are logged. |
| logFile (String) | Logging information can be sent to a file. This attribute specifies the path of the file to be used for logging purposes. |

Messages sent to the framework Logger are processed (i.e. logged) depending on message type. In other words, processMessage() logs messages depending on its type:

| Message Type | Description |
|---|---|
| String | Logs the message specified by the String parameter. The default log level is employed (`JtDEFAULT_LOG_LEVEL`). |
| JtLogMessage (Concept) | Logs the message associated to the `JtLogMessage` instance (MESSAGE association). `JtLogMessage` is a subclass of `JtConcept`. Optionally, the `JtLogMessage` instance may contain the log level (LEVEL association). |
| JtError (Concept) | Logs the message associated to the `JtError` instance (MESSAGE association). `JtError` is also a subclass of `JtConcept`. Error messages (`JtError`) are always logged regardless of log level (logLevel attribute). |
| JtWarning (Concept) | Logs the message associated to the `JtWarning` instance (MESSAGE association). `JtWarning` is also a subclass of `JtConcept`. Warning messages are always logged regardless |

| | |
|---|---|
| | of log level (logLevel attribute). |
| JtConcept (Concept) | Logs the concept (C) using the XML format. The default log level is employed (JtDEFAULT_LOG_LEVEL ). |

For convenience, the framework Logger is able to handle instances of any class. In other words, instances of any arbitrary class can be logged. If the class is not contained in the table above, the instance is converted to XML and logged – similar to what is done with Concepts (JtConcept class).

In general, all application components should share the same Logger responsible for the central management of logging information. The framework creates and registers a 'central' Logger which can be located via the Factory. Components that wish to use the framework Logger can retrieve it by using the following snippet:

```
// Locate the framework Logger
logger = (JtLogger)
    factory.lookupObject(JtFactory.jtLogger);
```

The following example demonstrates the use of the framework Logger based on its specification.

## 25.5.1 Example

```
/**
 * Provides logging capabilities for
 * the Conceptual framework. It is able
 * to log framework concepts and objects.
 */

public static void main(String[] args) {

        JtLogger logger = new JtLogger ();
        logger.setLogging(true);
        JtConcept reply;
        JtConcept weatherInformation;
        JtFactory factory = new JtFactory ();


        // Log a message

        logger.processMessage("Log message");

        // Log a message using explicit log level (default)

        logger.processMessage (new JtLogMessage
           ("Log message (default level - explicit)",
           JtLogger.JtDEFAULT_LOG_LEVEL));

        // The following message should not be logged
        // because it uses the minimum log level.

        logger.processMessage
            (new JtLogMessage (
                     "This message should not be logged",
                     JtLogger.JtMIN_LOG_LEVEL));

        // Change the log level (minimum level)

        logger.setLogLevel(JtLogger.JtMIN_LOG_LEVEL);

        logger.processMessage
            (new JtLogMessage (
                "Log message (minimum level - explicit)",
                JtLogger.JtMIN_LOG_LEVEL));

        // Change the log level (maximum level)

        logger.setLogLevel(JtLogger.JtMAX_LOG_LEVEL);

        logger.processMessage
            (new JtLogMessage (
                "This message should not be logged."));


        // Log an error message

        logger.processMessage
```

```
       (new JtError ("Log this error"));


    // Log an exception

    try {

      // generate an internal JtException

      throw new Exception ("Log this exception");

    } catch (Exception e) {
      reply = (JtConcept) logger.processMessage (e);
    }

    logger.processMessage(reply);


    // Log a warning message

    logger.processMessage
      (new JtWarning ("Log this warning"));


    logger.setLogLevel(JtLogger.JtDEFAULT_LOG_LEVEL);

    // Log a concept

    weatherInformation = new JtConcept ();
    factory = new JtFactory ();

    factory.setValue(weatherInformation,
                WeatherService.summary, "Sunny");
    factory.setValue(weatherInformation,
                WeatherService.maximum,
                new Integer (80));
    factory.setValue(weatherInformation,
                WeatherService.minimum,
                new Integer (67));
    factory.setValue(weatherInformation,
                WeatherService.precipitation,
                new Float (5.0));

    logger.processMessage(weatherInformation);

    // Search for the Logger component (invoked
    // by framework components).

    logger = (JtLogger)
      factory.lookupObject(JtFactory.jtLogger);
  }
```

## 25.6 Exception Handler

Framework component responsible for handling exceptions and errors. The built-in Exception Handler forwards errors and exceptions to the framework Logger. A custom exception handler can be easily incorporated by registering it. The reference Exception Handler is able to process two types of messages:

| Message Type | Description |
|---|---|
| Java Exception | Forward the exception to the framework Logger. |
| JtError | Forward the error to the framework Logger. |

In general, all application components should share the same handler responsible for the central management of exception and error information. The framework creates and registers a 'central' handler which can be located via the Factory. Components that wish to use the framework Exception Handler can retrieve it by using the following snippet:

```
// Locate the framework Exception Handler

exceptionHandler = (JtExceptionHandler)

factory.lookupObject(JtFactory.jtExceptionHandler);
```

### 25.6.1 Example

The example below demonstrates the use of the framework Exception Handler.

```
/**
 * Demonstrates the messages processed by the framework
 * Exception Handler.
 */
public static void main(String[] args) {

        JtExceptionHandler exceptionHandler =
                new JtExceptionHandler ();
```

270

```java
JtFactory factory = new JtFactory ();


// Locate the exception handler


exceptionHandler = (JtExceptionHandler)
  factory.lookupObject
    (JtFactory.jtExceptionHandler);

if (exceptionHandler == null) {
      System.err.print
        ("Unable to locate the Exception Handler");
      System.exit(1);
}

// Java Exception

exceptionHandler.processMessage
    (new Exception ("my exception"));


// Framework error

exceptionHandler.processMessage
    (new JtError ("my error"));


   }
```

## 25.7    Printer

Framework component responsible for printing capabilities. It is able to print detailed information about a concept (C) or component regardless of complexity. The XML format is usually employed since the entity being printed may represent a complex hierarchy. A framework Printer provides additional convenience while building, testing, and debugging applications. The standard output stream (stdout) is utilized.

Messages sent to the framework Printer are processed (i.e. printed) depending on message type:

| Message Type | Description |
|---|---|
| String | Print the message specified by the String parameter. |
| JtConcept (Concept) | Print the specified concept (C) using the XML format. Each one of the concept associations is printed. |
| Object and its subclasses | Print the specified object using the XML format. Each object attribute is printed. |

For convenience, the framework Printer is able to handle instances of any class. The following example demonstrates the use of the framework Printer.

### 25.7.1  Example

```
/**
 * Framework component responsible for printing the content of
 * components and concepts (C).
 */

 public static void main(String[] args) {

   JtFactory factory = new JtFactory ();
```

272

```
JtPrinter printer;
HelloWorld hello = new HelloWorld ();
JtConcept weatherInformation;

    printer = new JtPrinter ();

    weatherInformation = new JtConcept ();

    // Create a concept

    factory.setValue(weatherInformation,
                WeatherService.summary, "Sunny");
    factory.setValue(weatherInformation,
                WeatherService.maximum, new Integer (80));
    factory.setValue(weatherInformation,
                WeatherService.minimum, new Integer (67));
    factory.setValue(weatherInformation,
                WeatherService.precipitation,
                new Float (5.0));

    // Print the concept

    printer.processMessage(weatherInformation);

    // Print an Object

    hello.setGreetingMessage("Hello World");

    printer.processMessage(hello);

    // Print a String

    printer.processMessage("Print this string.");


}
```

## 25.8    Resource Manager (Properties File)

The Resource Manager is responsible for configuring components and concept (C) when they are created. Attributes are read from the framework properties resource file. The mechanism provides a consistent way of customizing applications without having to hard code attribute values. Moving to a new platform or environment becomes a matter of replacing the resource file with one appropriate for the new environment.

The Resource Manager is based on pure Java and able to transparently run on every Java platform. No platform-dependent APIs are employed for its implementation. It also facilitates localization and internationalization of framework applications. Several software features are usually configured via the Resource Manager. Among them:

- Application Context (Application name, platform, locale, etc)
- Logging capabilities
- Data Sources including SQLite Adapter
- JDBC driver
- Security and Encryption features (Cypher, KeyStores, etc.)
- JMS configuration parameters
- Web Service adapters (SOA)

The Factory implementation, part of the Conceptual framework, relies on the Resource Manager to initialize component/concept attributes during creation. A resource entry applies to a class, component, or concept (C). The following is the syntax employed:

*className.attribute:value*

or

*~entityID.attribute:value*

entityID represents the concept or component ID. When an entity with the specified ID or class is created by the Factory, the attribute is initialized with the value found in the properties file. A complete example of the resource file is shown below:

```
! Resource properties file

! Application Context

~jtContext.applicationName:myapplication

! Logging paramenters

!Jt.JtLogger.logging:true
!Jt.JtLogger.logLevel:0
!Jt.JtLogger.logFile:log.txt

! Hello World demo application

Jt.examples.HelloWorld.greetingMessage:Hi there ...


! The attribute can also be initialized by using the component ID
instead of  ! the class.

!~helloWorld.greetingMessage:Hi there ...


! Graphical User Interface

~commandDialog.message:Enter keyboard input . . . .
~commandDialog.positiveButtonLabel:OK
~commandDialog.negativeButtonLabel:Cancel

~exitDialog.message:Are you sure you want to exit?

~addUrlDialog.message:Add web page bookmark
~addUrlDialog.positiveButtonLabel:OK
~addUrlDialog.negativeButtonLabel:Cancel


! JDBC adapter (MySQL settings)

Jt.JtJDBCAdapter.user:root

Jt.JtJDBCAdapter.password:123456
Jt.JtJDBCAdapter.driver:com.mysql.jdbc.Driver
Jt.JtJDBCAdapter.url:jdbc:mysql://localhost/test
!Jt.JtJDBCAdapter.datasource:datasrc
```

! JMS Adapter (point-to-point)

```
Jt.jms.JtJMSQueueAdapter.queue:testQueue
Jt.jms.JtJMSQueueAdapter.connectionFactory:TestJMSConnectionFactory
Jt.jms.JtJMSQueueAdapter.timeout:1
```

! JMS Adapter (publish/subscribe)

```
Jt.jms.JtJMSTopicAdapter.topic:jtTopic
Jt.jms.JtJMSTopicAdapter.connectionFactory:TestJMSConnectionFactory
Jt.jms.JtJMSTopicAdapter.timeout:1
```

! Web Services Adapter

```
Jt.axis.JtWebServicesAdapter.url:http://www.domain.com/axis/service
s/JtAxisService
```

! Java Mail Adapter

```
Jt.mail.JtMail.server:serve.mydomain.com
Jt.mail.JtMail.username:user
Jt.mail.JtMail.password:password
Jt.mail.JtMail.port:587
```

! JNDI Adapter

```
Jt.jndi.JtJNDIAdapter.factory:weblogic.jndi.WLInitialContextFactory
Jt.jndi.JtJNDIAdapter.url:t3://localhost:7001
```

! Android Properties (platform specific)

```
!Jt.xml.JtXMLHelper.parserName:org.xmlpull.v1.sax2.Driver
!Jt.xml.JtSAXAdapter.parserName:org.xmlpull.v1.sax2.Driver
```

! Jt KeyStore (client application)

```
!Jt.security.JtKeyStore.password:password
!Jt.security.JtKeyStore.alias:Jt
!Jt.security.JtKeyStore.resourcePath:/com/example/helloandroid/JtCl
ient.ks
```

! Jt Asymmetric Cipher

```
!Jt.security.JtAsymmetricCipher.certificateName:Jt
!Jt.security.JtAsymmetricCipher.transformation:RSA/ECB/PKCS1Padding
```

! Jt Symmetric Cipher

```
!Jt.security.JtSymmetricCipher.algorithm:AES
!Jt.security.JtSymmetricCipher.transformation:AES
!Jt.security.JtSymmetricCipher.keySize:128
```

276

# 26. JAVA, J2EE, AND ANDROID EXAMPLES

## 26.1 Messaging

The following straighforward example illustrates the use of the concept of Messaging. A message is sent to the `helloWorldMessage` component which returns a reply message. Messaging is implemented using the Jt interface (`JtInterface`). This interface consists of a single method:

```
/**
 * Jt interface used for the implementation
 * of the concept of Messaging.
 */
public interface JtInterface  {

/**
  * Process a message and return a reply.
  */

  Object processMessage (Object msg);
}
```

Advanced object-oriented technologies provide features like Java generics which allow the types to be parameterized:

```
public interface JtInterface<Type,Type1>
             {Type1 processMessage (Type msg);}
```

External components can be integrated with the Jt framework by implementing the messaging interface.

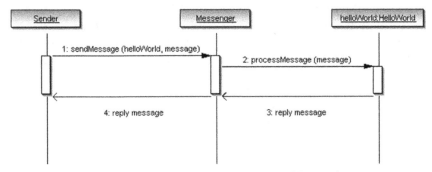

**HelloWorld Component based on Messaging.**

277

To utilize Messaging, framework components simply need to implement the information primitive: `processMessage (message)`.

The following straightforward Java class implements the method `processMessage (message)`. If the message parameter consists of the Strings "hi" or "hello", the method returns a greeting reply: "Hello World ... Welcome to Jt messaging".

As discussed earlier, a Messenger component is provided by the conceptual framework (`JtMessenger`). It allows you to send messages to framework components. A Factory component is also provided (`JtFactory`) which allows you to create components of a specific class. The framework also provides built-in logging capabilities via a Logging component (`JtLogging`): messaging between components is automatically logged. For the specific example being discussed, a component of the class `HelloWorldMessage` is created. The manipulation of framework components is straightforward; in particular, the implementation of Messaging. Additional examples will cover other aspects such as asynchronous and secure messaging. However, the general structure of every framework component will be the same to the one presented here. Obviously, the main component functionality is provided by the information primitive (processMessage ())

Components that leverage Concepts (C) – Messaging in particular – can be transparently accessed from distributed applications/components regardless of technology, platform, communication protocol, computer language and so forth. They are highly interoperable entities. Also, notice the impact on versioning challenges: no need for keeping and maintaining multiple versions of the component as long as the messaging implemented is backward compatible. In consequence, system scalability is also improved by relying on Concepts.

```
package Jt.examples;
import Jt.*;

/**
 * Demonstrates the use of MDP messaging.
 */

public class HelloWorldMessage implements JtInterface {
    public static final String JtCLASS_NAME =
        HelloWorldMessage.class.getName();
```

278

```
private JtLogger logger = null;
private JtFactory factory = new JtFactory ();


private static final long serialVersionUID = 1L;

private String greetingMessage = "
  Hello World ... Welcome to Jt messaging!";

public HelloWorldMessage() {


}

/**
 *  Set the greeting message to be displayed
 */

public void setGreetingMessage (String greetingMessage) {
    this.greetingMessage = greetingMessage;

}

/**
 *  Retrieve the greeting message
 */

public String getGreetingMessage () {
    return (greetingMessage);
}

    // Locate the framework Logger.

    private JtLogger locateLogger () {

            // Locate the framework Logger
            logger = (JtLogger)
              factory.lookupObject(JtFactory.jtLogger);

            // Create an instance if it cannot be found
            if (logger == null)
                    logger = new JtLogger ();

            return (logger);

    }

    // Handle errors

    private JtError handleError (String message) {

            if (message == null)
                    message = "framework error";


            // Log the error

            return ((JtError)
                logger.processMessage(new JtError (message)));
```

```
        }

        // Process object messages

        public Object processMessage (Object message) {

            // locate Logger component
            if (logger == null)
                    logger = locateLogger ();

            // Process the message

            if (message.equals("hi") || message.equals("hello"))
                return (greetingMessage);



            handleError ("Invalid message:" + message);
            return ("Invalid message:" + message);

        }


        /**
         * HelloWorld program. Demonstrates the use of MDP messaging.
         */

        public static void main(String[] args) {

            JtFactory factory = new JtFactory ();   // Jt Factory
            Object reply;
            HelloWorldMessage helloWorld;
            JtMessenger messenger = new JtMessenger ();


            // Create helloWorld (HelloWorldMessage class)

            helloWorld = (HelloWorldMessage) factory.createObject
                (HelloWorldMessage.JtCLASS_NAME);

            // Send the message

            System.out.println
                ("Sending a message to the helloWorld component:hi" );
            reply = messenger.sendMessage (helloWorld, "hi");

            // Print the reply message (Greeting)

            System.out.println ("Reply:" + reply);


        }

    }
```

## 26.2    Concept and Associations

A Concept (C) consists of a n-tuple of information associations: $C = \{(x1,y1), , (xn, yn)\}$. The Object abstraction is implemented via a language compiler or interpreter. Concepts can be implemented using similar capabilities. The Concept can be constructed and manipulated using a conceptual computer language or technology as follows:

C->x1 = y1;

C->x2 = y2;

....

C->xn = yn;


The semantics of "->" is similar to "." for Objects. It expresses the information association (or attribute). However, Concept associations are dynamic as opposed to fixed object attributes. The Concept construct (C) represents *pure* information – without information processing capabilities (no class methods).

Concepts (C) are implemented by the framework via the `JtConcept` class. The factory component (`JtFactory`) allows you to create and retrieve information associations. Two methods are provided: `setValue()` and `getValue()`. See framework Factory.


The following example creates a couple of Concepts and manipulates their associations. Framework messages represent concepts (C). For convenience and readability reasons, the framework defines a separate class named `JtMessage`, which inherits from `JtConcept`. Also for convenience, a message ID can be readily specified during the creation of the message. For instance, the following statement creates a new message and specifies its message ID:

```
msg = new JtMessage (JtComponent.JtREAD);
```

```java
/**
 * Concept abstraction. A concept is an ordered set
 * of information associations C = {a1,a2, ,an}
 * Concepts are implemented via a  factory
 * (Factory Method pattern). They can also be
 * implemented using compiler capabilities
 * (Conceptual language) which is more concise
 * and clear. Such implementation would be similar
 * to the implementation of the object abstraction.
 */

public static void main(String[] args) {

    JtFactory factory = new JtFactory ();
    JtMessage msg;

    JtPrinter printer = new JtPrinter ();

    JtConcept Sentence = new JtConcept (); // Sentence concept


    factory.setValue(Sentence, "adverb", "please");
    factory.setValue(Sentence, "article", "a");
    factory.setValue(Sentence, "verb", "make");
    factory.setValue(Sentence, "object", "reservation");

    // Print Concept (XML Format)

    printer.processMessage(Sentence);

    // A Message is also a concept.
    // The following message can be sent to
    // a GPS component to retrieve location information

    msg = new JtMessage (JtComponent.JtREAD);
    factory.setValue(msg, JtMessage.WHAT, "LOCATION");

    printer.processMessage(msg);

}
```

## 26.3    Live or Animated Component

The `JtComponent` class implements Live or Animated entities *(A = (f(m), I))* and hides the complexities associated with managing asynchronous messaging and traditional multithreading. In order to implement a Live/Animated component, you need to create a subclass of `JtComponent` and implement the appropriate information primitive.

The following example illustrates the use of the Live or Animated Entity. A timer component is implemented which keeps track of the time and runs using its own independent thread of execution. The timer simply inherits most of the required functionality from the framework `JtComponent` superclass.

As usual, the timer component implements the information primitive (`processMessage()`) to process incoming messages. The primitive needs to process a message (`UPDATE_TIME`) which tells the component to update its time attribute. After processing each `UPDATE_TIME` message, `processMessage()` adds a new one  to the message queue. As a result, the component is constantly updating itself.

The main component sends a `JtACTIVATE` message to start the timer. A standard framework message (`JtREMOVE`) tells the Live/Animated component to stop processing messages and perform housekeeping operations in preparation for the component to be discarded. The functionality is inherited from the framework superclass (`JtComponent`).

The framework Messenger is employed to transfer messages between components. It handles asynchronous messaging (`synchronous` attribute). In summary, Live/Animated entities and asynchronous messaging can be implemented in a straightforward fashion. Most of the required functionality is inherited from the framework which provides the information infrastructure. No multithreading/asynchronous APIs or artifacts are necessary. Live/Animated components can be transparently accessed via distributed interfaces, native APIs, and/or SOA services.

Plain Java/Android components can be readily converted to Animated/Live entities in order to handle incoming messaging.

```java
/**
 * Timer implementation based on the Animated or Live
 * Components. The timer runs using its own independent
 * thread of execution. Most of the asynchronous messaging
 * and threading functionality is implemented by the
 * Conceptual framework.
 */

public class TimerComponent extends JtComponent {

  private static final long serialVersionUID = 1L;
  public static final String JtCLASS_NAME =
    TimerComponent.class.getName();
  public static final String UPDATE_TIME = "UPDATE_TIME";
  private long tstart = 0L;          // t0
  private long tend;                 // t1
  private double time;               // Elapsed time in seconds (delta)
  private JtFactory factory = new JtFactory ();
  private JtLogger logger = null;   // Logger component

  public TimerComponent() {

  }

  // Locate the framework Logger.

  private JtLogger locateLogger () {

    // Locate the framework Logger
    logger = (JtLogger) factory.lookupObject(JtFactory.jtLogger);

    // Create an instance if it cannot be found
    if (logger == null)
      logger = new JtLogger ();

    return (logger);

  }

  /**
   * Retrieve the time attribute
   */

  public double getTime () {
    return (time);
  }

  /**
   * void operation
   *
   */
  public void setTime (double time) {

  }
```

284

```
private void updateTime () {

  if (tstart == 0L)
    tstart = (new Date()).getTime ();

  tend = (new Date ()).getTime ();
  time = (tend - tstart)/1000.0;

}

// Verify type of messaging

private boolean isSynchronous (Object message) {
  Boolean Bool;

  if (message == null)
    return (false);

  Bool = (Boolean) factory.getValue(message,
      JtMessage._SYNCHRONOUS);

  if (Bool == null)
    return (true);

  return (Bool.booleanValue());
}

// Process component messages

public Object processMessage (Object message) {

  Object msgid = null;
  JtMessage msg = (JtMessage) message;

  if (msg == null)
    return null;

  // locate Logger component
  if (logger == null)
    logger = locateLogger ();

  msgid = factory.getValue(msg, Jt.concept.JtMessage.ID);

  if (msgid == null)
    return null;

  // Add asynchronous messages to the message queue
  if (!isSynchronous (message)) {
    enqueueMessage (message);
    return null;
  }
```

```java
    // Start/Update the timer

    if (msgid.equals (TimerComponent.UPDATE_TIME) ||
        msgid.equals (JtComponent.JtACTIVATE)) {

      updateTime ();

      // Another UPDATE_TIME request is added to the message queue
      enqueueMessage(new JtMessage (TimerComponent.UPDATE_TIME));

      return (null);
    }


    // Let the superclass handle JtREMOVE (housekeeping is
    // performed)

    if (msgid.equals (JtComponent.JtREMOVE))
      return (super.processMessage (message));


    logger.processMessage (new JtError ("Invalid message:" +
    msgid));
    return (null);


}

static private char waitForInputKey () {
  char c = ' ';

  try {

    c = (char) System.in.read ();
    while (System.in.available () > 0)
      System.in.read ();

  } catch (Exception e) {
    e.printStackTrace ();
  }

  return (c);
}


public static void main(String[] args) {

  JtFactory factory = new JtFactory ();
  JtMessenger messenger = new JtMessenger ();
  TimerComponent timer;


  // Create the Timer component

  timer = (TimerComponent) factory.createObject
    (TimerComponent.JtCLASS_NAME);
```

286

```java
        System.out.println ("Press any key to start the timer ....");
        waitForInputKey ();
        System.out.println ("Timer started ....");

        // Start the timer component (Animated/Live Component).
        // The framework is responsible for implementing
        // the processing or threading mechanism. This message is
        // processed asynchronously via a message queue.

        messenger.setSynchronous(false);


        messenger.sendMessage (timer,
            new JtMessage (JtComponent.JtACTIVATE));

        System.out.println ("Press any key to stop the timer ....");
        waitForInputKey ();
        System.out.println (timer.getTime() + " second(s) elapsed.");

        // Stop the timer

        messenger.sendMessage (timer,
            new JtMessage (JtComponent.JtREMOVE));


    }


}
```

## 26.4　Group

A group represents a Concept (C). It can be expressed using the conceptual notation: G = {C1, C2, Cn} where $C_i$ is a concept. The framework defines an interface (CI) for the manipulation of groups. A factory component (JtFactory) is responsible for creating and manipulating groups (G).

For convenience and readability reasons, the framework defines a separate class named JtGroup, which inherits from JtConcept. As part of the conceptual interface (CI), three message types are defined to add, retrieve, and delete information from the group (G): JtADD, JtREAD, and JtDELETE correspondingly. Each message type is structured as follows:

| Message ID | Description |
| --- | --- |
| JtADD | Add a new member (MEMBER) to a group (GROUP). The member is added based on its ID attribute. This component ID needs to be provided for retrieving and deleting the member later on. |
| JtREAD | Retrieve a member (MEMBER) from a group (GROUP). Null is returned if the member cannot be found. |
| JtDELETE | Delete a member (MEMBER) from a group (GROUP). Null is returned if the member cannot be found. Otherwise, a reference to the deleted member is returned. |

A separate update message (JtUPDATE) is not required. To replace a group member, the user needs to delete the member and add a new one. Additionally, the message `JtREAD` has several modalities depending on the information to be retrieved:

| Message ID | Description |
|---|---|
| JtREAD (FIRST) | Retrieves the first member of the group (`GROUP`). The message includes the directive `FIRST` (`WHAT` attribute). Null is returned if the group is empty. |
| JtREAD (NEXT) | Retrieves the next member of the group (`GROUP`). The message includes the directive `NEXT` (`WHAT attribute`). The first member is retrieved, when the message is sent for the first time. Null is returned if the group is empty or the last member has been reached. |
| JtREAD (LAST) | Retrieves the last member of the group (`GROUP`). The message includes the directive `LAST` (`WHAT attribute`). Null is returned if the group is empty. |

Concepts, including Groups (G), are fluid abstractions (pure information) that can be transparently interchanged between heterogeneous systems/components regardless of technologies, computer languages, protocols, data representation, and so on. They also rely on a straightforward API implemented by a separate Factory component, usually part of a Conceptual framework. The separation between information and processing mechanism is one of the main factors behind the interoperability qualities exhibited by concepts (C).

The following example creates and manipulates a group of cities. For illustration purposes, the Printer component provided by the framework (JtPrinter), prints the group using the XML format.

```
/**
 * Group abstraction and its Conceptual Interface.
 * Concepts are implemented via a  factory
 * (Factory Method pattern). Concepts can also be
 * implemented using compiler capabilities
 * (Conceptual language) which is more compact
 * and clear. Such implementation would be similar
 * to the implementation of the object abstraction.
 */

public static void main(String[] args) {

    JtFactory factory = new JtFactory ();
    JtMessage msg;
    String memberId;
    Integer Size;
    String groupId;

    JtPrinter printer = new JtPrinter ();
    JtGroup cities = new JtGroup ("cities");

    JtConcept city = new JtConcept ();
    JtConcept city1 = new JtConcept ();


    factory.setValue(city, "POPULATION",
      new Integer (4000000));
    factory.setValue(city, JtFactory.ID, "Orlando");

    factory.setValue(city1, "POPULATION",
      new Integer (6000000));
    factory.setValue(city1, JtFactory.ID, "Seattle");



    // Add members to the group

    msg = new JtMessage (JtFactory.JtADD);

    factory.setValue(msg, JtFactory.GROUP, cities);
    factory.setValue(msg, JtGroup.MEMBER, city);

    factory.processMessage(msg);

    factory.setValue(msg, JtFactory.GROUP, cities);
    factory.setValue(msg, JtGroup.MEMBER, city1);

    factory.processMessage(msg);
    printer.processMessage(cities);
```

```java
Size = (Integer) factory.getValue(cities,
            JtGroup.SIZE);

if (Size != null && Size.intValue() == 2)
    System.out.println("JtGroup.SIZE:PASS");
else
    System.out.println("JtGroup.SIZE:FAIL");


groupId = (String) factory.getValue(cities, JtGroup.ID);

System.out.println("Group ID:" + groupId);

if ("cities".equals(groupId))
    System.out.println("JtGroup.ID:PASS");
else
    System.out.println("JtGroup.ID:FAIL");


// Check the group

msg = new JtMessage (JtFactory.JtREAD);
factory.setValue(msg, JtGroup.MEMBER, "Orlando");
factory.setValue(msg, JtFactory.GROUP, cities);
city = (JtConcept) factory.processMessage(msg);


if (city != null)
    System.out.println("JtADD:PASS");
else
    System.out.println("JtADD:FAIL");

printer.processMessage(city);



// Retrieve all the Members

printer.processMessage("Members:\n");

for (;;) {
    msg = new JtMessage (JtFactory.JtREAD);
    factory.setValue(msg, JtMessage.WHAT, JtGroup.NEXT);
    factory.setValue(msg, JtFactory.GROUP, cities);

    city = (JtConcept) factory.processMessage(msg);

    if (city == null)
        break;

    printer.processMessage(city);
}


msg = new JtMessage (JtFactory.JtREAD);
factory.setValue(msg, JtMessage.WHAT, JtGroup.FIRST);
factory.setValue(msg, JtFactory.GROUP, cities);
```

291

```java
city = (JtConcept) factory.processMessage(msg);

memberId = (String) factory.getValue(city, JtFactory.ID);


if ("Orlando".equals(memberId))
      System.out.println("JtREAD(FIRST):PASS");
else
      System.out.println("JtREAD(FIRST):FAIL");


msg = new JtMessage (JtFactory.JtREAD);
factory.setValue(msg, JtMessage.WHAT, JtGroup.LAST);
factory.setValue(msg, JtFactory.GROUP, cities);

city = (JtConcept) factory.processMessage(msg);

memberId = (String) factory.getValue(city, JtFactory.ID);


if ("Seattle".equals(memberId))
      System.out.println("JtREAD(LAST):PASS");
else
      System.out.println("JtREAD(LAST):FAIL");

// Delete a member from the group

msg = new JtMessage (JtFactory.JtDELETE);

factory.setValue(msg, JtFactory.GROUP, cities);
factory.setValue(msg, JtGroup.MEMBER, "Orlando");

factory.processMessage(msg);

// Check the group

msg = new JtMessage (JtFactory.JtREAD);
factory.setValue(msg, JtFactory.MEMBER, "Orlando");
factory.setValue(msg, JtFactory.GROUP, cities);
city = (JtConcept) factory.processMessage(msg);

if (city == null)
      System.out.println("JtDELETE:PASS");
else
      System.out.println("JtDELETE:FAIL");

// Print Group (XML Format)
printer.processMessage(cities);


// Retrieve first

msg = new JtMessage (JtFactory.JtREAD);
factory.setValue(msg, JtMessage.WHAT, JtGroup.LAST);
factory.setValue(msg, JtFactory.GROUP, cities);

city = (JtConcept) factory.processMessage(msg);
```

292

```java
        memberId = (String) factory.getValue(city, JtFactory.ID);

        if ("Seattle".equals(memberId))
                System.out.println("JtREAD(LAST):PASS");
        else
                System.out.println("JtREAD(LAST):FAIL");


        // Delete first

        msg = new JtMessage (JtFactory.JtDELETE);

        factory.setValue(msg, JtFactory.GROUP, cities);
        factory.setValue(msg, JtMessage.WHAT, JtGroup.FIRST);

        factory.processMessage(msg);

        Size = (Integer) factory.getValue(cities,
                        JtGroup.SIZE);

        if (Size != null && Size.intValue() == 0)
                System.out.println("JtDelete(FIRST):PASS");
        else
                System.out.println("JtDelete(FIRST):FAIL");

}
```

## 26.5   Dialog and MVC

The concept of Dialog represents the interchange of information between two or more entities. Such information exchange is accomplished via messaging between the parties involved. Dialog can be leveraged to implement MVC.

The following example illustrates the implementation of Dialog and MVC. There are three Live/Animated components running concurrently (Model, View, and Controller) and communicating via asynchronous messaging. The implementation of Live/Animated components is straightforward. A lot of the required functionality is reused or inherited from the Conceptual framework (JtComponent class). Multithreading artifacts and APIs are avoided.

| Live/Animated Component | Description |
|---|---|
| LocationController (Controller) | Responsible for coordinating all the interactions via Messaging: activates the GPS component (JtGPS) and forwards GPS/Location updates received to the View component. |
| Activity (View) | Responsible for updating the graphical user interface. |
| JtGPS (Model) | Responsible for retrieving GPS/Location information which is forwarded to the Controller. The source code can be found under Android specific components. |

```
/**
 * MVC Location Controller Class. Implementation
 * based on an Animated or Live component which
 * processes information (asynchronous messaging)
 * using an independent thread of execution.
 * Concepts are implemented via a factory
 * (Factory pattern).
 */

public class LocationController
        extends JtComponent {

    public static final String LOCATION_SERIAL = "12345";
    private JtLogger logger;
    private JtFactory factory = new JtFactory ();

    public LocationController() {
        // Locate framework Logger
        logger =
            (JtLogger)
          factory.lookupObject(JtFactory.jtLogger);
    }

    private void displayMessage (String msg) {
        JtMessage message =
            new JtMessage (JtComponent.JtDISPLAY);
        JtMessenger messenger =
            new JtMessenger ();

        if (msg == null)
            return;

        factory.setValue
            (message, JtMessage.CONTENT, msg);

        messenger.setSynchronous(false);
        sendMessageToUi (message);

    }
```

```
/*
 * Process reply from the GPS component in the
 * form of Location information.
 */

public Object processReplies
            (JtMessage message) {
   String subject;
   String textMessage = "";
   String via;
   String serial;

   if (message == null)
          return (null);

   subject =
     (String)
       factory.getValue
             (message, JtMessage.SUBJECT);

   if (subject == null)
          return (null);

   serial = (String)
       factory.getValue(message,
       JtMessage.SERIAL);

   // Match the message serial
   // with the one contained
   // in the reply message.

   if (!LocationController.LOCATION_SERIAL.equals (serial))
   // it does not match the message.
   return (null);


   if (subject.equals(JtGPS.PROVIDER_DISABLED)) {
          displayMessage
             ("Unable to retrieve location information."
             + " Location providers have been disabled." +
```

```
                "Please change phone settings and try again.");
        return (null);
    }

    textMessage += "lattitude = " +
      factory.getValue
        (message, JtGPS.LATITUDE) + "\n";
    textMessage += "longitude = " +
      factory.getValue
        (message, JtGPS.LONGITUDE) + "\n";

    if (subject.equals(JtGPS.LOCATION))
          displayMessage (textMessage);

    return (null);

  }


// Communicate with the GUI component to
// update the user interface.

private void sendMessageToUi
          (JtMessage msg) {
    JtMessenger messenger = new JtMessenger ();
    Object uiComponent;

    if (msg == null)
          return;

    uiComponent = factory.lookupObject
      (Controller.uiComponent);

    if (uiComponent == null) {
          logger.processMessage
            (new JtError ("Unable to locate component:" +
          Controller.uiComponent));
          return;
    }

    messenger.setSynchronous(false);
```

297

```
        messenger.sendMessage (uiComponent, msg);
    }


    /*
     * Activate GPS component to receive
     * location updates.
     */

    private void activateGPSComponent () {

        JtGPS gpsComponent;
        JtMessage msg = new
          JtMessage (JtComponent.JtACTIVATE);

        gpsComponent = new JtGPS ();

        // Add the serial to the request
        factory.setValue(msg, JtMessage.SERIAL, LOCATION_SERIAL);

        messenger.setSynchronous(false);
        messenger.sendMessage(gpsComponent, msg);

    }


    // Process component messages

    public Object processMessage (Object message)
    {

        JtMessage msg;
        Object msgId;
        Boolean isReply;
        Integer Button;
        Object type;

        msg = (JtMessage) message;

        msgId = (String)
          factory.getValue(msg, JtMessage.ID);
```

```
if (msgId == null)
        return (null);


logger.processMessage
    ("LocationController(msgId):"
    + msgId);


isReply = (Boolean)
      factory.getValue(msg,
        JtMessage.IS_REPLY);

// Process messages coming from
// the GPS component (location updates).

if (isReply != null
    && isReply.booleanValue())
        return (processReplies (msg));

// Activate GPS component (Model)

if (msgId.equals(JtObject.JtACTIVATE)) {
        activateGPSComponent ();
        return (null);
}


logger.processMessage
    (new JtError ("Invalid message Id:"
        + msgId));
return (null);


}


}
```

## 26.6    Distributed Proxy

The Conceptual framework provides access to distributed components and services via reusable Proxies. Framework Proxies hide the complexities associated with distributed and secure access (see Figure below). The same Proxy can be *reused* to access arbitrary components remotely. It is responsible for levering the framework in order to forward messages to the target component. Proxies usually communicate directly with a corresponding framework Adapter which is able to interface with the target technology or protocol. As the figure shows, the framework relies on a 'messaging pipeline' to transfer messaging from sender to receiver which are Live/Animated components *(A = ((f(m), I))*.

In general, framework Proxies need to be configured with the 'address' and the class – or 'name' – of the distributed component to be accessed. Perhaps, you may want to think of the phone book while you are looking to contact a specific class of service provider: class, name, phone, and address are listed so that communication can be established. A similar mechanism is required while configuring framework Proxies to communicate with remote components.

Secure access (encrypted and/or authenticated) is also supported. Design patterns like Proxy, Adapter and Façade are implemented based on Concepts including Messaging (see Design Pattern implementation). The concept construct (C) can be transparently interchanged between heterogeneous systems regardless of platform, technology, computer language, protocol, data representation, and so on.

The conceptual framework also provides built-in exception handling capabilities. Exceptions detected during distributed communication and/or execution are automatically propagated backwards, through the messaging pipeline, for handling by the sender component.

The following example demonstrates the use of the Proxy provided by the framework which supports the HTTP protocol. Several other reusable Proxies, applicable to common distributed technologies, are built-in as part of the framework including Axis, REST, and EJB. The framework can be readily extended by building custom Proxies for distributed technologies based on specific needs. Few additional components are required to interoperate with a new technology or protocol. Most of the needed functionality can be copied from existing framework Adapters, Proxies and Façades. Keep in mind that the framework is mainly responsible for transferring information (messaging) between sender and receiver components. While reducing overall complexity, Concepts also provide the framework with a high degree of interoperability between technologies, protocols, and computer languages.

HTTP Proxies are implemented via the `JtHttpProxy` class. The reusable HTTP Proxy needs a way of locating the distributed component. In order to do so, the URL is necessary (`setURL ()`). The class of component to be accessed also needs to be provided (`setClassname ()`). The specific example deals with a distributed component responsible for providing weather information: `Jt.examples.WeatherService`. After receiving the `JtREAD` message, the distributed component returns the information using the Concept construct (C). If an exception is detected during execution, it is returned to the calling component for handling. This is possible because of the framework's built-in propagation mechanism of Exceptions. Authenticated and encrypted access to distributed components is also fully supported.

By leveraging the Conceptual framework, communication with distributed components becomes straightforward – including secure access. Notice the absence of distributed artifacts and artificial primitives which add unnecessary complexity.

```java
public static void main(String[] args) {

JtFactory factory = new JtFactory ();
Object reply;
JtHttpProxy proxy;
JtConcept ctx;

String url =
  "http://localhost:8080/JtPortal/JtRestService";
JtMessenger messenger = new JtMessenger ();
JtMessage msg;
boolean bool;
JtPrinter printer = new JtPrinter ();

// Create an instance of the remote Proxy

proxy = (JtHttpProxy) factory.createObject
  (JtHttpProxy.JtCLASS_NAME);

// Specify URL and class name for the remote
// component

proxy.setUrl(url);
proxy.setClassname ("Jt.examples.WeatherService");

// Send the message (Read) to the distributed
// component that provides the Weather service.
// Weather information is retrieved.

reply = messenger.sendMessage (proxy,
            new JtMessage (JtFactory.JtREAD));

if (reply instanceof JtError) {
      System.out.println
        ("Service Invocation (JtREAD):FAIL");
      System.out.println ("Exception detected:");
      printer.processMessage(reply);
} else {
      System.out.println
        ("Service Invocation (JtREAD):PASS");
      printer.processMessage (reply);

}

proxy = (JtHttpProxy)
  factory.createObject (JtHttpProxy.JtCLASS_NAME);
proxy.setUrl(url);
proxy.setClassname
  ("Jt.examples.service.BankTeller");
proxy.setRestful(false);

messenger = new JtMessenger ();

// Specify that secure/encrypted messaging
// should be used. The Bank Teller component
// requires it.

messenger.setEncrypted(true);
```

```
// Authentication information

ctx = new JtConcept ();
factory.setValue(ctx, "username", "jt");
factory.setValue(ctx, "password", "messaging");

messenger.setContext(ctx);

// Send the message to the distribute
// teller component to retrieve account
// information. A concept (account)
// or an exception is returned.

msg = new JtMessage (JtComponent.JtREAD);
factory.setValue(msg,
  BankTeller.ACCOUNT, "12345678");

reply = messenger.sendMessage (proxy, msg);

if (reply instanceof JtError) {
  System.out.println
  ("Authenticated/Encrypted Service (JtREAD):FAIL");
      System.out.println ("Exception detected:");
      printer.processMessage(reply);
} else {
  System.out.println
  ("Authenticated/Encrypted Service (JtREAD):PASS");
      printer.processMessage (reply);

}
// Remove the proxy and all remote references.
// The remote framework component should be ready
// to be garbage collected after this operation.
bool = factory.removeObject(proxy);


if (bool)
      System.out.println("removeObject:PASS");
else
      System.out.println("removeObject:FAIL");


}
```

## 26.7   REST Service (Client)

```
/**
 * Demonstrates the invocation of a Restful Service.
 */

public static void main(String[] args) {

        JtFactory factory = new JtFactory ();
        JtRestService service;
        String url =
          "http://localhost:8080/JtPortal/JtRestService";

        Object reply;
        JtMessenger messenger = new JtMessenger ();
        JtMessage msg1;
        JtPrinter printer = new JtPrinter ();
        JtConcept ctx;


        service = (JtRestService)
        factory.createObject (JtRestService.JtCLASS_NAME);

        // Invoke the Weather service

        service.setUrl(url);
        service.setClassname ("Jt.examples.WeatherService");


        // Retrieve the information from the Weather service
        // (Read message).

        reply = messenger.sendMessage (service,
                      new JtMessage (JtFactory.JtREAD));

        if (reply instanceof JtException) {
                System.out.println ("Exception detected:");
                printer.processMessage(reply);
        } else {
                // Print weather information (XML format)
                printer.processMessage(reply);
        }


        // Authenticated service


        messenger = new JtMessenger ();

        // Specify that secure/encrypted messaging should be
        //used

        messenger.setEncrypted(true);

        service = (JtRestService)
        factory.createObject (JtRestService.JtCLASS_NAME);
        service.setUrl(url);
```

```
          service.setRemoteComponentId (null);

          service.setClassname
           ("Jt.examples.service.BankTeller");

          // Authentication information

          ctx = new JtConcept ();
          factory.setValue(ctx, "username", "jt");
          factory.setValue(ctx, "password", "messaging");


          // Send the message to the distribute teller
          // component to retrieve account information.
          // A concept (account or exception is returned).


          msg1 = new JtMessage (JtComponent.JtREAD);
          factory.setValue(msg1,
            BankTeller.ACCOUNT, "12345678");

          messenger.setContext(ctx);
          reply = messenger.sendMessage (service, msg1);
          // get rid of the authentication info
          messenger.setContext(null);
          factory.setValue(ctx, "password", "");


          if (reply instanceof JtException) {
                  System.out.println ("Exception detected:");
                  printer.processMessage(reply);
          } else
                  printer.processMessage(reply);


      }
```

## 26.8    Axis Web Service (Client)

Due to Turing-completeness, the Conceptual framework can be utilized to interface with arbitrary SOA technologies including AXIS.

Axis Proxies are implemented via the `JtAxisProxy` class. Like the other framework Proxies, the reusable Axis Proxy needs a way of locating the distributed component. In order to do so, the URL is necessary (`setURL ()`). The class of component to be accessed also needs to be provided (`setClassname ()`).

The specific example deals with a distributed component responsible for providing weather information: `Jt.examples.WeatherService`. After receiving the `JtREAD` message, the distributed component returns the information using the Concept construct (C). If an exception is detected, it is returned to the calling component for handling. This is possible because of the framework's built-in propagation mechanism of Exceptions. Authenticated and encrypted access to distributed components is also supported.

```
/**
 * Reusable framework Proxy for the Axis API. It allows the
 * interchange of messaging with distributed components based
 * on Axis web services. Arbitrary framework components can
 * be invoked via this proxy.
 */

  public static void main(String[] args) {

          JtFactory factory = new JtFactory ();

          Object reply = null;
          JtAxisProxy proxy;
          JtMessenger messenger;
          JtMessage msg;
          JtPrinter printer;
          JtConcept ctx;
          Boolean bool;


          messenger = new JtMessenger ();

          // Create a local proxy that references a
          // distributed component

          proxy = (JtAxisProxy)
            factory.createObject (JtAxisProxy.JtCLASS_NAME);
```

```java
        // Set the service url property (if it is not
        // present in the resource file)
        if (proxy.getUrl() == null)
                proxy.setUrl
("http://localhost:8080/axis/services/JtAxisService");

        proxy.setClassname ("Jt.examples.WeatherService");


        // Retrieve the information from the Weather
        // service (Read message).

        reply = messenger.sendMessage (proxy,
                        new JtMessage (JtComponent.JtREAD));

        printer = new JtPrinter ();

        if (reply instanceof JtError) {
                System.out.println ("Exception detected:");
                System.out.println
                   ("Service Invocation (JtREAD):FAIL");
                printer.processMessage(reply);
        } else {

                System.out.println
                   ("Service Invocation (JtREAD):PASS");
                // Print weather information (XML format)
                printer.processMessage(reply);
        }


        // Authentication information

        ctx = new JtConcept ();
        factory.setValue(ctx, "username", "jt");
        factory.setValue(ctx, "password", "messaging");

        proxy = (JtAxisProxy) factory.createObject
           (JtAxisProxy.JtCLASS_NAME);

        if (proxy.getUrl() == null)
                proxy.setUrl
("http://localhost:8080/axis/services/JtAxisService");

        proxy.setClassname
           ("Jt.examples.service.BankTeller");

        messenger = new JtMessenger ();

        messenger.setContext(ctx);
        // Specify that secure/encrypted messaging
        // should be used. The Teller component requires it.
        messenger.setEncrypted(true);
```

```
// Send the message to the distribute
// teller component
// to retrieve account information.
// A concept (account) or an exception
// is returned.


msg = new JtMessage (JtComponent.JtREAD);
factory.setValue(msg,
            BankTeller.ACCOUNT, "12345678");

reply = messenger.sendMessage (proxy, msg);

if (reply instanceof JtError) {
  System.out.println
  ("Authenticated/Encrypted Service (JtREAD):FAIL");
  System.out.println ("Exception detected:");
  printer.processMessage(reply);
} else {
  printer.processMessage (reply);
  System.out.println
  ("Authenticated/Encrypted Service (JtREAD):PASS");
}

// Remove the proxy and all remote references.
// The remote framework component
// should be ready to be garbage collected after
// this operation.

bool = factory.removeObject(proxy);

if (bool)
      System.out.println("removeObject:PASS");
else
      System.out.println("removeObject:FAIL");


ctx = new JtConcept ();
factory.setValue(ctx, "username", "jt");
factory.setValue(ctx, "password", "messaging1");

proxy = (JtAxisProxy) factory.createObject
  (JtAxisProxy.JtCLASS_NAME);

if (proxy.getUrl() == null)
      proxy.setUrl
("http://localhost:8080/axis/services/JtAxisService");

proxy.setClassname
  ("Jt.examples.service.BankTeller");

messenger = new JtMessenger ();

messenger.setContext(ctx);
// Specify that secure/encrypted messaging
// should be used. The Teller component requires it.
messenger.setEncrypted(true);
```

308

```
// Send the message to the distribute teller
// component to retrieve account information.
// A concept (account) or an exception is returned.

msg = new JtMessage (JtComponent.JtREAD);
factory.setValue(msg, BankTeller.ACCOUNT,
    "12345678");

reply = messenger.sendMessage (proxy, msg);

if (reply instanceof JtError) {
 System.out.println
   ("Authenticated Service (Invalid password):PASS");
 System.out.println ("Exception detected:");
 printer.processMessage(reply);
} else {
 printer.processMessage (reply);
 System.out.println
   ("Authenticated Service (Invalid password):FAIL");
}


}
```

## 26.9    Java Server Pages

The information pattern family and framework components based on them can be seamlessly integrated with Java Server Pages. The following example demonstrates the invocation of a framework component from a JSP page using Messaging.

```
<jsp:root version="1.2" xmlns:jsp="http://java.sun.com/JSP/Page"
xmlns:c="http://java.sun.com/jstl/core">
  <jsp:directive.page contentType="text/html; charset=ISO-8859-1"
/>
<jsp:directive.page import="Jt.*" />
<jsp:directive.page import="Jt.examples.*" />
<html>
<head>
<title>HelloWorld.jsp - Example of JSP support</title>
</head>
<body>

<!-- HelloWorld.jsp - Example of JSP support -->
<!-- Create the component factory  -->
<jsp:useBean id='factory' class='Jt.JtFactory' scope='request'/>
<!-- Create the helloWorld component -->

<jsp:scriptlet> HelloWorldMessage helloWorld = (HelloWorldMessage)
factory.createObject

(HelloWorldMessage.JtCLASS_NAME);
</jsp:scriptlet>

<!-- Implement the business logic by sending a message to the
component  -->

<jsp:scriptlet> String jtReply = (String) factory.sendMessage
                                    (helloWorld, "hi");
               request.setAttribute ("jtReply", jtReply);
</jsp:scriptlet>

<!-- View the reply message -->

<c:out value="${jtReply}"/>

</body>

</html>

</jsp:root>
```

310

# 27. Core Framework Components

## 27.1 Live/Animated Component (JtComponent.java)

The `JtComponent` class is the framework reference implementation of Live/Animated entities *(A = (f(m), I))* for Java and Android. The framework class hides the complexities associated with managing asynchronous messaging and traditional multithreading. It can be readily reused, through inheritance, by every component in the system which improves overall complexity, risk, cost, quality and timeframe (see Model Evaluation and Metrics). All forms of messaging are accommodated including synchronous, asynchronous and streaming.

`JtComponent` needs to maintain a queue of messages which are processed one at a time in the order in which they are received. The message queue is a common resource that can be accessed by several threads of execution concurrently. Such access needs to be controlled in order to avoid race conditions. Several control mechanisms are feasible. Java and Android manage this situation via thread synchronization.

Instances of `JtComponent` use their independent thread of execution. In order to do so, they implement the Runnable interface. The run method of the class is called after the thread is started.

The following are the main *internal* methods implemented by the reference framework class:

| Internal Method | Description |
|---|---|
| `activate ()` | Responsible for creating, configuring, and starting and independent thread of execution. It is invoked when the first message is received by the Live/Animated component. |

| `run ()` | After the independent thread is started, this method is invoked. It consists of a loop which is constantly extracting messages from the queue (`dequeueMessage ()`) and processing them using the information primitive. |
|---|---|
| `dequeueMessage ()` | Extracts the next message from the queue. |
| `suspendThread ()` | Suspend the component by calling wait() when the message queue is empty. Once a new message arrives, `notify()` is called and the component resumes processing messages. |
| `resumeThread ()` | Resume an idle component by calling `notify()` once a new message arrives for processing. |
| `requestStateTransition ()` | Manage the life cycle of the component which consists of several states: inactive, active, idle and stopped (see Table of States). |

The life cycle of a JtComponent instance consists of several states:

| State | Description |
|---|---|
| INACTIVE | Before the independent thread of execution is started. No messages have been sent to the component at this point. |

| | |
|---|---|
| ACTIVE | After the independent thread is started and while messages are being processed. The component thread is first started and configured once the first message arrives. |
| IDLE | The message queue is empty and the component is waiting for new messages to arrive. Once a new message is received, the component will become active again. |
| STOPPED | The component is not longer needed and has been stopped after receiving a `JtREMOVE` message. Housekeeping is performed as a result. |

Depending on the technology being used, other implementations of the concept of Live/Animated entity $(A = (f(m), I)$ are feasible. On the other hand, the main concepts will still apply: messaging and processing of information (information primitive) via an independent processing mechanism. Implementation of this streamlined set of concepts is straightforward and realistic.

## 27.2    Messenger (JtMessenger.java)

The framework Messenger is responsible for transferring messages between Live/Animated components – from component sender to the receiver. All modalities of messaging are supported including synchronous, asynchronous, distributed, and secure messaging. The Messenger relies on several support components for the implementation of security, encryption, authentication, and authorization of the messaging being exchanged.

For convenience, the following attributes control the behavior of the reference implementation of Messenger:

| Attributes | Description |
|---|---|
| synchronous (boolean) | Specifies whether asynchronous or synchronous messaging should be employed. Synchronous messaging is the default. |
| encrypted (boolean) | Enables or disables encrypted messaging. By default, no encryption is performed. |
| sessionKey (Key) | Specifies the session key to be used for message encryption. This key will be encrypted using the public key of the receiver. If no session key is specified (default), one is automatically generated by the framework. |

The following are the main internal methods implemented by the reference Messenger:

| Internal Method | Description |
|---|---|
| encryptMessage () | Encrypt the message via the framework cipher |

| | |
|---|---|
| | `(JtMessageCipher)` before forwarding it. |
| `decryptMessage ()` | Relie on the framework cipher (`JtMessageCipher`) to decrypt the reply message. |
| `sendMessage ()` | Forward the message to the receiver, or the next component part of the framework messaging pipeline, in case of distributed communication. All forms of messaging are handled including synchronous, asynchronous, distributed, and/or secure. |

## 27.3    Registry (JtRegistry.java)

Component responsible for maintaining the framework registry. This component also implements a naming mechanism to uniquely identify each component or Concept (C) being added to the registry. It allows framework components to locate and cooperate with each other; in particular in the context of applications based on distributed components/services. The framework Registry also supports the implementations of the Singleton pattern.

The following are the main internal methods implemented by the reference Registry:

| Internal Method | Description |
|---|---|
| add () | Add an entry to the framework Registry using a unique id (key). Components and Concepts (C) can be added to the Registry. |
| update () | Updates a registry entry. |
| lookup () | Retrieves an entry from the framework Registry using its associated key. Null is returned if the entry is not found in the Registry. |
| remove () | Removes the specified entry from the framework Registry. |

The framework Register handles proper concurrent access (i.e. synchronized) of registry information. All framework components interface with the same Registry instance. Such access is mainly performed indirectly via the framework Factory (lookup, create, remove, and so forth).

316

The Registry class may be reused for general-purpose applications. The following conceptual interface (CI) and associated messages are provided. The component can be readily incorporated as part of distributed applications and processes.

| Message ID | Description |
| --- | --- |
| JtCREATE | Add a new entry to the Registry (INSTANCE attribute) using the specified key (KEY). A framework error is returned if the entry already exists unless the message includes additional directives. If RETURN_IF_ALREADY_EXISTS is specified, the existing entry is returned. If REPLACE_IF_ALREADY_EXISTS is specified, the entry is overridden. An approriate framework error is also returned when the operation fails.for any other reason |
| JtREAD | Retrieve the entry associated with the specified key (KEY). Null is returned if the entry does not exist in the Registry. |
| JtUPDATE | Update the registry entry associated with the key (KEY) using the specified instance (INSTANCE). If the entry does not exist or the operation fails, a framework error is returned. |
| JtDELETE | Delete the registry entry associated with the key (KEY). A framework error is returned if the entry does not exist or the operation fails. |

## 27.4    Factory (JtFactory.java)

JtFactory relies on several framework components to support its functionality which mainly entails the creation and update of components and concepts (C):

| Classes | Description |
| --- | --- |
| JtGroupFactory.java | Implements the handling of Groups (G). |
| JtRegistry.java | Implements a component Registry and supports the implementation of Singletons. |
| JtResourceManager.java | Handles the configuration of components and concepts (C) during creation based on resources stored in the properties file. |
| JtFactoryHelper.java | Provides support for the clone operation, part of the framework implementation of the Prototype pattern. |
| | |

The following are the main *internal* methods implemented by the reference framework Factory class:

| Method | Description |
| --- | --- |
| initializeFramework() | Initialize the Conceptual framework. Instances of the framework Logger, Exception Handler, and Resource manager are created, configured, and added to the |

| | |
|---|---|
| | Registry. |
| `register()` | Relies on the framework Registry to register a component. |
| `setProxyValue()` | Set the attribute value of a distributed component through its local Proxy. |
| `getProxyValue()` | Retrieve the attribute value of a distributed component through its local Proxy. |
| `registerSingletonInstance()` | Relies on the framework Registry to register a Singleton instance. |
| `lookupSingletonInstance()` | Relies on the framework Registry to retrieve a Singleton instance. |
| `loadEntityResources()` | Relies on the framework Resource Manager to configure an instance by loading its property values during creation. |
| `removeProxy()` | Perform housekeeping operations when the remote Proxy is not longer needed. |
| `setAssociation()` | Set concept association (C). |
| `retrieveAssociation()` | Retrieve concept association. |

## 27.5    Memory or Information Repository

Live or Animated entities ($A = (f(x), I)$) rely on a memory subcomponent to provide information ($I = \{G_1, , G_n\}$ storage capabilities. The concept of Memory or Information Repository and the associated interface can be readily implemented using relational database technologies (RDBMS). On the other hand, by leveraging Concepts, the application does not need to be concerned as how persistency is implemented – arbitrary persistency technologies and mechanisms can be employed (see Conceptual Framework - Core Components).

The reference implementation of Memory based on RDBMS consists of the following support components:

| Component | Description |
|---|---|
| JtSQLAdapter.java | Component responsible for storing and retrieving conceptual information ($I=\{G1, , Gn\}$) using the SQL API. It relies on the JDBC Adapter (if supported) to interface with the relation database. |
| JtJDBAdapter.java | Framework Adapter to interface with JDBC API. It is supported by most implementations based on pure Java. |
| JtSqliteAdapter.java | Android does not support the JDBC API. Instead, it implements the SQLite API. This component supports the RDBMS implementation of the Memory concept on the Android platform. |

## 27.6 Logger (JtLogger.java)

The framework Logger and its conceptual interface have been discussed in previous sections (see Framework Core Components). The reference implementation consists of the following internal methods:

| Internal Method | Description |
|---|---|
| log () | Logs an entry. A logging level is specified. For clarity and readability the XML format is employed when appropriate. processException() and processError() rely on this method. |
| encodeInstance () | Encode entry using the XML representation. |
| processException () | Log a Java exception. |
| processError () | Log a framework error (JtError). |

## 27.7 Printer (JtPrinter.java)

The framework Printer and its conceptual interface have been covered in earlier sections (see Framework Core Components). The reference implementation consists of the following internal methods:

| Internal Method | Description |
|---|---|
| encodeInstance () | Encodes instance using the XML representation. For clarity and readability XML is employed when appropriate. |
| printBuffer () | Prints a buffer (byte[]). XML representation is not required. |

## 27.8 Resource Manager (JtResourceManager.java)

As discussed earlier, the Resource Manager is responsible for configuring components and concept (C) when they are first created. Attributes are read from the framework properties resource file or stream. The following are the main internal methods implemented by the reference Resource Manager:

| Internal Method | Description |
|---|---|
| `loadResourcesFromStream ()` | Read resource entries from the input stream associated with the framework properties file (`Jt.properties`). |
| `parseEntityResource ()` | Parse input line containing a resource entry that corresponds to a specific component or concept. |
| `parseClassResource ()` | Parse input line contatining a resource entry associated with a class. |
| `loadComponentResources ()` | Initialize component using its associated resources. |
| `loadConceptResources ()` | Initialize concept (C) using its associated resources. |

# 28.    Support Components

## 28.1    Group Factory (JtGroupFactory.java)

Support component responsible for managing groups. A group is a Concept that can be respesented as G = {C1, C2, Cn}. The framework factory relies on this component for the implementation of Group related capabilities. The following conceptual interface (CI) is provided:

| Message | Description |
|---------|-------------|
| ADD | Add a member (MEMBER) to a group (GROUP). For maximum flexibility, Groups may consists of framework components, concepts (C), and regular objects. |
| READ | Retrieve a member (MEMBER) from a group (GROUP). MEMBER specifies the ID of the member to be retrieved. Instead of a member ID, the message may contain the following directives: a) FIRST – retrieve the first member in the group. b) NEXT – retrieve the next member. c) LAST – retrieve the last member. d) POSITION – retrieve the member located at the specified position in the group. |
| DELETE | Delete a member (MEMBER) from a group (GROUP). |

| | MEMBER specifies the ID of the member to be deleted. Instead of a member ID, the message may contain the following directives: a) FIRST – delete the first member in the group. b) LAST – delete the last member. c) POSITION – delete the member located at the specified position in the group. |
|---|---|

No UPDATE message is required. DELETE and ADD messages can be combined to update the group membership. The following are the main internal methods implemented by the reference GroupFactory:

| Internal Method | Description |
|---|---|
| addMember() | Add a new member to a group. |
| retrieveMember () | Retrieve a group member based on the specified ID. |
| deleteMember () | Delete the specified member (ID) from the group. |
| retrieveFirstMember(), retrieveNextMember(), retrieveLastMember(), retrieveMemberAtPosition() | Retrieve first, next, last, and the member at the specified position correspondingly. A group header is kept which contains the current position in the group. |
| deleteFirstMember(), deleteLastMember(), deleteMemberAtPosition () | Delete first, last, and the member located at the specified position correspondingly. |

Groups (G), like other concepts (C), can be transferred between heterogeneous applications and components regardless of platform, computer language, protocol, and so forth. Information and information processing mechanism are fully decoupled. They can be readily transferred between heterogeneous systems using any arbitrary data representation including XML and binary formats.

## 29. Distributed Component and Service Model
## 29.1 Remote Façade (JtRemoteFacade.java)

The framework Façade (JtRemoteFacade) is mainly responsible for forwarding messages to the appropriate distributed component. It is also responsible for providing access control and message security (authentication and encryption) through several support components (subcomponents).

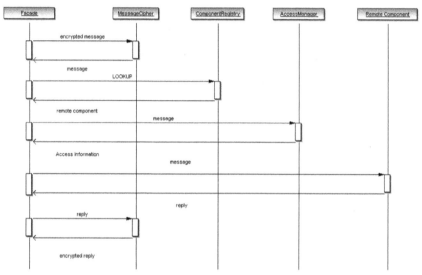

**Secure access to distributed components and services based on Concepts (server side)**

The following are the components involved:

| Component | Description |
|---|---|
| MessageCipher | Component responsible for decrypting the input message and encrypting the reply message. This component can be configured to use a specific encryption scheme. This component is only applicable when secure messaging is being utilized. |

| Registry | Allows the Façade to register and look up distributed components by ID. |
|---|---|
| AccessManager | Responsible for granting/denying access to distributed components. When needed, it authorizes and authenticates the messages received. If the access manager is unable to authenticate the message, it never reaches the intended receiver. |

The following are the main *internal* methods implemented by the reference framework Façade:

| Internal Method | Description |
|---|---|
| decryptMessage () | Utilize the message cipher to decrypt secure incoming messages. |
| verifyAccess () | Relies on the Access Manager for the verification of authorized access to the distributed component. |
| authenticateMessage() | Authenticate the incoming message. |
| encryptMessage () | Relies on the message cipher to encrypt replies when secure messaging is being employed. |
| generateUniqueId () | Generate unique ID for the distributed component when needed. The ID is returned to the client during the initialization of the distributed Proxy. It allows subsequent access to the distributed component via its Proxy. |

The framework supports a straightforward naming mechanism for distributed components based on component ID and class. As part of the conceptual interface (CI), several message types are defined to manipulate distributed components and its attributes: `JtCREATE`, `JtSEND_MESSAGE`, `JtGET_VALUE`, `JtSET_VALUE`, and `JtDELETE` correspondingly. These messages are leveraged by framework Proxies that provide access to distributed components. Each message type is structured as follows:

| Message ID | Description |
|---|---|
| `JtCREATE` | Create a component of a specific class (CLASSNAME) and return a generated component ID. The new component is added to the internal component registry, maintained by `JtRemoteFacade`. This message is usually utilized by Proxies during initialization. The life span of the new component is temporal. It will exist until the distributed Proxy is discarded (`JtREMOVE` message). A framework error is returned if the operation fails. |
| `JtSEND_MESSAGE` | Forward the message (MESSAGE) to a distributed component (COMPONENT) for processing. The reply message is returned unless the operation fails in which case an error is returned. |
| `JtSET_VALUE` | Set the value of the component attribute specified by ATTRIBUTE. String values are automatically converted to the appropriate type by the framework. COMPONENT specifies the component ID. A framework error (`JtError`) is returned if the operation fails. |

| JtGET_VALUE | Retrieve the value of the component attribute specified by ATTRIBUTE. COMPONENT contains the component ID. If the operation fails, a framework error is returned. |
|---|---|
| JtLOOKUP | Locate a distributed component based on its component ID (COMPONENT). This message is usually utilized by Proxies during initialization. The operation does not apply to the internal registry. Only the framework component registry is checked. Null is returned if the component cannot be found. If the operation fails, a framework error is returned. |
| JtREMOVE | Removes the component (COMPONENT) from the internal registry maintained by JtRemoteFacade. A framework error is returned if the operation fails. |

The conceptual interface (CI) described above is independent of platform, technology, protocol, computer language, data representation, and so forth. By leveraging Concepts, arbitrary technology pieces can be transparently integrated into a unified and interoperable environment. The framework messaging pipeline is highly reusable: usually a single Proxy and Adapter is all that is required to support a new client technology. The rest of the information infrastructure remains unchanged.

## 29.2   Message Cipher (JtMessageCipher.java)

Framework support component responsible for encrypting and decrypting messages as part of secure communication between distributed components. The message cipher relies on several additional support components which have dual responsibilities (client and server side).

329

| Support Component | Description(client side) | Description (server side) |
|---|---|---|
| Symmetric Cipher (JtAsymmetric) | Encrypt messages using a session key which can be provided or automatically generated. The symmetric cipher is responsible for generating the session key if one is not provided. Decrypt reply messages using the same session key. | Decrypt messages using the encrypted session key passed as part of the message. The session keys needs to be decrypted beforehand as described below. |
| Asymmetric Cipher (JtSymmetric) | Encrypt the session key using the public key of the recipient (server). The encrypted key is sent as part of the message to the remote computer. | Decrypt the session key using the private key of the receiver (server). Once the session key is decrypted, it can be utilized to decrypt the message itself via the symmetric cipher. |

The following are the main internal methods implemented by the reference Message Cipher:

| Internal Method | Description |
|---|---|
| encryptMessage () | Encrypt the message using the session key. If no session key is provided, one is automatically generated. |
| decryptMessage () | Decrypt the message. First, it decrypts the session key before using it for decrypting the actual message. |

330

## 29.3    Access Manager (JtAccessManager.java)

The framework Access Manager (AM) controls the messaging access to distributed components. By default no access is granted to any distributed framework class or component unless it is explicitly enabled via the AM configuration file. Access to distributed framework components can be enabled/disabled and specified to be encrypted and/or authenticated.

| ENABLED | Enables the messaging access to a distributed component, class, or package. |
|---|---|
| ENCRYPTED | Messaging must be encrypted using the appropriate session key in order to be processed by the distributed receiver. Otherwise, it is rejected by the framework because of a security violation. The session key is automatically encrypted using the framework public key. |
| AUTHETICATED | Messaging must contain valid authentication information like username and password. Otherwise, it is rejected by the framework because of a security violation. For tight security, authenticated messaging should be employed in conjunction with encrypted messaging. |

Additional features can be incorporated as part of the framework Access Manager. For instance, access can be granted based on user, role, and/or group. In conjunction with the capabilities provided by the framework, distributed components may readily implement custom security mechanisms (encryption/authentication) over the messaging being exchanged. The framework Access Manager relies on a configuration file or database which contains a group of access entries like the following:

```
<Entry>
  <classname>Jt.examples.MyClass</classname>
  <enabled>true</enabled>
</Entry>
```

The previous entry enables messaging access to the class named Jt.examples.MyClass. Access can be specified to be encrypted:

```
<Entry>
  <classname>Jt.examples.MyClass</classname>
  <enabled>true</enabled>
  <encrypted>true</encrypted>
</Entry>
```

Access can also be specified to be encrypted and authenticated:

```
<Entry>
  <classname>Jt.examples.MyClass</classname>
  <enabled>true</enabled>
  <encrypted>true</encrypted>
  <authenticated>true</authenticated>
</Entry>
```

Instead of a class name, a component ID can be specified as part of the access entry:

```
<Entry>
  <entryId>myComponent</entryId>
  <enabled>true</enabled>
  <encrypted> </encrypted>
  <authenticated>true</authenticated>
</Entry>
```

332

The previous entry enables access to the component named `myComponent`. Messaging access is specified to be encrypted and authenticated. Finally, access can be granted to a package of classes by using wild characters. The following entry enables encrypted access to all the classes that belong to the package `Jt.service`.

```
<Entry>
  <classname>Jt.services.*</classname>
  <enabled>true</enabled>
  <encrypted>true</encrypted>
</Entry>
```

An entry can be easily extended to deal with additional access features (roles, usernames, etc.) . The following are the main *internal* methods implemented by the reference Access Manager:

| Internal Method | Description |
|---|---|
| readConfigFile () | Read access entries from a configuration file, stream, or database. |
| retrieveClassAccessEntry () | Retrieve the access entry associated to a specific class. |
| retrieveComponentAccessEntry () | Retrieve the access entry associated to a specific component. |

# 30.   HTTP Components

## 30.1   HTTP Proxy (JtHttpProxy.java)

The Conceptual framework provides access to distributed components via Proxies. The following framework class implements a reusable HTTP proxy for Java and Android. The implementation of framework Proxies for other technologies is very similar.

**Framework's messaging pipeline**

The following are the main internal methods implemented by the reference HTTP Proxy:

| Method | Description |
|---|---|
| `intializeProxy ()` | Initialize the Proxy: 1) Create an instance of the framework Adapter (`JtHttpAdapter`). 2) Request the creation of an instance of the distributed class (if classname is provided). Otherwise, attempt to locate the distributed component based on component ID (remoteComponentId). |
| `processMessage ()` | Mainly responsible for sending incoming messages to the HTTP Adapter so they can be forwarded to the distributed component – through the framework's messaging pipeline. It relies on |

334

| | the framework Messenger which also provides secure messaging capabilities. |
|---|---|

## 30.2    HTTP Adapter (JtHttpAdapter.java)

The conceptual framework implements the Adapter design pattern to interface with a diverse variety of technologies. The main purpose of Adapter is the transformation of messages between sender and receiver so they can communicate.

The JtHttpAdapter class is the framework Adapter responsible for distributed component communication via the HTTP protocol. For convenience, messages are converted to the XML format. However, arbitrary data representations can be employed including binary and custom formats. The HTTP Adapter is usually employed in conjunction with the HTTP Proxy as part of the framework's messaging pipeline (see JtHTTPProxy.java). All forms of messaging are supported including synchronous, asynchronous, and secure (authenticated and/or encrypted).

The following are the main *internal* methods implemented by the reference HTTP Adapter:

| Internal Method | Description |
|---|---|
| sendRemoteMessage () | Forwards the message to a distributed component by posting it as an HTTP request via the framework's messaging pipeline. |

## 30.3    URL Handler (JtURLHandler.java)

The HTTP Adapter (JtHTTPAdapter) relies on the URL handler (JtURLHandler), as a support class, to post HTTP requests.

The following are the main *internal* methods implemented by the URL handler. doPost() is the only method leveraged by the HTTP Adapter.

| Internal method | Description |
|---|---|
| doPost () | Perform the HTTP POST request specified by CONTENT. |

## 30.4    Framework Servlet (JtServlet.java)

The Conceptual framework can interface with Web servers via several well-known technologies including JSPs and Java servlets. A single Java servlet (JtServlet) is able to provide the communication mechanism between distributed components by transporting the required messaging. The JtServlet component is part of the framework messaging pipeline. It is responsible from forwarding messages, coming from the client component, to the framework distributed façade (JtRemoteFacade) which in turn routes them to the appropriate distributed component.

The following are the main *internal* methods implemented by JtServlet.

| Internal method | Description |
|---|---|
| doPost () | Framework messages can be transferred via HTTP requests to the Web server (POST and GET). doPost() is invoked when a HTTP POST request is received. It transfers incoming messages to the distributed façade (JtRemoteFacade) for routing to the appropriate remote component. |
| convertXMLToObject () | Transforms an XML message to its corresponding Java representation. For convenience, framework messages are transferred |

| | using the XML format. Arbitrary formats are feasible. |
|---|---|
| | |

Notice that a single universal servlet is required to support the framework information infrastructure and distributed inter-component communication via the HTTP protocol.

# 31.    Axis Components

## 31.1    Axis Proxy (JtAxisProxy.java)

As discussed earlier, the Conceptual framework provides access to
distributed components via Proxies. The JtAxisProxy class implements a
reusable Proxy for the Axis technology which deals with SOA services.
The implementation of all framework Proxies is very similar. The same
methods and concepts apply (see HTTP Proxy for a complete
description). The main difference is that the Axis Proxy communicates
directly with an adapter specific for Axis (see Axis Adapter).

## 31.2    Axis Adapter (JtAxisAdapter.java)

Framework client-side component responsible for interfacing with the
Axis API which implements SOA services. It provides a mechanism of
communication between distributed components and applications.

For convenience, messages are converted to the XML format. However,
arbitrary data representations can be employed including binary and
custom formats. The Axis Adapter is employed in conjunction with the
Axis Proxy as part of the framework's messaging pipeline (see
JtAxisProxy.java).

The following are the main *internal* methods implemented by the
reference Axis Adapter:

| Internal Method | Description |
|---|---|
| sendRemoteMessage () | Forwards the message to a distributed component by relying on the AXIS API for SOA services. |

## 31.3 Axis Server Adapter (JtAxisServerAdapter.java)

Framework server adapter part of the messaging pipeline responsible for interfacing with Axis technology (SOA services). It communicates directly with the framework remote facade (see JtRemoteFacade.java) which forwards messages to distributed components. Incoming messages are converted to Java instances before being forwarded. Reply messages are converted from Java to XML.

For convenience, messages are transferred using the XML format. On the other hand, arbitrary data representations can be supported by the Conceptual framework including binary and custom formats.

Configuring the interface between Axis and the conceptual framework is straightforward. A single descriptor, based on the information primitive, is required to interface with Axis technology. No additional complexity needs to be introduced.

## 32. J2EE Components and Patterns

### 32.1 EJB Proxy (JtEJBProxy.java)

Component responsible for implementing a reusable Proxy for the EJB technology. The implementation of all framework Proxies is very similar. The same methods and concepts apply (see HTTP Proxy for a complete description). The main difference is that the EJB Proxy communicates directly with an adapter specific for EJB (see EJB Adapter). Very few built-in components are required to connect the Jt Conceptual framework with the EJB technology. Concepts are leveraged for the reusable implementation of J2EE design patterns: J2EE Service Locator, J2EE Session Façade, J2EE Business delegate, and J2EE Value Object.

### 32.2 EJB Adapter (JtEJBAdapter.java)

Framework adapter responsible for interfacing with the EJB technology. It communicates through a single session bean (JtSessionFacade.java) with the framework remote facade (see JtRemoteFacade.java) which forwards messages to distributed components.

| Internal Method | Description |
|---|---|
| retrieveSessionFacade () | Retrieve EJB implementation of the J2EE session Façade pattern. |
| sendRemoteMessage () | Forward the message to a distributed component by communicating with the framework session facade. |

340

## 32.3  J2EE Session Façade Pattern (JtSessionFacadeEJB.java)

EJB session bean responsible for the implementation of the J2EE session Façade Pattern. Such implementation is based on Concepts. It communicates with the remote façade to forward messages to distributed components (see JtRemoteFacade.java).

The conceptual paradigm makes the implementation of J2EE session Façade straightforward. A single EJB bean is required. Three EJB classes and one descriptor are involved as part of the EJB 2.1 specification (see Table below). The EJB 3.0 implementation is also straightforward. Most of the messaging pipeline provided by the Conceptual framework can be transparently reused. Just a few additional components need to be incorporated in order to achieve interoperability: Proxy, Adapter, and Façade. Actually, arbitrary protocols, platforms, technologies, and computer languages can seamlessly interoperate when Concepts are leveraged.

| Classes | Description |
|---|---|
| JtSessionFacade.java | EJB Remote interface. |
| JtSessionFacadeHome.java | EJB Home interface. |
| JtSessionFacadeEJB.java | Component that implements the EJB SessionBean interface. |
| ejb-jar.xml | EJB descriptor. |

## 32.4    J2EE Session Façade (JtSessionFacade.java)

```
/**
 * Remote interface for JtSessionFacade.
 */

public interface JtSessionFacade
    extends javax.ejb.EJBObject
{

    /**
     * Process a message. EJB Implementation of the
     * information primitive. A single method is
     * required.
     */

    public java.lang.Object
        processMessage(java.lang.Object message )
            throws java.rmi.RemoteException;

}
```

## 32.5    J2EE Session Façade (JtSessionFacadeHome.java)

```
/**
 * Home interface for JtSessionFacade.
 */
public interface JtSessionFacadeHome
extends javax.ejb.EJBHome
{
    public static final String
        COMP_NAME="java:comp/env/ejb/JtStateful";
    public static final String JNDI_NAME="JtStateful";

    public JtSessionFacade create()
      throws

    javax.ejb.CreateException,java.rmi.RemoteException;

}
```

## 32.6    J2EE Business Delegate (JtBusinessDelegate.java)

Framework implementation of the J2EE Business Delegate design pattern. This component is mainly responsible for forwarding the message to the distributed component via EJBAdapter and JtSessionFacade. It reuses the functionality provided by the EJB Proxy (JtEJBProxy.java).

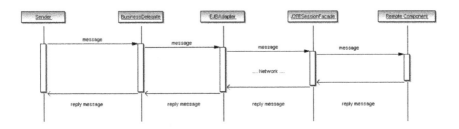

An example application to communicate with a distributed component is included as part of the source distribution. The logic is very similar to the one used by other applications based on framework Proxies.

```java
/**
 * Jt implementation of the J2EE Business Delegate pattern.
 * It inherits from JtEJBProxy.
 */

public class JtBusinessDelegate extends JtEJBProxy  {

        public static final String JtCLASS_NAME =
          JtBusinessDelegate.class.getName();
        private static final long serialVersionUID = 1L;


        public JtBusinessDelegate () {
        }


        /**
         * Demonstrates all the messages processed by
         * JtBusinessDelegate.
         */

        public static void main(String[] args) {

                JtFactory factory = new JtFactory ();
                JtBusinessDelegate businessDelegate;
```

```
    String tmp;
    Object reply = null;


    // Create an instance of JtBusinessDelegate

    businessDelegate = (JtBusinessDelegate)
    factory.createObject
      (JtBusinessDelegate.JtCLASS_NAME);

    businessDelegate.setClassname
      (HelloWorldMessage.JtCLASS_NAME);


    // The JtBusinessDelegate component is ready to
    // be used. Set an attribute value of a remote
    // component via the local JtBusinessDelegate.

    factory.setValue (businessDelegate,
                "greetingMessage",
                "Hello there....");

    tmp = (String) factory.getValue (businessDelegate,
    "greetingMessage");

    System.out.println ("greetingMessage:" + tmp);


    // Send a message to the remote component

    reply = factory.sendMessage (businessDelegate,
                           "hi");


    // Display the reply

    System.out.println ("reply:" + reply);


    // Remove the business delegate

    factory.removeObject (businessDelegate);

  }

}
```

## 32.7 EJB deployment descriptor (ejb-jar.xml)

The following represents the deployment descriptor required for deploying the single framework session bean. Carefully consider that a single straightforward descriptor is required regardless of the number of distributed components involved as part of the application. The simplication is a direct consequence of the conceptual approach based on messaging and a single information primitive.

```
<?xml version="1.0" encoding="UTF-8"?>
<!DOCTYPE ejb-jar PUBLIC "-//Sun Microsystems, Inc.//DTD
Enterprise JavaBeans 2.0//EN" "http://java.sun.com/dtd/ejb-
jar_2_0.dtd">

<ejb-jar >
    <display-name>Single Jt Session Bean</display-name>
    <enterprise-beans>

        <!-- Session Beans -->
        <session >

            <ejb-name>JtSessionFacade</ejb-name>

            <home>Jt.ejb.JtSessionFacadeHome</home>
            <remote>Jt.ejb.JtSessionFacade</remote>
            <ejb-class>Jt.ejb.JtSessionFacadeEJB</ejb-class>
            <session-type>Stateful</session-type>
            <transaction-type>Container</transaction-type>

        </session>

    </enterprise-beans>

    <assembly-descriptor >
    </assembly-descriptor>

</ejb-jar>
```

You may also need a descriptor specific to your application server. The descriptor below applies to WebLogic Server. Besides the descriptors, the configuration file for the framework Access Manager (JtAccessManager.xml) which allows granting of distributed access, must be part of the application Jar file.

```xml
<?xml version="1.0" encoding="UTF-8"?>

<!DOCTYPE weblogic-ejb-jar PUBLIC "-//BEA Systems,
Inc.//DTD WebLogic 6.0.0 EJB//EN"
"http://www.bea.com/servers/wls600/dtd/weblogic-ejb-
jar.dtd">

<weblogic-ejb-jar>
 <description> Jt Session Bean </description>
   <weblogic-enterprise-bean>
      <ejb-name>JtSessionFacade</ejb-name>
      <stateful-session-descriptor>
      </stateful-session-descriptor>
      <reference-descriptor>
      </reference-descriptor>
      <jndi-name>JtSessionFacade</jndi-name>
   </weblogic-enterprise-bean>
</weblogic-ejb-jar>
```

# 33.    ANDROID-SPECIFIC COMPONENTS

## 33.1    Interactive Voice Recognition (IVR)

```java
/**
 * Voice Recognizer component for the Android
 * platform (reference implementation).
 * Concurrency and asynchronous messaging capabilities
 * are inherited from the framework class. This class
 * implements a conceptual interface that communicates
 * with the Android IVR API. It can be readily
 * replaced by another platform-specific component
 * using the same conceptual interface without
 * any impact on the rest of the system.
 */

public class JtVoiceRecognizer extends JtComponent  {

        private static final long serialVersionUID = 1L;
        public static final String JtCLASS_NAME =
          JtVoiceRecognizer.class.getName();
        public static final int REQUEST_CODE_ID = 1234;
        public static final String  PROMPT = "PROMPT";
        public static final String  SENTENCE = "SENTENCE";
        public static final String  SPEECH = "SPEECH";
        public static final String  MATCHES = "MATCHES";


        private JtFactory factory = new JtFactory ();
        private JtLogger logger;


        public JtVoiceRecognizer() {

        }

        // Start voice recognition

        private void activateComponent (Object message) {
                JtActivityManager manager;
                JtMessage msg = new JtMessage
                  (JtComponent.JtACTIVATE);
                Intent intent = new
                  Intent(RecognizerIntent.ACTION_RECOGNIZE_SPEECH);
                String prompt;

                if (message == null)
                        return;

                intent.putExtra
                  (RecognizerIntent.EXTRA_LANGUAGE_MODEL,
                   RecognizerIntent.LANGUAGE_MODEL_FREE_FORM);
```

```
            prompt = (String) factory.getValue(message,
                            JtVoiceRecognizer.PROMPT);

            if (prompt != null)
                    intent.putExtra
                    (RecognizerIntent.EXTRA_PROMPT, prompt);


            manager = new JtActivityManager ();


            factory.setValue(msg,
                            JtActivityManager.INTENT, intent);
            factory.setValue(msg,
                            JtActivityManager.FOR_RESULT,
                            new Boolean (true));
            factory.setValue(msg,
                            JtActivityManager.REQUEST_CODE,
                            JtVoiceRecognizer.REQUEST_CODE_ID);

            manager.processMessage(msg);

    }

    // Retrieve the framework Logger

    private void locateLogger () {


            logger = (JtLogger)
              factory.lookupObject(JtFactory.jtLogger);

            if (logger == null) {
                    System.err.println
                      ("Unable lo locate Logger");
                    logger = new JtLogger ();
            }


    }

    /**
     * Process component messages:
     * <ul>
     * <li>JtACTIVATE - Start listening by invoking the Android
     * IVR API.
     * </ul>
     */

    @Override
    public Object processMessage(Object message) {

            Object msgId;

            if (message == null)
                    return (null);

            locateLogger ();
```

```java
        msgId = (String) factory.getValue
          (message, JtMessage.ID);

        if (msgId == null) {
                logger.processMessage
                (new JtError ("Invalid message Id:"
                  + null));
                return (null);
        }

        // Activate the component
        if (JtComponent.JtACTIVATE.equals(msgId)) {
                activateComponent (message);
                return (null);
        }

        if (JtComponent.JtREMOVE.equals(msgId)) {

                // Forward the message to the
                // superclass
                super.processMessage(message);
                return (null);
        }

        return (logger.processMessage
                (new JtError ("Invalid message Id:" +
                msgId)));

     }


}
```

## 33.2    Telephony

```
/**
 * Framework component for the Android telephony API
 * (reference implementation). A conceptual interface
 * is implemented. This Android component can be readily
 * replaced by another platform-specific component
 * using the same conceptual interface without
 * any impact on the rest of the system. Minimum software
 * changes (if any) are needed.
 */


public class JtPhone implements JtInterface {

        public static final String JtCLASS_NAME =
                JtPhone.class.getName();
        public static final String CALL = "CALL";
        public static final String NUMBER = "NUMBER";
        public static final String TIMESTAMP = "TIMESTAMP";

        public static final String JtOFFHOOK = "JtOFFHOOK";
        public static final String JtIDLE = "JtIDLE";
        public static final String JtRING = "JtRING";

        public static final String LISTENER = "LISTENER";

        public static final long RING_DELTA = 3000L;

        public static final String CURRENT_ACTIVITY =
                "CURRENT_ACTIVITY";

        public static final String toastComponent =
                "toastComponent";


        private static final long serialVersionUID = 1L;
        public JtLogger logger;

        private JtInterface controller;
        private JtPhone thisObject;

        JtFactory factory = new JtFactory ();

        public JtPhone () {
                thisObject = this;
        }


        private Context retrieveAppContext () {

                Object context;

                context = (JtConcept)
                factory.lookupObject(JtFactory.jtContext);
```

350

```
        if (context == null) {
                processError ("Invalid Jt context");
                return (null);
        }

        return ((Context) factory.getValue(context,
                        JtPhone.CURRENT_ACTIVITY));
}

// Handle errors

private Object processError (String errorMsg) {

        if (logger == null || errorMsg == null)
                return (null);

        return (logger.processMessage
                        (new JtError (errorMsg)));
}

// Retrieve framework Logger

private void locateLogger () {


        logger = (JtLogger)
        factory.lookupObject
        (JtFactory.jtLogger);

        if (logger == null) {
                System.err.println
                ("Unable lo locate Logger");
                logger = new JtLogger ();
        }

}

// Display message via the GUI component

private void displayMessage (String message) {
        JtMessenger messenger = new JtMessenger ();
        JtMessage msg =
                new JtMessage (JtComponent.JtACTIVATE);
        Object uiComponent;

        if (message == null || message.equals(""))
                return;

        uiComponent =
                factory.lookupObject(JtFactory.uiComponent);

        if (uiComponent == null) {
                logger.processMessage
                (new JtWarning
                  ("Unable to locate UI component"));
                return;
        }
```

```
                factory.setValue(msg, JtMessage.MESSAGE, message);
                factory.setValue(msg, JtMessage.WHAT,
                                JtPhone.toastComponent);

                messenger.setSynchronous(false);
                messenger.sendMessage(uiComponent, msg);

        }

        // Place a call

        private Object call(Object message) {
                JtActivityManager manager;
                JtMessage msg =
                        new JtMessage (JtComponent.JtACTIVATE);
                String phoneNumber;
                String tmp;

                if (message == null)
                        return (null);

                manager = new JtActivityManager ();

                phoneNumber = (String)
                factory.getValue(message, JtPhone.NUMBER);

                tmp = "tel:" + phoneNumber;

                try {
                        Intent callIntent =
                                new Intent(Intent.ACTION_CALL);
                        callIntent.setData(Uri.parse(tmp));

                        factory.setValue(msg,
                                        JtActivityManager.INTENT,
                                        callIntent);

                        manager.processMessage(msg);
                        return (null);
                } catch (Exception ex) {
                        displayMessage ("Unable to place call.");
                        return (logger.processMessage(ex));
                }
        }

        // Forward message to MVC Controller

        private void forwardToController (JtMessage msg) {
                JtMessenger messenger;

                if (msg == null || controller == null)
                        return;

                messenger = new JtMessenger ();

                messenger.setSynchronous(false);
                messenger.sendMessage(controller, msg);
```

```java
}

// Start listening

private Object activateListener(Object message) {
        Context context;

        context = retrieveAppContext ();

        if (context == null) {
          processError
                ("unable to retrieve current activity.");
          return (null);
        }

        TelephonyManager tm = (TelephonyManager)
        context.getSystemService
        (Context.TELEPHONY_SERVICE);

        if (message != null) {

                controller = (JtInterface)
                factory.getValue(message,
                        JtMessage.REPLY_TO);

                if (controller == null) {
                        processError
                        ("Invalid Controller:null");
                        return (null);
                }

        }




        PhoneStateListener mPhoneListener =
                new PhoneStateListener() {
                public void onCallStateChanged(int state,
                        String incomingNumber) {

        JtMessage msg;

        logger.processMessage ("State:" + state);


        try {
                switch (state) {

                // Phone is ringing
                case
                TelephonyManager.CALL_STATE_RINGING:

                  msg = new JtMessage
                  (JtPhone.JtRING);
```

```java
            if (controller != null) {
                factory.setValue(msg,

                    JtPhone.NUMBER,

                    incomingNumber);
                factory.setValue(msg,

                    JtPhone.TIMESTAMP,

                    new Date ());
                factory.setValue(msg,

                    JtMessage.FROM,

                    thisObject);
                forwardToController (msg);
            } else {
                processError
                    ("Invalid controller:null");
                return;
            }

            logger.processMessage
                ("Incoming number:" +

                    incomingNumber);
            break;
        // Off the hook
        case
          TelephonyManager.CALL_STATE_OFFHOOK:

            msg = new
            JtMessage (JtPhone.JtOFFHOOK);
            if (controller == null) {

                processError
                    ("Invalid controller:null");
                return;

            }

            factory.setValue(msg,
                JtMessage.FROM, thisObject);

            forwardToController (msg);

            logger.processMessage ("State:" +

"TelephonyManager.CALL_STATE_OFFHOOK");

            break;
        // Idle
        case
          TelephonyManager.CALL_STATE_IDLE:

            msg = new JtMessage
              (JtPhone.JtIDLE);
```

```
                    if (controller == null) {

                      processError
                        ("Invalid controller:null");
                          return;

                    }

                    factory.setValue(msg,
                            JtMessage.FROM,
                        thisObject);

                forwardToController (msg);

                logger.processMessage
                  ("JtPhone (state):" +

                "TelephonyManager.CALL_STATE_IDLE");

                  break;
                default:
                  logger.processMessage
                    ("JtPhone(state):"
                                            +

                  state);

                }
              } catch (Exception e) {
                      logger.processMessage (e);
              }
          }
    };

    int events =
    PhoneStateListener.LISTEN_SIGNAL_STRENGTH |
    PhoneStateListener.LISTEN_CALL_STATE |
    PhoneStateListener.LISTEN_CALL_FORWARDING_INDICATOR
    |
    PhoneStateListener.LISTEN_MESSAGE_WAITING_INDICATOR
    | PhoneStateListener.LISTEN_SERVICE_STATE;

    try {
            tm.listen(mPhoneListener, events);
            return (null);
    } catch (Exception ex) {
            return (logger.processMessage (ex));
    }
}
```

```java
/**
 * Process component messages.
 * <ul>
 * <li>CALL - Place a phone call.<br>
 *     NUMBER: phone number
 * <li>JtACTIVATE<br>
 *     WHAT:LISTENER. Start listening for events: ring,
 * off the hook, and Idle.
 * </ul>
 */

public Object processMessage(Object message) {

        Object msgId;
        String what;


        if (message == null)
                return (null);

        msgId = (String) factory.getValue
          (message, JtMessage.ID);

        if (msgId == null)
                return (null);


        locateLogger ();

        if (msgId.equals(JtComponent.JtACTIVATE)) {

                what = (String) factory.getValue(message,
                                JtMessage.WHAT);

                if (JtPhone.LISTENER.equals(what))
                        return (activateListener (message));
                else
                        return
                         (processError
                        ("Invalid message (JtACTIVATE): WHAT"
                                        + msgId));

        }

        if (msgId.equals(JtPhone.CALL))
                return (call (message));


        return (processError
                        ("Invalid message Id:" + msgId));
}

}
```

## 33.3 SMS Interface

```
/**
 * Framework component for the Android SMS API
 * (reference implementation). It implements
 * a straightforward conceptual interface.
 * This Android component can be readily
 * replaced by another platform-specific component
 * using the same conceptual interface without
 * any impact on the rest of the system. Minimum
 * software changes (if any) are needed.
 */

public class JtSMS extends JtComponent  {


        private static final long serialVersionUID = 1L;
        public static final String JtCLASS_NAME =
                JtSMS.class.getName();
        private Object context;
        private JtFactory factory = new JtFactory ();
        private JtLogger logger;

        public static final String PHONE_NUMBER = "PHONE_NUMBER";
        public static final String MESSAGE = "MESSAGE";
        public static final String JtSEND = "JtSEND";

        public static final String toastComponent =
                "toastComponent";

        public static final String CURRENT_ACTIVITY =
                "CURRENT_ACTIVITY";


        public JtSMS() {

        }



        // Retrieve framework Logger

        private void locateLogger () {

                logger = (JtLogger)
                  factory.lookupObject(JtFactory.jtLogger);

                if (logger == null) {
                        System.err.println
                          ("Unable lo locate Logger");
                        logger = new JtLogger ();
                }

        }
```

```java
/**
 * Returns the context.
 */

private Context retrieveAppContext () {

        Object context;

        context = (JtConcept)
          factory.lookupObject(JtFactory.jtContext);


        if (context == null) {
                logger.processMessage
                (new JtError ("Invalid Jt context"));
                return (null);
        }


        return ((Context) factory.getValue(context,
                    JtSMS.CURRENT_ACTIVITY));
}

// sends SMS message

private Object sendSMS(JtMessage message)
{
        String phoneNumber;
        String msg;
        String SENT = "SMS_SENT";
        SmsManager sms;
        ArrayList<String> arrayMsg;

        if (message == null)
                return (null);

        locateLogger ();

        context = retrieveAppContext ();

        if (context == null) {
                logger.processMessage
                (new JtError
                  ("unable to retrieve current activity"));
                return (null);
        }

        phoneNumber = (String)
        factory.getValue(message, JtSMS.PHONE_NUMBER);

        if (phoneNumber == null || phoneNumber.equals("")) {
                logger.processMessage
                (new JtError
                        ("Invalid message (phoneNumber)"));
                return (null);
        }

        phoneNumber = phoneNumber.trim();
```

```java
if (phoneNumber.equals("")) {
  logger.processMessage
  (new JtError
                ("Invalid message (phoneNumber)"));
  return (null);
}

msg = (String) factory.getValue(message,
                JtSMS.MESSAGE);

if (msg == null || msg.equals("")) {
        logger.processMessage
        (new JtError (
                "Invalid message (text message)."));
        return (null);
}

msg = msg.trim();

if (msg.equals("")) {
        logger.processMessage
        (new JtError
                ("Invalid message (text message)."));
        return (null);
}

PendingIntent sentPI =
        PendingIntent.getBroadcast((Context)context,
                        0,
                        new Intent(SENT), 0);


if (sentPI == null) {
        logger.processMessage (new
                JtError ("Invalid sentPI: null"));
        return (null);
}

logger.processMessage ("sentPI:" + sentPI);

//---when the SMS has been sent---
((Context) context).registerReceiver
    (new BroadcastReceiver(){
        @Override
        public void onReceive(Context context,
                        Intent arg1) {
                switch (getResultCode())
                {
                case Activity.RESULT_OK:
                  logger.processMessage
                  ("Text message has been sent.");
                        break;
                default:
                        logger.processMessage
                        ("Text message failed:" +

                                getResultCode());
                        break;
                }
```

```
                    }
        }, new IntentFilter(SENT));


        sms = SmsManager.getDefault();
        try {

                arrayMsg = sms.divideMessage(msg);

                // Check max size
                if (arrayMsg.size() == 1)
                        sms.sendTextMessage(phoneNumber,
                                null, msg, sentPI, null);
                else
                        sms.sendMultipartTextMessage
                                (phoneNumber,
                                null, arrayMsg, null, null);
                displayMessage (msg);
                return (null);
        } catch (Exception ex) {
                displayMessage
                  ("Unable to send SMS message.");
                return (logger.processMessage (ex));
        }
}

// Display message via the GUI component

private void displayMessage (String message) {
        JtMessenger messenger = new JtMessenger ();
        JtMessage msg = new
          JtMessage (JtComponent.JtACTIVATE);
        Object uiComponent;


        if (message == null || message.equals(""))
                return;

        uiComponent =
          factory.lookupObject(JtFactory.uiComponent);

        if (uiComponent == null) {
                logger.processMessage
                (new JtWarning
                        ("Unable to locate UI component"));
                return;
        }


        factory.setValue(msg,
                        JtMessage.MESSAGE, message);
        factory.setValue(msg,
                        JtMessage.WHAT,
                        JtSMS.toastComponent);

        messenger.setSynchronous(false);
        messenger.sendMessage(uiComponent, msg);


}
```

```java
private Object processError (String errorMsg) {

        if (logger == null || errorMsg == null)
                return (null);

        return (logger.processMessage
                        (new JtError (errorMsg)));
}

/**
 * Process component messages.
 * <ul>
 * <li>JtSEND - Send a SMS message.<br>
 * PHONE_NUMBER: recipient's phone number.<br>
 * MESSAGE: message to be sent.<br>
 * </ul>
 */

public Object processMessage (Object message) {
        Object Id;

        if (message == null)
                return (null);

        locateLogger ();

        Id = factory.getValue(message,
                        JtMessage.ID);

        if (Id == null)
                return (processError
                        ("Invalid message Id:" + null));

        if (JtSMS.JtSEND.equals (Id))
                return (sendSMS ((JtMessage) message));

        return (processError
                        ("Invalid Message Id:" + Id));

}

/**
 * Demonstrates the messages processed by the
 * SMS component.
 */

public static void main(String[] args) {

        JtFactory factory = new JtFactory ();

        JtSMS sms;
        JtMessage msg =
                new JtMessage (JtSMS.JtSEND);
```

361

```
        // Create the SMS component

        sms = (JtSMS)
          factory.createObject(JtSMS.JtCLASS_NAME);

        // Send a Text message

        factory.setValue(msg, JtSMS.PHONE_NUMBER,
                    "9991111111");
        factory.setValue(msg, JtSMS.MESSAGE,
                    "Text message");

        sms.processMessage(msg);
    }


}
```

## 33.4 Text-To-Speech (TTS)

```java
/**
 * Framework Text-to-Speech component for the
 * Android platform (reference implementation).
 * Concurrency and asynchronous messaging capabilities
 * are inherited from the framework class. This class
 * implements a conceptual interface that communicates
 * with the Android TTS API. A couple of messages
 * are required for a reference implementation: speak and
 * stop speaking. This Android component can be readily
 * replaced by another platform-specific component using the
 * same conceptual interface without any impact on the
 * rest of the system. Minimum software changes (if any)
 * are needed.
 */
public class JtTextToSpeech extends JtComponent implements
TextToSpeech.OnInitListener,
TextToSpeech.OnUtteranceCompletedListener {

  private static final long serialVersionUID = 1L;
  public static final String JtCLASS_NAME =
    JtTextToSpeech.class.getName();

  private TextToSpeech mTts;
  private boolean initialized = false;
  private JtFactory factory = new JtFactory ();
  private JtLogger logger;
  private Object replyTo = null;
  private boolean initialStatus = true;

  public static String jtTTSComponent = "jtTTSComponent";

  public static final String JtSPEAK = "JtSPEAK";
  public static final String JtSTOP_SPEAKING = "JtSTOP_SPEAKING";
  public static final String SENTENCE = "SENTENCE";
  public static final String QUEUE_MODE = "QUEUE_MODE";
  public static final String CURRENT_ACTIVITY = "CURRENT_ACTIVITY";

  public static final String UTTERANCE_COMPLETED =
    "UTTERANCE_COMPLETED";

  public static final int QUEUE_FLUSH = TextToSpeech.QUEUE_FLUSH;
  public static final int QUEUE_ADD = TextToSpeech.QUEUE_ADD;

  public static final String toastComponent = "toastComponent";

  public static final Long TIMEOUT = 1000L;

  public JtTextToSpeech() {

  }
```

```
// Shutdown TTS

public void remove () {
  if (mTts != null) {
    mTts.stop();
    mTts.shutdown();
  }
}


public void onInit(int status) {

  logger.processMessage ("JtTextToSpeech: onInit()");

  if (mTts == null) {
    logger.processMessage
    (new JtError
     ("Could not initialize TextToSpeech (mTts==null)."));
    displayMessage
    ("Unable initialize. Language is not available.");
    initialized = false;
    initialStatus = false;
    return;
  }

  if (status == TextToSpeech.SUCCESS) {
    // Set preferred language to US English.
    // Note that a language may not be available,
    // and the result will indicate it.
    int result = mTts.setLanguage(Locale.US);

    if (result == TextToSpeech.LANG_MISSING_DATA ||
        result == TextToSpeech.LANG_NOT_SUPPORTED) {
      // Language data is missing or the language is not
      // supported.
      logger.processMessage
      (new JtError ("Language is not available."));
      displayMessage
      ("Unable initialize component.Language is not available.");
      initialStatus = false;
    } else {

      initialized = true;

      logger.processMessage
        ("JtTextToSpeech: initialization complete.");

      // The TTS engine has been successfully initialized.

      initialStatus = true;
    }
```

```java
  } else {

    // Initialization failed.
    displayMessage
    ("Unable initialize component. Language is not available.");
    logger.processMessage
    (new JtError ("Could not initialize TextToSpeech."));
    initialStatus = false;
  }


}


// Display message via the GUI component

private void displayMessage (String message) {
  JtMessenger messenger = new JtMessenger ();
  JtMessage msg = new JtMessage (JtComponent.JtACTIVATE);
  Object uiComponent;

  if (message == null || message.equals(""))
    return;

  uiComponent = factory.lookupObject(JtFactory.uiComponent);

  if (uiComponent == null) {
    logger.processMessage
    (new JtError ("Unable to locate UI component"));
    return;
  }

  factory.setValue(msg, JtMessage.MESSAGE, message);
  factory.setValue(msg, JtMessage.WHAT,
      JtTextToSpeech.toastComponent);


  messenger.setSynchronous(false);
  messenger.sendMessage(uiComponent, msg);

}


// Speak

private void speak(String message, int queueMode) {

  HashMap<String, String> params = new HashMap<String, String>();
  params.put(TextToSpeech.Engine.KEY_PARAM_UTTERANCE_ID,
   message);

  if (mTts == null)
    return;

  mTts.setOnUtteranceCompletedListener(this);
```

```java
// Drop all pending entries in the playback queue.
if (queueMode != TextToSpeech.QUEUE_FLUSH &&
    queueMode != TextToSpeech.QUEUE_ADD)
  queueMode = TextToSpeech.QUEUE_FLUSH;

mTts.speak(message,
    queueMode,
    params);
}


public void onUtteranceCompleted(String utteranceId) {
  JtMessenger messenger = new JtMessenger ();
  JtMessage msg =
    new JtMessage (JtTextToSpeech.UTTERANCE_COMPLETED);

  logger.processMessage ("onUtteranceCompleted:" + utteranceId);

  if (replyTo != null) {
    messenger.setSynchronous(false);
    factory.setValue(msg,
        JtMessage.SUBJECT, utteranceId);
    factory.setValue(msg,
        JtMessage.IS_REPLY, new Boolean (true));
    messenger.sendMessage (replyTo, msg);
  }

}

// Sleep for a while

private void sleep (long period) {

  try {
    Thread.sleep (period);
    logger.processMessage ("sleep:" + period);
  } catch (Exception e) {
    logger.processMessage (e);
  }

}

private Context retrieveAppContext () {

  Object context;

  context = (JtConcept)
   factory.lookupObject(JtFactory.jtContext);

  if (context == null) {
    logger.processMessage
    (new JtError ("Invalid Jt context"));
    return (null);
  }

  return ((Context)
      factory.getValue(context,
```

```
                JtTextToSpeech.CURRENT_ACTIVITY));
}


// Initialize component

private boolean initialize () {

  Context context;

  logger.processMessage
  ("JtTextToSpeech: Initialize .... " + this);

  context = retrieveAppContext ();

  if (context == null) {
    logger.processMessage
    (new JtError
      ("unable to retrieve current activity"));
    return (false);
  }


  initialStatus = true;

  mTts = new TextToSpeech((Context) context,
      this  // TextToSpeech.OnInitListener
  );

  // Wait until initialized or Error detected

  while (!initialized && (initialStatus == true))
    sleep (JtTextToSpeech.TIMEOUT);

  return (initialStatus);

}

// Stop speaking

private void stopSpeaking () {
  if (mTts == null)
    return;

  if (mTts.stop() != TextToSpeech.SUCCESS)
    return;

}

/**
 * Process component messages:
 * <ul>
 * <li>JtSPEAK - Speak a sentence (SENTENCE).<br>
 * QUEUE_MODE: a) QUEUE_ADD. Add message to the queue.
 * b) QUEUE_FLUSH (default). Flush the queue and add the
 * new message.
 * <li>JtSTOP_SPEAKING - Stop speaking.
 * <li>JtREMOVE - Remove the TTS component (proper housekeeping
 * is performed).
```

367

```
 * </ul>
 */

@Override
public Object processMessage(Object message) {

  JtMessage mdpMsg;
  Object msgId;
  String sentence;
  Integer QueueMode;
  Object tmp;

  if (message == null)
    return (null);

  // Locate the Logger component

  logger = (JtLogger) factory.lookupObject(JtFactory.jtLogger);

  if (logger == null) {
    System.err.println
    ("Unable to locate Logger component");
    logger = new JtLogger ();
  }

  logger.processMessage
  ("JtTextToSpeech.processMessage:" + message);

  if (message instanceof JtMessage) {

    msgId = (String) factory.getValue (message, JtMessage.ID);


    // Initialize the component
    if (JtComponent.JtINITIALIZE.equals(msgId)) {
      if (!initialized)
        initialize ();

      return (null);
    }

    // Component is ready to be discarded
    if (JtComponent.JtREMOVE.equals(msgId)) {
      remove ();

      // Forward message to the
      // superclass
      super.processMessage(message);
      return (null);
    }
  }

  if (!initialized) {
    initialize ();

    if (!initialized)
      return (null);
  }
```

368

```java
if (message instanceof JtMessage) {

  mdpMsg = (JtMessage) message;
  msgId = (String)
  factory.getValue (mdpMsg, JtMessage.ID);

  if (msgId == null)
    return (null);


  if (JtTextToSpeech.JtSTOP_SPEAKING.equals(msgId)) {
    stopSpeaking ();
    return (null);
  }

  if (JtTextToSpeech.JtSPEAK.equals(msgId)) {
    sentence = (String)
    factory.getValue (mdpMsg, JtTextToSpeech.SENTENCE);

    QueueMode = (Integer)
    factory.getValue (mdpMsg, JtTextToSpeech.QUEUE_MODE);

    if (QueueMode == null)
      QueueMode = new Integer (JtTextToSpeech.QUEUE_FLUSH);

    if (sentence == null) {
      logger.processMessage
      (new JtError ("Invalid message (null sentence)"));
      return (null);
    }

    tmp = factory.getValue (mdpMsg, JtMessage.REPLY_TO);

    if (tmp != null)
      replyTo = tmp;

    speak (sentence, QueueMode.intValue());

  }

  logger.processMessage
  (new JtError ("Invalid message:" + message));
  return (null);
}

if (!(message instanceof String)) {
  logger.processMessage
  (new JtError ("Invalid message:" + message));
  return (null);
}

speak ((String) message, JtTextToSpeech.QUEUE_FLUSH);

return (null);

}

}
```

## 33.5    Location and GPS Interface

```
/**
 * Framework component for the Android Location and GPS API
 * (reference implementation). A conceptual interface
 * is implemented. This Animated/Live component can be readily
 * replaced by another platform-specific component
 * using the same conceptual interface without any
 * impact on the rest of the system. Minimum software
 * changes (if any) are needed.
 */


public class JtGPS extends JtComponent
implements LocationListener {


  private static final long serialVersionUID = 1L;
  public static final String JtCLASS_NAME = JtGPS.class.getName();
  public static final String LOCATION = "LOCATION";

  public static final String ACCURACY = "ACCURACY";
  public static final String LATITUDE = "LATITUDE";
  public static final String LONGITUDE = "LONGITUDE";
  public static final String PROVIDER = "PROVIDER";
  public static final String SPEED = "SPEED";
  public static final String ALTITUDE = "ALTIDUDE";
  public static final String TIME = "TIME";

  public static final String PROVIDER_DISABLED =
    "PROVIDER_DISABLED";
  public static final String PROVIDER_ENABLED = "PROVIDER_ENABLED";

  public static final String CURRENT_ACTIVITY = "CURRENT_ACTIVITY";
  public static final String SERIAL = "SERIAL";
  public static final String toastComponent = "toastComponent";

  private Object context;
  private JtFactory factory = new JtFactory ();
  private JtLogger logger;
  private boolean networkProviderEnabled = true;
  private boolean gpsProviderEnabled = true;
  private long minTime = 0L;
  private float minDistance = (float) 0.0;
  private Object replyTo = null; // Send reply to this component
  private String serial = null;
  private Object currentLocation =null;
  private LocationManager locationManager;
  private boolean status = false;
  private boolean repeat = false;
  private boolean synchronousMessaging = true;
  private boolean gpsDisabled = false;
  private boolean networkDisabled = false;
```

```java
public JtGPS() {

}


/**
 * Returns the value of the networkProviderEnabled flag
 * which specifies whether or not location updates should
 * be requested from the network provider.
 */

public boolean isNetworkProviderEnabled() {
  return networkProviderEnabled;
}

/**
 * Sets the networkProviderEnabled flag.
 */

public void setNetworkProviderEnabled
(boolean networkProviderEnabled) {
  this.networkProviderEnabled = networkProviderEnabled;
}

/**
 * Returns the value of the isGpsProviderEnabled flag which
 * specifies whether or not location updates should be
 * requested from the GPS provider.
 */

public boolean isGpsProviderEnabled() {
  return gpsProviderEnabled;
}

/**
 * Sets the networkProviderEnabled flag.
 */

public void setGpsProviderEnabled(boolean gpsProviderEnabled) {
  this.gpsProviderEnabled = gpsProviderEnabled;
}


/**
 * Returns the current location.
 */

public Object getCurrentLocation() {
  return currentLocation;
}

/**
 * void operation
 */

public void setCurentLocation(Object curentLocation) {

}
```

```java
/**
 * Returns the time (in milliseconds) between location
 * updates.
 */

public long getMinTime() {
  return minTime;
}

/**
 * Specifies the time (in milliseconds) between
 * location updates. To obtain notifications as frequently
 * as possible, set parameter to 0.
 */

public void setMinTime(long minTime) {
  this.minTime = minTime;
}


/**
 * Returns the minimum distance between location
 * updates.
 */

public float getMinDistance() {
  return minDistance;
}

/**
 * Specifies the minimum distance between location
 * updates. To obtain notifications as frequently
 * as possible, set parameter to 0.
 */

public void setMinDistance(float minDistance) {
  this.minDistance = minDistance;
}

/**
 * Specifies whether or not the component
 * should keep listening for location updates
 * after the first update.
 */

public boolean isRepeat() {
  return repeat;
}

public void setRepeat(boolean repeat) {
  this.repeat = repeat;
}

/*
 * Start listening for Location updates
 */

private Object activate (Object message) {
```

372

```
    Location location;
    Boolean Bool;

    replyTo = factory.getValue(message,
        JtMessage.REPLY_TO);
    serial = (String) factory.getValue(message,
        JtGPS.SERIAL);

    Bool = (Boolean) factory.getValue(message,
        JtMessage._SYNCHRONOUS);

    if (Bool != null)
      synchronousMessaging = Bool.booleanValue();

    gpsDisabled = false;
    networkDisabled = false;

    // Acquire a reference to the system Location Manager

    try {
      locationManager = (LocationManager)
      ((Context) context).getSystemService
      (Context.LOCATION_SERVICE);

      // Register the listener with the Location Manager
      // to receive location updates
      if (networkProviderEnabled)
        locationManager.requestLocationUpdates
        (LocationManager.NETWORK_PROVIDER,
            minTime, minDistance, this);

      if (gpsProviderEnabled)
        locationManager.requestLocationUpdates
        (LocationManager.GPS_PROVIDER, minTime,
            minDistance, this);

      location =
        locationManager.getLastKnownLocation
        (LocationManager.NETWORK_PROVIDER);
      logger.processMessage ("JtGPS(lastKnownLocation) ....");
      logLocation (location);
      status = true;
      return (null);
    } catch (Exception ex) {
      displayMessage ("Unable to start GPS component.");
      return (logger.processMessage (ex));
    }

}

private void removeListener () {
  // Remove the listener previously added
  try {
    locationManager.removeUpdates(this);
    status = false;
    logger.processMessage ("removeListener");
  } catch (Exception ex) {
    logger.processMessage (ex);
```

373

```
    }
  }

  private Context retrieveAppContext () {

    Object context;

    context = (JtConcept)
    factory.lookupObject(JtFactory.jtContext);


    if (context == null) {
      logger.processMessage
      (new JtError ("Invalid Jt context"));
      return (null);
    }

    return ((Context)
        factory.getValue(context,
          JtGPS.CURRENT_ACTIVITY));
  }

  // Retrieve the framework Logger

  private void locateLogger () {


    logger = (JtLogger)
    factory.lookupObject(JtFactory.jtLogger);

    if (logger == null) {
      System.err.println("Unable lo locate Logger");
      logger = new JtLogger ();
    }

  }

  // Display message via the GUI component

  private void displayMessage (String message) {
    JtMessenger messenger = new JtMessenger ();
    JtMessage msg = new JtMessage
    (JtComponent.JtACTIVATE);
    Object uiComponent;


    if (message == null || message.equals(""))
      return;

    uiComponent = factory.lookupObject(JtFactory.uiComponent);

    if (uiComponent == null) {
      logger.processMessage
      (new JtWarning ("Unable to locate UI component"));
      return;
    }

    factory.setValue(msg, JtMessage.MESSAGE, message);
    factory.setValue(msg, JtMessage.WHAT,
```

374

```
        JtGPS.toastComponent);

    messenger.setSynchronous(false);
    messenger.sendMessage(uiComponent, msg);

}

/**
 * Process component messages.
 * <ul>
 * <li>JtACTIVATE - Activate component to start listening
 * for location updates.
 * <li>JtDEACTIVATE - Deactivate component.
 * <li>JtREMOVE - Remove component.
 * </ul>
 */

public Object processMessage (Object message) {

    Object msgId;

    if (message == null)
        return (null);

    locateLogger ();

    if (!(message instanceof JtMessage)) {
        logger.processMessage
        (new JtError ("Invalid message format."));
        return (null);
    }


    context = retrieveAppContext ();

    if (context == null) {
        displayMessage
        ("Unable to start GPS component: context is missing.");
        logger.processMessage
        (new JtError ("Invalid context (null):"));
        return null;
    }

    msgId = factory.getValue(message, JtMessage.ID);

    /*
     * Start listening for Location updates
     */

    if (msgId.equals(JtComponent.JtACTIVATE)) {
        if (status)
            removeListener ();
        return (activate (message));
    }

    if (msgId.equals(JtComponent.JtDEACTIVATE)) {
        removeListener ();
        return (null);
```

```
    }

    if (msgId.equals(JtComponent.JtREMOVE)) {
      removeListener ();

      // Forward the message to the
      // superclass
      super.processMessage(message);
      return (null);
    }

    return (logger.processMessage
        (new JtError ("Invalid message Id:" +
            msgId)));


}

// Log the current location

public void  logLocation (Location location) {
  if (location == null) {
    logger.processMessage ("JtGPS(location): null");
    return;
  }
  logger.processMessage("Accuracy:" + location.getAccuracy());
  logger.processMessage("Latitude:" + location.getLatitude());
  logger.processMessage("Longitude:" + location.getLongitude());
  logger.processMessage("Provider:" + location.getProvider());
  logger.processMessage("Speed:" + location.getSpeed());
  logger.processMessage("Altitude:" + location.getAltitude());
  logger.processMessage("Time:" + location.getTime());
}


// Location update

public void onLocationChanged(Location location) {

  JtMessage message = new JtMessage (JtGPS.LOCATION);
  JtMessenger messenger = new JtMessenger ();

  logger.processMessage("onLocationChanged:" + location);
  if (location == null)
    return;
  if (synchronousMessaging)
    messenger.setSynchronous(true);
  else
    messenger.setSynchronous(false);

  // Returns the GPS information as
  // a concept (message).


  factory.setValue(message,
      JtMessage.SUBJECT, JtGPS.LOCATION);
  factory.setValue(message,
      JtMessage.IS_REPLY, new Boolean (true));
  factory.setValue(message,
```

376

```java
        JtGPS.LATITUDE, new Double (location.getLatitude()));
    factory.setValue(message,
        JtGPS.LONGITUDE, new Double (location.getLongitude()));
    factory.setValue(message,
        JtGPS.ACCURACY, new Double (location.getAccuracy()));
    factory.setValue(message,
        JtGPS.PROVIDER, location.getProvider());
    factory.setValue(message,
        JtGPS.ALTITUDE, new Double (location.getAltitude()));
    factory.setValue(message,
        JtGPS.SPEED, new Double (location.getSpeed()));
    factory.setValue(message,
        JtGPS.TIME, new Long (location.getTime()));

    // Serial to be matched by the component
    // requesting Location information.
    factory.setValue(message, JtGPS.SERIAL, serial);

    if (replyTo != null) {

      messenger.sendMessage(replyTo, message);

      if (!repeat)
        removeListener ();
    }
    currentLocation = message;
    logLocation (location);

}

public void onProviderDisabled(String provider) {
    JtMessenger messenger = new JtMessenger ();
    JtMessage message = new JtMessage (JtGPS.LOCATION);

    logger.processMessage("onProviderDisabled:" + provider);

    if (LocationManager.NETWORK_PROVIDER.equals(provider))
      networkDisabled = true;

    if (LocationManager.GPS_PROVIDER.equals(provider))
      gpsDisabled = true;

    if (!(networkDisabled && gpsDisabled))
      return;

    // Both providers are disabled. Notify the user.

    factory.setValue(message,
        JtMessage.SUBJECT, JtGPS.PROVIDER_DISABLED);
    factory.setValue(message,
        JtMessage.IS_REPLY, new Boolean (true));

    if (replyTo != null)
      messenger.sendMessage(replyTo, message);


}

public void onProviderEnabled(String provider) {
```

```java
    logger.processMessage("onProviderEnabled:" +
        provider);
}

public void onStatusChanged(String provider, int status, Bundle
extras) {

    logger.processMessage ("onStatusChanged(" + provider + "):"
        + status);

}


}
```

# REFERENCES

1. Boole, G. *An Investigation of the Laws of Thought on Which are Founded the Mathematical Theories of Logic and Probabilities.* Macmillan. Reprinted with corrections, Dover Publications, New York, NY, 1958.

2. Galvis, A. *Messaging Design Pattern and Pattern Implementation.* 17th conference on Pattern Languages of Programs - PLoP 2010.

3. Turing, A. *Computing Machinery and Intelligence.* Mind 1950.

4. Galvis, A. *Process Design Pattern and a Realistic Information Model.* 18th conference on Pattern Languages of Programs (writers' workshop) - PLoP 2011.

5. Galvis, A. *Messaging Design Pattern and Live or Animated Objects.* 18th conference on Pattern Languages of Programs (writers' workshop) - PLoP 2011.

6. Lamport, L. *The implementation of Reliable Distributed Multiprocess Systems.* Computer Networks. 1978.

7. Hewitt, C. E. *Viewing Control Structures as Patterns of Passing Messages.* MIT. Artificial Intelligence Laboratory. A.I. Memo 410, December 1976.

8. Galvis, E. A. and Galvis D. E. *Concepts and a Realistic Information Model.* Submitted for publication.

9. Gregor Hohpe and Bobby Woolf. *Enterprise Integration Patterns: Designing, Building, and Deploying Messaging Solutions.* Addison-Wesley, 2004.

10. Galvis, E. A. *Jt - Java Pattern Oriented Framework, An application of the Messaging Design Pattern.* IBM Technical Library, 2010.

11. Gamma, E. et al. *Design Patterns: Abstraction and Reuse of Object-Oriented Design.* ECOOP '93 Proceedings of the 7th European Conference on Object-Oriented Programming.

12. Fielding, R. T. Architectural Styles and the Design of Network-based Software Architectures. Ph.D. Dissertation. University of California, 2000.

13. Bih, J. *Service Oriented Architecture (SOA) a new paradigm to implement dynamic e-business solutions.* ACM ubiquity, August, 2006.

14. Henning, M. *Rise and Fall of CORBA.* ACM queue, June, 2006.

15. Loughran S. et al. *Rethinking the Java SOAP Stack.* IEEE International Conference of Web Services (ICWS) 2005. Orlando, USA, 2005.

16. Schneider, F. B. *Implementing fault-tolerant services using the state machine approach: A tutorial.* ACM Computing Surveys. 1990.

17. Michael B. et al. *BPELJ:BPEL for Java.*BEA Systems Inc. and IBM Corp.USA, 2004.

18. Wollrath, A. et al. *A distributed Object Model for the Java System.* Proceeding of the USENIX 1996. Toronto, Canada, 1996.

19. Ambler, S. W. *Process Patterns: Building Large-Scale Systems Using Object Technology.* SIGS Books/Cambridge University Press, July 1998.

20. Goth, G. *Critics say Web Services need a REST.* IEEE distributed systems online. Vol. 5. No. 12, 2004.

21. Sowa, J. *Cognitive Architectures for Conceptual Structures,* Proceedings of ICCS 2011, Heidelberg: Springer, 2011, pp. 35-49.

22. Roberts, S. on George Boole. *The Isaac Newton of logic.* The Globe and Mail. March 27, 2004.
http://www.theglobeandmail.com/life/the-isaac-newton-of-logic/article1129894/?page=1

23. Von Newman, J. *First Draft of a Report on the EDVAC.* 1945.

24. Chen, P. *The Entity-Relationship Model--Toward a Unified View of Data.* In Communications of the ACM, 1(1).1976.

25. Newell, A. and Simon, H. *Computer Science as Empirical Inquiry: Symbols and Search.* In Communications of the ACM, 19 (3).1976.

26. Backus, J. *Can Programming Be Liberated From the von Neumann Style?* 1977 Turing Award Lecture.

27. Sowa, J. *Conceptual graphs for a database interface.* IBM Journal of Research and Development, vol. 20, no. 4, pp. 336-357. 1976

28. Nilsson, N. *The Physical Symbol System Hypothesis: Status and Prospects.* In M. Lungarella, et al., (eds.), 50 Years of AI, Festschrift, LNAI 4850, pp. 9-17, Springer, 2007.

29. Granger R. *Essential circuits of cognition: The brain's basic operations, architecture and representation.* University of California Irvine and Dartmouth College. 2006.

30. *Stanford Encyclopedia of Philosophy.* http://plato.stanford.edu/

31. Tegmark, Max. *The Mathematical Universe.* Foundations of Physics 38 (2): 101–150. 2008.

32. Newell, A.*Unified Theories of Cognition*, Harvard University Press. 1994.

33. Fodor, J. *The Language of Thought*, Harvard University Press. 1975.

34. Johnson-Laird, P. *Mental models: Towards a cognitive science of language, inference, and consciousness.* 1983.

35. *Survey of the State of the Art in Human Language Technology.* Cole R. Editor. 1997.

36. Gamma, E. et al. *Design Patterns: Elements of Reusable Object-Oriented Software.* Addison-Wesley Professional, Reading, MA, 1994.

37. Chidamber S. and Kemerer C. *A metrics suite for object-oriented design.* IEEE Trans. on Software Engineering, June 1994.

38. Basili, V. et at. *A Validation of Object-Oriented Design Metrics as Quality Indicators.* IEEE Trans. on Software Engineering, October 1996.

39. Rosenberg, L. et al. *Risk-based object oriented testing.* Twenty Fourth Annual Software Engineering Workshop, NASA, 1999

40. Tegarden, D. et al. *A software complexity model of object-oriented systems.* Decision Support Systems: The International Journal, January 1993.

41. Lorenz, M. et al. *Object-Oriented software metrics*, Prentice-Hall. 1994.

42. Lie, W. et at. *Object-oriented metrics that predict maintainability.* Journal of Systems and Software. February 1993.

43. Wooldridge, M. *Multiagent Systems: Introduction (2nd Edition).* John Wiley & Sons. 2009.

44. Krueger, C. W. *Software reuse*. ACM Computing Surveys, 24(2), June 1992.

45. Henry Lieberman and Hugo Liu. *Feasibility Studies for Programming in Natural Language*. End-User Development, Springer, 2005

# APPENDIX

## A.  Traditional Application Interfaces (APIs)

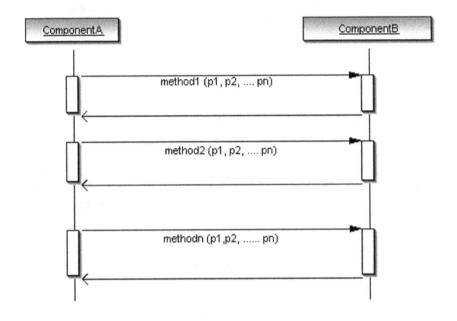

**Fig. 1. Traditional Application Interface**

This section was initially included for the benefit of the people who reviewed the work and requested a complete comparison. The diagram above represents a conventional API (function/method invocation) and its associated parameters. The conventional approach does not rely on messaging. It is overlooked. Component functionality and communication mechanism are tightly coupled. They cannot be changed independently.

The resulting shortcomings become evident – especially in the context of distributed/multithreaded OO technologies and models. Some of the problems related to traditional APIs (procedure calling and parameter passing) have been discussed by authors with comprehensive insight into the matter [26]. The lack of "conceptual usefulness" is also discussed, in regards to "concepts that help us to formulate and reason about processes".

For comparison purposes the statement made by Alan Kay and others should be carefully considered: "We can note in passing that one of the biggest problems in the development of object-oriented SW architectures, particularly in the last 25 years, has been an enormous over-focus on objects and an under-focus on **messaging** (most so-called object-oriented languages don't *really* use the looser coupling of messaging, but instead use the much *tighter gear meshing of procedure calls* – this hurts scalability and interoperability)." Alan Kay et al.

**Coupling**: Participant components are tightly coupled. There is no separation between component functionality provided by the API, information being transferred, and communication mechanism. Changes to the component API (method/function signature) require all the dependent components to be *simultaneously* changed. Some languages provide method overloading which partially alleviates the issues. However, it may be difficult to discern which method is being called. Methods with a large number of parameters may be required some of which are not always used. The information primitive, part of a realistic conceptual interface, requires a single parameter (message) and a straightforward set of predefined message types.

In general, traditional APIs are tied to specific computer language or technology and such functionality cannot be readily reused as part of heterogeneous systems without a considerable amount of effort. All method parameters must be rigidly passed regardless of whether or not they are needed for processing. A message, on the other hand, is represented as a concept: $M=\{a1, a2, , an\}$ which provides versatility and is able to encapsulate the exact structure and amount of information required – without redundancy. Messages can take all types of forms depending on the information to be transferred. It mimics the natural language where sentences (messages) can have all sorts of structures depending on what needs to be expressed.

**Reusability:** Traditional APIs present reusability limitations. In general, components cannot be reused individually because of dependencies on other components. It is usually necessary to include a complete monolithic library of components (jar) which impacts the overall application size. Versioning challenges also have a negative impact on reusability. A matching version of the component library is required because traditional APIs do not share the versioning versatility exhibited by conceptual interfaces based on messaging. Such requirement is the source of additional complexity/cost since it introduces the need for keeping and maintaining multiple versions of the component library. It is not uncommon for a system to fail because of version incompatibilities. The topic is discussed in more detail as part of this section.

As mentioned above, traditional APIs are tied to specific computer language or technology. Typical traditional APIs cannot be readily reused as part of distributed applications, SOA services, BPEL/BPM processes and concurrent applications.

**Encapsulation**: Components that rely on traditional APIs are not totally encapsulated as shown above. A web of dependencies gets created. Changes to the traditional API (method/function signature) require all the dependent components to be *simultaneously* changed. The API becomes difficult to maintain. Instead of single/straightforward message, the API may require a large number of parameters. A message is able to encapsulate the exact amount of information required for communication. The traditional API is rigid and requires all the parameters to be passed whether or not they are needed for processing.

**Multithreading artifacts**: Conventional APIs require the implementation of separate multithreading logic which is time consuming, complex, and error-prone. Software defects are difficult to avoid, reproduce and isolate (thread management, synchronization, race conditions, deadlocks, etc). The implementation or reuse of the Live/Animated component abstraction for concurrent processing is not feasible.

**Versioning**: Projects based on traditional APIs usually require separate versions of the software to be created, maintained, and merged which can be convoluted, taxing and prone to error. It becomes hard and cumbersome to prevent bugs from occurring. Each project member is required to keep a copy for individual use, since changes made by other team members, to the traditional component APIs, are likely to prevent the software from compiling and running. Because of tight coupling, changes to the API (method signature), require simultaneous changes to multiple components.

At several points during the project life, the individual versions need to be merged in order to incorporate the changes made by every team member. The process of creating, maintaining and merging several versions can be costly, cumbersome, and unreliable. It is fairly easy to introduce bugs due to incompatible changes. Because of all the component dependencies, it becomes hard to keep accurate track of all the software updates and complicated web of component interdependencies. The problem gets severely exacerbated as the number of team members, components, and dependencies increases.

**Distributed Component and Services**: Traditional APIs cannot be readily included as part of distributed applications or SOA services. Distributed access to conventional APIs cannot be implemented via a reusable remote proxy. The conventional approach requires the implementation of a separate set of distributed artifacts for each remote component. This includes the required stubs/skeleton classes, WSDL descriptors, or similar artifacts. In general, the functionality required to establish communication between local and remote components cannot be reused.

Consider that a production system probably needs to handle a substantial amount of distributed components and concurrent threads of execution. The complexity associated with such distributed/multithreaded application quickly becomes hard to manage under traditional APIs. Remote components need to handle multiple procedure/method calls with multiple parameters each (p1 ... pn). The approach becomes fairly complicated since we need to consider the stub/skeleton classes, IDLs, WSDL descriptors or similar constructs that are required to implement remote procedure/method invocation. Parameter/method changes require a fair amount of work in terms of maintaining the additional constructs (i.e. artifacts).

**Scalability:** Traditional APIs present scalability limitations[2]. Because of coupling, client and server software need to be upgraded at the same time which is usually complicated for large installations and/or operations running 24/7.

**BPM/BPEL applications and processes:** Conventional BPEL/BPM approaches inherit complexities, limitations, and shortcomings because of their reliance on *artificial* abstractions, distributed constructs, and multithreading. Their associated primitives present complexity, interoperability issues, and implementation challenges. As a consequence of the proposed model and single information primitive, the BPEL parallel primitives (activities) become redundant and the source of unnecessary complexity: <flow>. Many other BPEL primitives become redundant as well: <pick>, <receive>, <reply>, and <correlation>.

Traditional APIs cannot be readily reused as part of BPEL/BPM processes. As discussed earlier, traditional APIs also require complicated multithreading artifacts for the implementation of concurrent processing. Such functionality cannot be reused via a framework and the Animated/Live component abstraction.

**QA/Testing process:** Traditional APIs, not based on messaging, cannot be tested by sending messages to fully independent components and verifying the expected reply messages, via test hardness (black-box testing). Because of coupling and API dependencies it may also be hard to test components as independent units. In general, there is the need to include testing code inside the component code which can be time consuming and lead to the unexpected introduction of software defects.

**Logging and Debugging:** Under a messaging paradigm, messages can be logged automatically. By taking a look at the messages being interchanged and automatically logged, the user is usually able to quickly track down the message/component that is causing the problem (with minimum or no extra effort). Traditional APIs on the other hand, often present the need for print/logging statements inside the code which can be time consuming and error-prone.

**Access Control and Security**: Implementing access control and security becomes more complicated under conventional APIs because of coupling and the lack of a common messaging interface. Message-level security is, in general, not feasible. Transport level security is often required, which is computationally expensive.

**Lack of Interoperability**: Due in great part to the lack of decoupling, conventional APIs present interoperability limitations. The solution is tightly coupled to a specific language, technology and/or platform. Platforms, languages, and technologies cannot be freely incorporated within the context of a process. Considerable time and effort is required for the implementation of heterogeneous SOA systems. On the other hand, the proposed model is independent of technology and platform. Animated/Live components can interoperate freely as part of heterogeneous applications. Notice that no artifacts or component changes are needed to make Animated/Live components interoperable within the context of distributed applications/services.

**Obsolescence:** Because of dependencies on specific language or technology, traditional APIs are more likely to become obsolete once the technology is replaced by newer ones. Traditional APIs are less adaptable to changing requirements. Consider that a large number of systems have had to go through expensive and involved conversions once the underlying language or technology became obsolete. Such platform changes are costly and produce limited benefits when it comes to new software functionality. Most of the resources are usually spent on getting the software to provide the same or similar level of functionality under a new platform.

Traditional APIs and components are not readily exposable as SOA services, or via distributed component access, which may become a likely requirement as computer systems become more and more interconnected. A similar situation occurs when traditional APIs need to become part of business processes and technologies (BPEL/BPM) – or when concurrent processing is required. It also becomes more difficult to employ native interfaces, like JNI, as part of applications that rely on heterogeneous languages in order to avoid expensive software conversions.

Man-machine interfaces via voice recognition, a form of messaging, are becoming more common these days. Traditional APIs, not based on the conceptual approach, are rigid and ill-equipped to handle these changing requirements. Conceptual interfaces on the other hand are more adaptable to evolving requirements and less likely to become outdated.

**Exception/Error handling**: Handling of errors and exceptions can become complicated when dealing with traditional APIs. For instance, the graphical user interface (GUI) may need to report the error/exception detected by a remote component or service. Many layers of components may be involved. A mechanism to propagate the exception all the way back to the GUI is required.

Under traditional multithreaded/distributed approaches, such mechanism is difficult to implement. It usually requires changes to the multiple components and methods which in turn involves corresponding modifications to the distributed artifacts. As discussed earlier, such software modifications require a fair amount of work and effort. A reusable propagation mechanism is usually not feasible. The proposed model, on the other hand, makes a framework and messaging pipeline feasible. New components can be seamlessly plugged in. Errors and exceptions can be automatically propagated by the framework to the sender using the common messaging interface.

**Complexity, Cost and Timelines:** all the factors listed above have a negative impact on overall software complexity and therefore on project cost and timelines.

**Quality, risk, and software maintenance:** Overall complexity and all the other factors listed previously have a negative impact on quality, risk, and software maintenance activities.

## B. Comparison with other approaches and technologies including the Actor Model

"In these times brimming with excitement, our task is nothing less than to discover a *new, broader*, notion of computation, and to understand the world around us in terms of information processing." Grzegorz Rozenberg and Lila Kari

This appendix describes some of the main differences between the proposed approach and other approaches including the Actor model. It is mainly provided for the benefit of the people who have requested a detailed comparison. We will rely on its mathematical model summarized as follows.

a) **Information machine (A):** An automatic machine able to perform computations via the information primitive which defines the machine's single function (or purpose). The machine A is Turing complete.

f) **Information primitive**: Single function *processInformation (message)* where the message represents conceptual information (C).

g) **Concept (C)**: pure information expressed by a single language Construct, $C = \{a1, a2, , a_n\}$ where $a1, a2, , a_n$ are information associations.

For comparison purposes, let us propose criteria based on the following main aspects:

**Completeness:** The proposed approach is able to accommodate *all* the concepts found in reality. The mathematical concepts (3) found in the model itself mirror the ones leveraged by the conceptual mind: a) Entity or machine with a single function or purpose. b) Processing of information expressed by single function (primitive). c) Information in the form of Concepts (C). This represents a streamlined and complete set: Turing Completeness has been demonstrated via formal proof (see chapter on Information Machines and Turing Completeness). A compact set of natural concepts (3) can be applied to solve, in a comprehensive and natural fashion, an otherwise complex problem. No additional abstractions or primitives are required as part of the straightforward model based on nature.

**Simplicity**: This aspect can be compared by using the number of primitives and abstractions required by the mathematical model. The proposed approach relies on three (3) main concepts: Turing-complete information machine, single information primitive, and single concept construct (C).

Additionally, based on the conceptual approach, straightforward metrics of conceptual complexity can be proposed. Given an arbitrary model, applied to a problem or application domain (D) defined as a set of concepts (including abstractions and associated primitives):

$D = \{C1, C2, , Cn\}$  C1, ,Cn represent concepts (including primitives)

a) *Number of Main Concepts(NMC)*:  NMC = Cardinality (D)

This metric is similar in semantics to NKC (number of key classes) applied to the realm of concepts (C) [ 41]. A main concept is defined as one that is not part of any other concept. In the case of the proposed information machine, there are three main concepts involved: NMC = 3. A message is not a main concept because it represents information – already counted as part of the concept of information which is a 'broader' entity.

The problem/application domain (D) can be visualized as a graph: Concepts (C) represent the nodes and the associations represent the edges of the graph. An additional metric can be proposed based on the size of the graph (size (D)):

b) *Size of the Problem Domain (Problem Size)*: Size (D)

Notice that NMC is equal to the order of the graph: NMC = Order (D). For the particular problem of information processing, the graph can be visualized as an equilateral triangle with all three edges interconnected by associations. The size of the problem can be calculated: Size (D) = 3.

391

c) *Conceptual Complexity (Complexity)*: Complexity (D) = $\sum$ Complexity (Ci); i <= n

The complexity of a particular concept (C) can be measured based on the associations with other concepts in the domain (D): the edges of the graph ($e_1$, $e_m$) connected to the concept (C).

Complexity (Ci) = $\sum$ Complexity (ej); j <= m

If all edge complexities are considered to be unity, then the conceptual complexity is equal to the size of the problem/application domain (D): Complexity (D) = Size (D). Intuitively speaking, it can be said that the complexity of a problem/application domain (D) can be roughly measured by using problem size as defined by Size (D). For our particular problem domain, Complexity (D) = Size (D) = 3.

It is widely accepted that simplicity is a theoretical, scientific, and engineering virtue. The principle is known as Occam's razor: All other things being equal, simpler theories are better. Through the years, it has been stated in multiple forms:

"If a thing can be done adequately by means of one [concept], it is superfluous to do it by means of several; for we observe that nature does not employ two instruments [concepts] where one suffices". St. Thomas Aquinas.

"Nature is pleased with simplicity, and affects not the pomp of superfluous causes [concepts]." Isaac Newton.

Excuse the liberty of employing the term concept when appropriate. The term is applicable, in particular, to the natural concepts applied to processing of information. Notice that the complexity metrics provided above represent a way in which simplicity can be quantified. The chapter dealing with Model Evaluation discusses additional metrics.

An arbitrary model (M) is a concept that can be expressed as the graph of abstractions (i.e. concepts) included in the model:

M = {C1, , Cn}

Based on Occam's razor, and all things being the same, the theoretical model that maximizes simplicity represents a better model. The proposed metrics Complexity (M), Size (D) and NMC can be employed to quantify the aspect of simplicity. Furthermore, Biomimetics tells us that Mother Nature knows best as expressed by natural concepts and related model(s). It is evident that nature excels in terms of simplicity as far as information processing is concerned. Therefore, computer software must follow. A great degree of complexity in software is just unnatural and caused in large part by unrealistic/redundant abstractions, primitives, and APIs (i.e. artifacts). Obviously, *information* technologies, including software technologies, should be focused on the fundamental concept of information. To gain substantial improvements, software must mirror nature's design and solution to the challenge or 'problem' of information processing: conceptual mind!

**Efficiency:** This aspect can also be evaluated based on the number of abstractions and primitives that are part of the model and its associated implementation. The proposed model leaves no room for unnecessary redundancy and inefficiencies: single information primitive and single concept construct(C). Three (3) concepts in total define the Turing-complete information machine. These three concepts are implementable entities that mirror the ones leveraged by the conceptual mind. The number of class components (NC/NMC) is also significantly reduced since most entities represent Concepts (C) unable to process information. Additional efficiency metrics are part of the section dealing with Model Evaluation and Metrics.

Economy and efficiency are also associated with Occam's razor :

"Nature does not multiply things [concepts] unnecessarily; that she makes use of the easiest and simplest means [concepts] for producing her effects; that she does nothing in vain, and the like." Galileo Galilei.

"Rudiments [Concepts] or principles must not be unnecessarily multiplied." Immanuel Kant.

Notice the correspondence between Occam's razor and the proposed model: one information machine defined by single information primitive and single concept construct (C). It seems obvious that nature has a fixation with the number one: zero redundancy or inefficiency. "Nature does not multiply [Concepts] unnecessarily ...".

**Effectivity:** Due to Turing completeness, the proposed approach can be leveraged for the comprehensive implementation of arbitrary information technologies and models. Areas of application include SOA, OO, Component Framework, distributed component models/technologies, BPEL/BPM/ESB technologies, and Concurrent/Parallel architectures. The approach is also very effective in solving, in a natural fashion, complex problems found in the real world related to information processing. The implementation of traditional multithreaded/distributed applications is a complex undertaking, costly, and hampered by risks/issues: a) Complexity. b) Strong coupling. c) Lack of encapsulation and reusability. d) Scalability and interoperability limitations. e) Complex quality issues that include race conditions, deadlocks, thread management defects, and so on. The proposed approach can be leveraged to solve these issues in a comprehensive fashion.

**Mathematical Foundations**: Backus provided criteria for classifying models of computing [26]. Such classification is a useful tool that can also be applied to compare the proposed model. Mathematical foundation is one of the fundamental aspects: "Is there an elegant and concise mathematical description of the model? Is it useful in proving helpful facts about the behavior of the model? Or is the model so complex that its description is bulky and of little mathematical use?"

Absolutely. As shown above, a very concise and straightforward mathematical model that clearly expresses all the concepts associated with the model and their interrelationships (Complexity (D) = 3). Model elegance is synonymous with the syntactic simplicity (Occam's razor) achieved by the model. It measures the number and conciseness of the model's basic concepts. Furthermore, consider that providing a comprehensive mathematical *model* is not the focus of many of the *systems* and *technologies* discussed in this appendix. Such systems and

394

technologies are based on conventional programming languages/APIs which mathematical foundations are "complex, bulky, not useful" [26].

The proposed approach provides a complete mathematical foundation for every single level of organization: an object/component, a service, a process, an application, a system, a computer, and arbitrary groups of these entities. For instance, a component can be modeled using its precise mathematical definition: $A = (f(m), I)$. So can a full-blown computer that mirrors the mind: $(A = (f(m), I))$.

A process/system/application can be mathematically modeled as a collection of these information machines or components ($\{A_1, , A_n\}$ where $A_i = (f(m), I))$ working concurrently (or in parallel) and communicating via messaging. Arbitrary aspects of the world around us can be realistically and accurately modeled in a concise mathematical fashion – in particular, the mind's cognitive/AI abilities ('intelligent software'). Notice that no new primitives, APIs, or artifacts are required. They only contribute to unnatural redundancy and complexity.

**Clarity and conceptual usefulness of programs**. This element is also included by Backus as part of his criteria: "Are programs of the model clear expressions of a process or computation? Do they embody *concepts* that help us to formulate and reason about processes?"

Absolutely. Actually, the conceptual approach is based on a streamlined group of realistic concepts extracted and mirrored from reality. In other words, the conceptual approach incorporates exactly the same concepts found in real-world processes. In particular, consider the concepts part of the information pattern family. There is a one-to-one correspondence between reality and the concepts employed. No artificial abstractions, primitives, and APIs are part of the model, including "the complex machinery of procedure declarations" associated with traditional APIs and parameter passing [26].

As a consequence, the implementation is clear and conceptually useful. This aspect is related to the level of abstraction. It is widely accepted that higher levels of abstraction are conducive to software improvements [26, 11, 44]. By mirroring the conceptual mind, the proposed approach operates at a high level: conceptual level.

The entities contained in the mathematical model represent high level concepts: Information, Animated/Live entity, and information primitive. Program based on conventional programming languages/APIs can be moderately clear, *are not very useful conceptually* [26]. The complete criteria proposed by Backus can be found in the chapter dealing with Model Evaluation and Metrics.

You might wonder how the proposed paradigm is directly related to software problems, like software maintenance for example. Although it should sound redundant, every *information* technology is about the fundamental concepts of information and information processing. The terms being utilized makes it unequivocal and accurate. In a strategic sense, identifying, targeting, and framing the critical problem(s) is as important, and often more important, than finding solutions. Problems around these technologies must be framed using the appropriate paradigm, concepts, and context.

The main focus must be on the fundamental concept of information, not software. Computer software represents the vehicle by which the fundamental purpose can be achieved: processing of information. Furthermore, nature already provided the best known model and solution for information related challenges and problems: conceptual mind. In consequence, by mirroring the mind's conceptual framework, software can be improved in many respects including level of abstraction, overall complexity, encapsulation, reusability, versioning, coupling, maintainability, interoperability, cost, timeframe, and so on (see Model Evaluation and Metrics).

"Present account of models of computation highlights several topics of importance for the development of new understanding of computing and its role: natural computation and the relationship between the model and physical implementation, interactivity as fundamental for computational modeling of concurrent *information processing systems* such as living organisms and their networks, and the new developments in logic needed to support this generalized framework. Computing understood as *information processing* is closely related to natural sciences; it helps us recognize connections between sciences, and provides a **unified approach** for modeling and simulating of both living and non-living systems." Gordana Dodig-Crnkovic

396

**Realism and Correspondence**: Conceptualization represents the identification or extraction from reality of all the concepts relevant to the application or problem domain (D). Carefully consider that nature and its processes already exhibit an inherent design and a set of associated natural concepts. In order to achieve true correspondence and realism, we must mirror the natural design as part of the software design and implementation. Obviously, there is no point in 'reinventing' a design that already exists. The imitation of the natural design via conceptualization is an attainable goal, consistent with Biomimetics, which produces benefits in the realm of software engineering. A similar principle applies to man-made processes which already have and inherent design and may need to be automated as part of computer systems.

To attain true correspondence, there must be one-to-one correspondence between the implemented abstractions and the concepts extracted from conceptualization. In other words, the collection of abstractions should perfectly match the extracted concepts (D) in terms of quantity (NMC) and their individual semantics. Careful attention should be paid to whether or not the real entity is able to process information since concepts (C) are passive entities with no information processing capabilities.

By the same token, model, implementation, *and reality* must correspond. For instance, the implementation of the messaging concept must be realistic: message, sender, receiver, and messaging mechanism are decoupled and independent entities. Gear meshing of procedure calls (artifact) should never be confused or mischaracterized as true messaging. Consider Alan Kay's comments. Many traditional APIs do not rely on messaging. Since there is no realistic correspondence, it is not an uncommon misconception to think that the technology/application is relying on messaging when gear meshing of procedure calls is being employed.

Animated/Live entities (information machine abstraction) are the only known entities in the universe able to process information. The other concepts, related to information processing, are tightly intertwined (i.e. associated) with the concept of Animated/Live entity: concurrency, parallelism, and fault tolerance. Realistically speaking, they do not exist separately but as part of the natural order and design.

397

In reality, multiple Animated/Live entities or information machines are able to work cooperatively and concurrently (in parallel). Messaging is also related to concurrency and Animated/Live entities since it is the only realistic mechanism of communication: information is always transferred via messaging in order to be processed. To achieve fault tolerance, redundancy at one or multiple levels is feasible: Animated/Live entity, message, information association, dialog, and so forth.

In summary, all the concepts related to information processing operate in unity and harmony. They also orbit around the main concept of Animated/Live entity. Complex processes can be put in place by relying on multiple Animated/Live entities in a realistic fashion. Concurrency, parallelism, and fault tolerance are readily accommodated by the proposed model without increasing complexity. Conceptual Complexity as measured by problem size remains *unchanged* (Complexity (D) = Size (D) = 3). No new primitives, APIs, or language constructs are necessary.

In particular, multithreading/distributed APIs, primitives, and artifacts are effectively removed since they do not correspond with natural concepts. Such artifacts, primitives, and APIs represent the source of unnecessary complexity and inefficiencies. In agreement with Occam's razor, they are superfluous and need to be 'shaved away'.

The aspects or correspondence and realism are founded on solid philosophical and scientific grounds as expressed by the Correspondence Theory of Truth[30]. Actually, it can be argued once again that in pursuing realism and correspondence with natural concepts, we effectively improve or perhaps optimize all the previous aspects because of Biomimetics principles. By carefully observing the natural mind, we should conclude that the concepts part of the model match the ones leveraged by nature in regards to information processing.

Based on the natural characteristics exhibited by the approach, Mother Nature is a tough competitor – probably unequaled. It sets a really high standard (Golden standard) in terms of efficiency, completeness (Turing Complete), effectively, and simplicity (Complexity (D) = 3). Three natural concepts including one information primitive and one concept construct (C). They constitute a Turing-complete set of reusable concepts applicable to arbitrary information challenges, models, and technologies.

The evaluation of the proposed model based on tangible software engineering metrics and empirical studies represents additional evidence (see Model Evaluation and Metrics).

As mentioned before, the terms object and component are often used interchangeably. From an information standpoint, the fundamental aspect is whether the object or component is able to process information in the real world. If so, the object or component is modeled by the Animated/Live abstraction (information machine). In reality, most entities are unanimated objects or components, unable to process information.

In regards to the Actor model, it should be stated that the model was initially created during the 70's, which obviously puts it at a disadvantage. A lot of software technology advances have come to pass since that time – specifically in the areas of Object Oriented methodologies, design patterns, and software modeling. More than 40 years later, there is a better understanding of software models, principles and abstractions. On the other hand, the Actor model provides a rigorous theoretical framework for asynchronous messaging.

The Actor model relies on several abstractions, assumptions, primitives and implementation aspects that do not mirror reality. The model makes the assumption that the message delivery is guaranteed (fairness). As a consequence mailboxes are infinite. Such assumption has been the source of criticism. It seems artificial, unrealistic, and not really required. The potential loss of information is a fact of life. However, there are control mechanisms, consistent with the realistic information model, that can be put in place in order to provide redundancy, reliability, fault tolerance and ultimately ensure delivery of *critical* information. Fairness assumptions pose challenges that may have hindered the applicability of the Actor model.

Every single entity is modeled as an actor in the context of the Actor model. Even messages are artificially represented using actors, which has been criticized as dogmatic and the source of complexity. We have come to understand that reality is much more than a narrow and limited concern.

There are many concepts and abstractions that are part of the real world: variety of design patterns, messaging in all its forms, gravity, force, other natural laws, etc. When the Actor model was created, the modern understanding of these abstractions was very limited.

A complete model must show awareness, accommodate, integrate and actively employ all these abstractions. Otherwise the model is limited, consisting of a narrow view of the real world. The original Actor model was not studied and specified from a modern OO perspective, not available at the time of its conception.

The Actor model uses the concept of *behavior*. Each time an Actor accepts a message, a replacement *behavior* is computed. This abstraction is probably unrealistic and redundant within the context of object-oriented technologies. It has also been the source of criticism. It introduces complexity and overhead associated with having additional abstractions and primitives. Behavior is already handled by the component functionality provided by its internal functions or methods. In other words, the component will behave according to the information received (inputs), its internal state and its collection of functions or methods. In reality, the concept of behavior is already an intrinsic aspect associated with an object. No separate abstraction and associated set of primitives need to be modeled and implemented.

Another example would be the required use of the *acquaintance* abstraction which fits reality within a specific set of scenarios. On the other hand, an accurate representation needs to recognize that for most messaging scenarios, an additional *acquaintance* abstraction is not really necessary. In the context of a complete distributed component/service model, acquaintances and their associated primitives are not required. Similar issues apply to many other abstractions found in the Actor model (*cell, continuation, future, task*, etc), which probably come as a result of the limited knowledge available during the 70's, in terms of modern object-oriented technologies and design patterns. The information pattern family does not present these issues, since it does not make use of redundant abstractions and primitives.

Animated/Live components are able to model all forms of messaging without limitations: synchronous, asynchronous, streaming, distributed, two-way messaging, combinations of these forms, etc. Synchronous and

400

asynchronous messaging present advantages and disadvantages depending on the application. There are many areas of application where the simplicity of synchronous messaging is recommended and asynchronous messaging is not required. Other applications are best served by using a combination of synchronous, asynchronous and other forms of messaging which may include streaming. Actually, there are many applications where a combination of synchronous and asynchronous messaging incorporates the strengths of both worlds. For example, Service Oriented models/technologies (SOA).

The invocation of a web service can usually be modeled as a simple synchronous operation (message exchange). Using asynchronous messaging for a Web service invocation would be feasible. On the other hand, it would introduce an additional degree of complexity. Synchronous messaging represents a better fit for this type of sequential application. Typically, the sender (calling component) needs to wait for the service response before proceeding with its own computations. There is an inherently synchronous aspect to this modality of interaction.

Asynchronous behavior is best suited for applications, or modules, that require parallelism or concurrent processing. For practical purposes, sequential behavior can be modeled by simple and straightforward synchronous messaging. Many pattern implementations, based on messaging, only require synchronous messaging.

The pure Actor model is based on asynchronous messaging. The coordination of Actors has been criticized for its complexity. In general, asynchronous messaging present complications and should not be used for all circumstances. Animated components provide transparent support for all modalities of messaging. An Animated/Live component can transparently process synchronous and asynchronous messaging which combines the best characteristics of both approaches and avoids complexity.

The actor model requires the concept of *receptionist* which is also useful for a specific set of applications. On the other hand, this abstraction and associated primitives should not always be required. Distributed Animated components may be accessed without the need for a *receptionist*.

In reality, a message can be sent directly to an Animated component without the need of intermediaries. Such intermediaries may or not be part of the model and implementation.

The Actor model uses the concept of *mail address* to interchange messages between actors. An actor may obtain the target's mail address from one of three sources:

a) It was known to the actor from the start, when the actor was first created.

b) It came within a message sent to the actor.

c) It was defined by the actor when it created another actor.

Animated components can send messages to any other component (local or remote) without restrictions. Other components may provide the directory services required to locate remote components. Any straightforward naming mechanism can be modeled depending on the requirements of the application being implemented. For instance, services provided by Animated/Live components can be accessed by using the URL associated to the target component.

In summary, several abstractions, assumptions, primitives, and implementation considerations present challenges that have been criticized and probably hindered the widespread use of the model. The original Actor model acknowledges open issues regarding its implementation, specifically in terms of the messaging mechanisms. Pure Actors are based on asynchronous communication. Aspects such as secure/authenticated messaging, SOA services, and fault tolerance are not part of the scope of pure Actors.

In contrast, the proposed model is founded on a modern understanding of software engineering models and principles. Founded on natural concepts, it is able to deal with all aspects of information processing including SOA services, secure/authenticated messaging, interoperability, and fault tolerance. All modalities of messaging are naturally accommodated including synchronous, asynchronous, streaming, local/distributed messaging, two-way messaging, secure messaging, and combinations of these forms.

The proposed mathematical model is distinctly different in terms of abstractions, single concept construct (C), single information primitive, and overall realistic approach mirrored from the conceptual mind. Founded on natural concepts, the model/implementation does not rely on artificial abstractions, primitives, or distributed constructs.

Relying on artificial abstractions and primitives is not an issue associated exclusively with the Actor model. Obviously there are advantages to looking at specific areas and finding targeted solutions which is consistent with the Reductionism approach. It allows us to gain additional understanding about particular areas or problems. Tangible progress has been achieved this way. On the other hand, while targeting a specific area of knowledge there is the risk of missing the forest for the trees or putting the blinders on so to speak. As a consequence, the big picture and main concepts can be missed. Redundancy of primitives, constructs, and APIs is also common when relying on fragmented and/or partial perspectives.

Consider gear meshing of procedure calls (traditional APIs), multithreading, and distributed artifacts. Such artifacts bring forth issues and limitations. Also, they add unnecessary complexity and are ultimately redundant (Complexity (D) = 3). Instead of a fully integrated system able to process information, like the conceptual mind, the technology solution may become a complex patchwork of technologies and artifacts. To achieve a comprehensive solution, a Holistic view should also be leveraged which is consistent with Aristotle's quote: the whole is more than the sum of its parts.

Event technologies focus on the transference of events, usually as part of GUI applications. An event constitutes just one type of concept associated with one type of messaging: transference of events. GUI technologies represent a single area of application. Aspects such as object orientation, SOA services, distributed components/messaging, security, and fault tolerance are not usually within the scope of Event technologies.

Also, keep in mind, that implementations of typical Event technologies usually rely on APIs based on traditional artifacts like gear meshing of procedure calls and multithreading. In contrasts, the proposed Turing-complete model is not restricted to a specific type of concept, messaging, and/or application domain. In a sense, the concept of messaging represents a generalization with a broader scope applicable to the special area of events. The model is able to deal, in a natural fashion, with arbitrary information technology aspects: object orientation, SOA services, distributed components/messaging, security, and fault tolerance. No artificial abstractions or primitives are incorporated. Event technologies can be implemented by levering the proposed approach.

A similar situation occurs with message-oriented middleware technologies (MOM), like JMS. EJB message beans are based on JMS. These technologies are focused on transferring messages between distributed applications in the context of Enterprise Application Integration (EAI) . MOM *technologies* do not focus on providing a mathematical model. Aspects such as object orientation, communication between local application components, SOA services, synchronous messaging, and fault tolerance, are not part of their scope.

MOM APIs are usually proprietary, platform/language/vendor dependent, and based on traditional artifacts like gear meshing of procedure calls. The overhead required for these technologies is considerable which makes them unsuitable for most component technologies and communication – both local and distributed. In other words, it is not practical to employ MOM technologies as the basis for the typical object/service oriented architectures including distributed component/service implementations. They mainly focus on the enterprise application level (EAI) as opposed to the object/service level.

In contrast, the proposed Turing-complete approach is not restricted to a particular area of application, or problem domain. A complete mathematical model is provided based on single Animated/Live component (information machine), information primitive, and single language construct (C). It is also able to deal, in a natural fashion, with arbitrary information technology aspects including object orientation, communication between local application components, SOA services, synchronous messaging, and fault tolerance. No artificial abstractions, primitives or APIs are incorporated. MOM technologies can be implemented using the proposed straightforward approach.

By the same token, Multi-Agent systems focus on a specific area of agency. There is no universally accepted definition of the term agent although there has been debate and controversy on the subject [43]. In general, an agent represents a computer system that is capable of independent action on behalf of its user or owner (i.e. autonomous) [43]. Historically, the concept of agent can be traced back to the Actor model. Multi-Agent *systems* do not focus on providing a unified mathematical formulation, precise realistic representation based on the mind's conceptual framework, or integrated model based on natural concepts. Multiple perspectives, agent definitions, and implementations are feasible under the umbrella of Multi-Agent systems.

Typically, aspects such as SOA services are not within their scope. System implementation usually relies on traditional APIs, gear meshing of procedure calls, multithreading, and distributed artifacts. In contrast, there is a single conceptual model based on a realistic approach mirrored from the mind (Complexity (D) = 3) and precise mathematical foundation: information machine abstraction (Animated/Live entity), information primitive, and single concept construct (C).

Due to Turing completeness, the proposed conceptual model can be leveraged for the implementation of Multi-Agent systems: the Animated/Live entity, which has a precise mathematical definition, can readily implement the Agent abstraction. Implementations of the conceptual paradigm must be based on the same unified mathematical model and concepts making them fully compatible and interoperable regardless of technology, platform, protocol, and/or computer language. Consider that the conceptual mind can be instructed to act as an agent on behalf of a third party (user or owner). Agency would be one special modality, part of the multiple ways in which the mind can be employed.

Most of the distributed component/service technologies, including SOA related technologies, rely on gear meshing of procedure calls and distributed artifacts. An alternative approach called Representational State Transfer (REST) has been proposed. REST represents a style of software architecture for distributed systems, instead of a model.

Aspects such as object orientation, fault tolerance, model/implementation realism, and mathematical model based on natural concepts, are not part of the main scope. REST is tightly coupled with the HTTP semantics. In contrast, the proposed approach is technology/platform agnostic. Instead of natural concepts, REST is based on several abstractions including Resources and State Representations. It presents several advantages when compared with distributed component/service technologies based on distributed artifacts: 1) simplicity, 2) generality of interface, 3) scalability. The generality of interface discussed by REST [12] appears to be a sound idea with a variety of benefits.

The proposed model shares the advantages of REST in terms of simplicity, scalability, and generality of interface. On the other hand, the proposed model identifies messaging as the realistic interface (natural concept) able to provide accurate and complete representation of the real world (i.e. correspondence): local and distributed entities use messaging in order to communicate with each other.

Process Algebras (Process Calculus) focus on the process abstraction, communication, and related operations as part of their mathematical models. Aspects such as object orientation, SOA services, model/implementation realism based on natural concepts (including Live/Animated entities), are not part of their scope. There are several process Algebras. In contrast, there is only one Conceptual model. The proposed Turing-complete approach incorporates all the concepts found in reality (including the concept of process). It is able to provide a straightforward mathematical foundation for every abstraction, at every level of organization: object/component, service, process, application, system, computer, and arbitrary groups of these entities.

Consider that realistically speaking, Live/Animated entities, and their interactions through messaging, are ubiquitous constituents of many processes in the real world. The proposed mathematical model is also distinctly different in terms of abstractions, single information primitive, and overall realistic approach mirrored from the mind (Complexity (D) = 3). Abstractions, primitives, and implementation are in correspondence as well.

In summary, the conceptual approach is clearly different from other approaches in several aspects including Mathematical formulation, Turing-complete information machine, single information primitive, single concept construct (C), realistic approach based on natural concepts (Complexity(D) = 3), holistic correspondence, conceptual framework mimicked from the mind, applicability to arbitrary technologies, and single unified/realistic implementation. It presents a holistic view of reality and information. The proposed approach, mirrored from the conceptual mind, is not limited to a problem domain, area of application, or level of organization: an object/component, a service, a process, an application, a system, a computer, and arbitrary groups of these entities. It also provides a complete mathematical foundation for every level of complexity: an object, a service, a process, an application, a system, a computer, and arbitrary groups of these entities.

The same mathematical concepts (i.e. natural concepts) are applicable to each level which avoids the need for adding new primitives, constructs, artifacts, or APIs. Therefore, the 'natural' approach does not share the challenges and problems associated with technologies based on artificial abstractions, primitives, and APIs. The Turing-complete approach is also able to implement and integrate, in a realistic fashion, the individual abstractions studied by other models/technologies (at every level). A holistic and unified perspective of information, also avoids overlaps, redundancy, and inefficiencies. It should be emphasized that providing a complete *model*, including mathematical formulation, is not the goal or focus of the aforementioned *technologies* and *systems* (The Actor approach and Process Algebras represent models).

"To solve nearly any problem, we must both reduce [conceptualize] the problem to its component parts [concepts], and then provide a solution to the problem as a whole. In doing so, we use both reductionism and holism in partnership." Chris Masterjohn

"It is necessary to remark that there is an ongoing synthesis of computation and communication into a **unified** process of *information processing*. Practical and theoretical advances are aimed at this synthesis and also use it as a tool for further development. Thus, we use the word computation in the sense of *information processing* as a whole. Better theoretical understanding of computers, networks, and other information processing systems will allow us to develop such systems to a higher level. " Mark Burgin.

Nature does not present itself as a fragmented collection of abstractions. On the contrary, in agreement with Occam's razor, it consists of an effective and efficient (streamlined) set of natural concepts that act in unity and harmony as part of a whole within the order of nature. In particular, in terms of the concepts associated with information processing, as part of a complete unit: the conceptual mind.

To gain a comprehensive understanding, concepts need to be studied independently *and* as part of a holistic unit (family or forest of concepts). Both perspectives offer significant benefits. In particular, by using a holistic perspective, the risks of redundancy and missing fundamental concepts or the larger picture are avoided. Independents concepts are extracted through conceptualization. From a conceptual and realistic perspective, once extracted they need to be analyzed both independently and as part of a whole expressed in the form of a complete mathematical model which presents the interrelationships (graph of associations) between all involved concepts.

## C. Cognitive/AI Models (related work)

It should be stated that the proposed paradigm can be applied to logical reasoning, conceptual processing (C), and related *conscious* cognitive abilities, because they can be modeled, understood, and explained by a precise mathematical formulation $(A = (f(m), I))$. However, the approach is general and flexible enough to be extended to other cognitive areas. The following comparison will be based on the scope just defined. I should also state that this area of application is still work in progress. The improvements derived from the application of the model to software engineering in general can be evaluated and measured in quantitative terms (see Appendix on Model Evaluation and Metrics).

The specific cognitive/AI area represents only one among multiple areas of application. Consider that natural concepts are ubiquitous and extend beyond a specific area of application. Natural concepts represent mathematical entities with wide applicability. For instance, the concept of messaging, like the mathematical concepts of a number and set, has wide applicability. Notice that similar to other mathematical entities, the exact same mathematical concept takes a variety of forms in the real world.

Unified Theories of Cognition (UTC) focus on the specific areas of cognition and artificial intelligence. UTC does not focus on providing a unified mathematical formulation based on the mind's conceptual framework, or integrated information model founded on natural concepts and applicable to arbitrary information/software technologies. According to UTC, the mind functions as a single system. The conceptual paradigm can be characterized as a valid UTC candidate because it models key cognitive abilities. It also operates as a single unified system $(A = (f(m), I))$.

In contrast with UTC, the proposed approach is based on a precise mathematical Turing-complete model: information machine $(A = (\beta(m), I))$. The conceptual paradigm, naturally and holistically explains several key cognitive abilities including logical reasoning (Boole's $\beta$-function), symbol utilization (C), memory, learning of conceptual/non-conceptual information, goal (procedure) oriented behavior (P) and knowledge representation (I/C). Motor control can also be realistically accommodated.

409

For instance, the mind communicates with other components of the body using messaging although no conceptual information is exchanged. Such components can also be modeled using the same natural/mathematical concepts and formulation: $A = (f(m), I)$. Notice that information, as expected, is a fundamental concept part of all conscious cognitive abilities.

From a logical and mathematical perspective, the conceptual paradigm is founded on a solid footing: Boole's Algebra of Logic which he characterized as The Laws of Thought. His remarkable conclusions, as applied to the conceptual model, are logical and demonstrable via formal mathematical proof (see demonstration of the Conceptual Deductive Approach). The timeless contributions of Boole's brilliant and *logical* mind, far ahead of his time, should be weighed [22].

From the cognitive psychology perspective, information processing is at the core. In agreement with the proposed model, cognitive psychology views the human mind as an information processor, like a modern computer, interacting with its environment [25]. Such view has also become the dominant view in modern psychology.

From a conceptual perspective, reasoning literally means "to form conclusions, judgments, or inferences from facts or premises". Logical processing of information (i.e. reasoning), the fundamental concept implemented by the machine, has been mathematically formalized by Boole's Algebra of Logic (Laws of Thought). This should also give you a sense of the expressiveness, conciseness, accuracy, and power of the natural language as the ultimate tool for transferring information (i.e. concepts) – a match for the conceptual mind that hosts it. Human languages have evolved for ages and become highly precise and 'logical' tools for transferring concepts.

The concept "logical processing of information" can be utilized to express an otherwise complex idea in an accurate, concise, and logical fashion - perhaps almost mathematical, in terms of accuracy and precision, when looked at from a conceptual standpoint. Let us not forget the tight connection between human languages and the formal mathematical language. Both are symbolic representations of the same reality and are governed by the same logical rules expressed by Boole's Algebra of Logic. Both seek a realistic and accurate representation.

410

The concept of learning literally means acquiring new knowledge which can be mathematically modeled using set theory, a Boolean algebra. Problem solving means using generic or ad hoc methods (procedures (P)), in an orderly manner, for finding solutions to problems.

"The idea of a learning machine may appear paradoxical to some readers. How can the rules of operation of the machine change? They should describe completely how the machine will react whatever its history might be, whatever changes it might undergo. The rules are thus quite time-invariant. This is quite true. The explanation of the paradox is that the rules which get changed in the learning process are of a rather less pretentious kind, claiming only an ephemeral validity. The reader may draw a parallel with the Constitution of the United States." Alan Turing [3].

Boole's Algebra of Logic ($\beta$-function) represents the Constitution that provides the machine with abilities of logical reasoning: The Laws of Thought, which are time-invariant. On the other hand, the information ($I$) learned in the form of concepts (C), is ephemeral – including learned procedures (P) to solve problems or perform tasks. The mathematical formulation clearly shows it: $A=(\beta(m), I)$. An important point is the alleged existence of rules that are time-invariant, innate if you will.

In summary, the proposed paradigm is consistent with several related perspectives on cognition: UTC's view of the mind as a single unified system (UTC Candidate), mathematical/logical perspective represented by Boole's Laws of Though, cognitive psychology, psychology, philosophical conceptualism/realism, Turing's time-invariant rules ('constitution of thinking'), Biomimetics, and conceptual perspective. It should be clear from observation of reality that the same natural concepts (mathematical entities) leveraged by the conceptual machine apply to the mind. The proposed paradigm is also in agreement with Occam razor. Indeed, the simplest and easiest concepts: logical processing of information ($A=(\beta(m), I)$).

"Nature does not multiply things [concepts] unnecessarily; that she makes use of the easiest and simplest means [concepts] for producing her effects; that she does nothing in vain, and the like." Galileo Galilei.

"Rudiments [Concepts] or principles must not be unnecessarily multiplied." Immanuel Kant.

On the other hand, the Society of the Mind (SOM) presents an alternative approach:

"The functions performed by the brain are the products of the work of thousands of different, specialized sub-systems, the intricate product of hundreds of millions of years of biological evolution." Marvin Minsky.

The agent abstraction is introduced to refer to the simplest individuals that populate such society of the mind:

"No single one of these little agents knows very much by itself, but each recognizes certain configurations of a few associates and responds by altering its state. " Marvin Minsky.

Having multiple subcomponents part of the brain is consistent with ongoing research including the Society of the Mind. Based on the proposed conceptual approach, a group of information machines can be readily accommodated – living inside the mind, interchanging information via messaging, and performing multiple functions: $\{A1, A2, , An\}$ where $(A_i = (f(m), I))$. Consider that the mind performs functions besides the ones associated with logical reasoning. Think that the whole body consists of a set of associated organs (components) interchanging information through the same natural concepts. They can also be modeled using a group of information machines: $\{A1, A2, ,An\}$ where $(A_i = (f(m), I))$.

The Society of the Mind also focuses on the specific area of cognition and artificial intelligence. It does not focus on providing an integrated model based on natural concepts (i.e. mathematical entities), unified mathematical formulation, or unified model for that matter. In contrast, the proposed approach provides a Turing-complete mathematical foundation able to model and naturally explain a wide variety of cognitive/AI functions including logical reasoning, learning, memory, and language processing. Founded on natural concepts and the mind's conceptual framework, it is applicable to arbitrary information/software

412

technologies. In agreement with Occam's razor, instead of multiple SOM agents only one conceptual machine is strictly necessary for performing logical processing of information (reasoning): "Nature does not multiply things [concepts] unnecessarily;" In contrast with the SOM agent, a conceptual machine is a single 'intelligent' entity (unit) capable of logical reasoning, self-sufficient, able to communicate/learn arbitrary amounts of concepts (C) including procedures to solve problems, and as powerful as a computer in terms of processing power (Turing-complete).

Other components/functions of the mind can be simply modeled using information machines. Keep in mind that the difference between Boole's conceptual machines $A=(\beta(m), I)$ and information machines $A=(f(m), I)$ is the ability to process conceptual information in a logical fashion. Such organization would explain the widely accepted belief that only a single thought can be consciously entertained at any given time. The same applies to conversations and performing tasks: it is also widely accepted that we can focus on doing one thing at a time. However, switching from task to task can be done very rapidly which gives the sense – probably an illusion – of multiple tasks being done concurrently.

Ongoing research supports the 'popular' beliefs grounded in common sense. For instance, Earl Miller, a neuroscientist at MIT, says that "for the most part, we simply can't focus on more than one thing at a time." By the same token, if only one thought or task can realistically be performed at any given time, *only one* conceptual machine is necessary as part of the mind, communicating with less 'intelligent' components $(A=(f(m), I))$ responsible for performing other brain functions. Your personal computer (smartphone) is capable of performing only one task at a time. The Central Processing Unit (CPU) executes one instruction at any given time although the speed of processing gives the illusion of multiple tasks being performed simultaneously.

Based on concepts, symbols, and Algebra of Logic, the conceptual approach is clearly different from connectionism. Conceptually, logical reasoning, entity recognition, and motor skills are very different from each other: separate concepts altogether. The way in which you carry a *logical* argument is completely different from the function of recognizing a face/symbol, or riding your bike. The former skill can be completely explained in logical and conceptual terms: Mary married Mr. Boole; that is how we reason that she became his wife.

In contrast, entity recognition and motor skills cannot be reasoned in the same fashion, so to speak. However these functions are complementary and work cooperatively. For instance, you may rely on certain aspects of logical reasoning to help face/symbol recognition: He looks like my friend because of the green eyes and black hair. The round shape looks like the letter O.

"Which approach is best to pursue? That is simply a wrong question. Each has virtues and deficiencies, and we need integrated systems that can exploit the advantages of both." Marvin Minsky

"Most serious of all is what we might call the Problem of Opacity: the knowledge embodied inside a network's numerical coefficients is not accessible outside that net. This is not a challenge we should expect our connectionists to easily solve." Marvin Minsky

The aforementioned views are consistent with implementation connectionists who hold that the brain neural network implements a symbolic processor at a higher and more abstract level. Their research is aimed at figuring out how symbolic processing can be accomplished on a foundation of a neural network [30]. It is not very difficult to visualize and/or theorize about straightforward ways in which the web (graph) of information/knowledge ($I = \{C1, , Cn\}$), part of the conceptual machine ($A=(\beta(m), I)$), could be mapped onto the brain's neural network. Both structures are isomorphic.

In theory, the biological neural network is perhaps just an ultrafast information superhighway designed to store/transport non-conceptual and conceptual knowledge (C). No much more would be required, at the bio-neural level, to support the straightforward conceptual computing model. On the other hand, notice that the same natural concepts apply to all aforementioned skills: information and processing of information.

A key difference is the type of information being manipulated (conceptual vs. non-conceptual). Logical reasoning is strictly based on conceptual information. Ponder that a neuron, like the mind, can be completely specified using the same mathematical concepts: ($A=(f(m), I)$). A neuron is an analog information machine (mini-machine). Obviously, the 'implementation' is different although the concepts are

414

the same: function ($f(m)$), information stored ($I$), and type of message ($m$).

In summary, the conceptual approach is distinctly different from other AI/Cognitive approaches in several aspects including Mathematical formulation, Turing-complete information machine, conceptual machine ($A=(\beta(m),\ I)$), single information primitive, single concept construct (C), realistic approach based on natural concepts, conceptual framework mimicked from the mind, applicability to arbitrary computing technologies, and single unified/realistic implementation.

# INDEX

# Q

Quality, 15, 58, 72, 74, 84, 218
   mission critical applications, 137

# R

Realism, 10, 12, 24, 35
   exaggerated, 12
   moderate, 12
Realistic Information Model (REAL), 8–12
Redundancy, 14
Remote Procedure Call (RPC), 113
Representational State Transfer (REST), 26, **405**
Reusability, 57, 70, 115
   lack of, 52, 66

# S

Scalability, 14, 67, 71, 84
   limitations, 38, 52, 66
Security, 73, 175–78
   authentication, 175
   encryption, 175
Service Oriented Architecture (SOA). *See* Distributed Compontent and Service Model
Simplicity, 23, 391–93
Society of the Mind (SOM), 412
Software Architectures
   compared to Concepts, 202
Software maintenance, 74, 218
Software metrics

Application size, 213
Coupling between object classes (CBO), 213
Depth of the inheritance tree (DIT), 211
Method level complexity, 210
Number of children (NOC), 211
Number of classes (NC), 210
Number of key classes (NKC), 210
Weighted methods per class (WMC), 210

# T

Testing, 58, 72
   black box, 72
thing-in-itself, 11
Turing
   Learning machine paradox, 188
   machine, 183
Turing complete, 183–89

# U

Unanimated object, 11, 34, 149, 196, 198, 217
Unified Modeling Language (UML), 29, 72, 217
Unified Theories of Cognition (UTC), 409
Universal. *See* conceptualism

# V

Versioning, 26, 72, 204

419

## About the Author

Mr. Galvis has had several roles over a period of more than 15 years in the computer industry. Roles include Computer Scientist at research facilities and responsibilities as a technical consultant and architect for several major corporations. He has also authored several papers published in technical conferences and journals.

www.ingramcontent.com/pod-product-compliance
Lightning Source LLC
Chambersburg PA
CBHW071357050326
40689CB00010B/1677